BOY CLINTON

THE POLITICAL BIOGRAPHY

R. EMMETT TYRRELL, JR.

REGNERY PUBLISHING, INC.
Washington, D.C.

Library of Congress Cataloging-in-Publication Data

Tyrrell, R. Emmett.
    Boy Clinton: the political biography / by R. Emmett Tyrrell.
        p. cm.
    Includes index.
    ISBN 0-89526-439-0 (alk. paper)
        1. United States—Politics and government—1993-   2. Clinton,
Bill, 1946-   . 3. Political corruption—United States.   I. Title.
E885.T97   1996
973.929'092—dc20   96-8371
                                                           CIP

Published in the United States by
Regnery Publishing, Inc.
An Eagle Publishing Company
422 First Street, SE, Suite 300
Washington, DC 20003

Distributed to the trade by
National Book Network
4720-A Boston Way
Lanham, MD 20706

Printed on acid-free paper.
Manufactured in the United States of America

10 9 8 7 6 5 4 3 2 1

Books are available in quantity for promotional or premium use. Write to
Director of Special Sales, Regnery Publishing, Inc., 422 First Street, SE,
Suite 300, Washington, DC 20003, for information on discounts and terms
or call (202) 546-5005.

For Kenneth Lynn, the perfect prof

And Valerie Lynn, the perfect woman

CONTENTS

ACKNOWLEDGMENTS

AT THE OUTSET I want to acknowledge that this book is the consequence of Erwin Glickes's prudent skepticism toward the pert ignoramuses of my generation who in the late 1960s took over many fine universities, degrading them and driving wise faculty members such as himself elsewhere. Erwin left Columbia for the world of publishing, where he performed with great distinction until his untimely death. Even while flourishing as a publisher he never forgot what this snotty sliver of my generation did to American learning; when he saw the Clintons in the White House he invited me to lay bare their essential nonsensicality. Thus this is another salvo in an intergenerational battle that those of us who see America as a good democracy have been waging against those of our peers who see America as a Golden Goose to be plucked. I wish Erwin had lived to appraise the final product.

Since I began working on this book in 1993, the *American Spectator*, the magazine I founded at Indiana University in 1967 to confront student radicalism, has grown from a circulation of 30,000 to a high point of 340,000, making it the largest intellectual review in the country, which is to say, the world. I acknowledge my debt to Bill and Hillary, but also to my marvelous staff whose members have overseen that growth, stepping in when I was, say, on an expedition to Arkansas or reviewing various criminal codes or composing this monograph. Publisher Ron Burr presided over the magazine with his usual businesslike mastery of detail. The noble Wladyslaw Pleszczynski, ably supported by Chris Caldwell and M. D. Carnegie, kept the editorial department humming in time of crisis and time of bliss. Investigative reporters David Brock and Danny Wattenberg uncovered much that certain people would rather not hear about, and James Ring Adams, our financial investigator, did that and also assisted me in uncovering and explicating Byzantine financial dealings that might have bankrupted Byzantium and left the emperor in the hoosegow. All their labors have assisted me in recreating the Clinton miracle.

Researchers Pedro Manzana, George Neumayr, and Tracy Robinson were very helpful, and the amazing Pedro was great fun to work with. George and my son, P. D. Tyrrell, performed splendidly, reading my changes into the manuscript during its final period of fine tuning. Then came the indefatigable and fastidious Tracy, volunteering her own time to review endnotes with selfless care. I have had the perfect secretaries. Jenny Woodward, in retirement now, read the text for error. Lonnie Rewis stuck by me through the whole ordeal, seeing to it that Jenny was left few errors to detect. Yet Lonnie did so very much more, and she deserves my especial gratitude. We have an all-purpose genius in our office by the name of Catherine Campbell, whose grace and kindness are legendary; as always I am grateful for the literary counsel of the dear Miss Myrna Larfnik, who to my surprise has remained unmarried all these years.

Beyond my immediate colleagues I want to acknowledge my agent, Lois Wallace, who steps in during grim moments and performs above the call of duty. She is a pro. Two superb journalists helped in many ways: the queen's gift to the colonies, Ambrose Evans-Pritchard, and John Corry, one of the great journalists of his generation, who has now come down from New York to give the *American Spectator* still more firepower. Jack Hinton and Dave Henderson brought their varied talents to my project, and Andrew

Whist of *Libertad* brought his friendship. The Lynns, Kenneth and Valerie, were always helpful, and then came the colleagues of Regnery Publishing. Following in the great tradition of his father Henry, Alfred Regnery, the president and publisher of Regnery Publishing, runs the most professional publishing house I have ever been associated with. Not surprisingly my editor there, Richard Vigilante, has proven to be my best editor. To all of the above, my gratitude.

One final acknowledgment. I want to thank those selfless Arkansans who helped me with information and critical insights. Arkansas is now the most maligned state in the Union. Yet I have found the vast majority of Arkansans to be uniquely friendly, decent, and law abiding. Theirs is a beautiful state, blessed by nature but not always by history. Arkansans deserve better than the political corruption now on display. I hope what I have written will be of some assistance to the many brave and industrious Arkansans now endeavoring to bring about reform. To them I am very grateful.

RET

McLean, Virginia

April 27, 1996

INTRODUCTION

A LL THE SCANDALS OF the Clinton presidency have their
genesis in Arkansas, even the foreign campaign donations
that played such a large role in his 1996 reelection. Did the Clinton
White House misuse the FBI to gather political intelligence on
some nine hundred citizens? Did it abuse its power by leaning on
the FBI to malign the employees of the White House Travel
Office? Turn to Chapter 6 of this book, and read how Arkansas state
troopers were regularly asked to gather political intelligence for the
governor. Did the Clintons attempt to turn hitherto unpolitical
offices of the federal government into political operations and
financial plums for cronies? Turn to Chapters 5, 6, and 8, and you
will see them doing the very same back home.

The financial irregularities of Campaign '96 are not particularly
surprising either. Only in the last days of the campaign did America's
mainstream press become aware of foreign involvement from such
shadowy figures as Indonesia's Riady family and the Lippo group.
Yet, as you will see in Chapter 5, the Riadys' activity in Arkansas was
observable from the 1980s, as was the fundraising for Clinton by
Charlie Trie, who did it amidst the chop suey and egg rolls of his Little Rock oriental eatery (Fu Lin, a play on Foo Lin?) back then and
amidst peculiar Asian contacts later, in 1992 and 1996.

Mochtar Riady and his son James infiltrated Arkansas in a serious
way when their Lippo Holding Company purchased a substantial

piece of Arkansas's Worthen bank on February 14, 1984. They became partners with the powerful Stephens family of Little Rock, owners of the largest privately owned investment bank outside of Wall Street.

Though coming from the far corners of the globe, both the Stephens family and the Riadys had similar characteristics. They were hustlers who rose fast from nowhere to amass their billions. Wilton R. Stephens began his family's fortune in the late 1920s peddling Bibles to the rustics in rural Arkansas. By the early 1930s he upgraded his product to discount bonds. Mochtar Riady's billions do not go so far back. He began in Jakarta in 1956 and perhaps under more cosmopolitan circumstances than the rural salesman from Arkansas. Old Mochtar's point of origin was a bicycle shop. By 1985 both had extended their operations from Little Rock and Jakarta to Hong Kong, Thailand, and even China. When Arkansas pension funds took a $60 million hit in 1985, owing to Governor Clinton's cronyism and shoddy regulatory practices, the Stephens–Riady axis rushed to rescue the fund and, not incidentally, the Boy Governor's career. Naturally the Stephenses and the Riadys were ready with cash for the 1992 presidential campaign as well as the 1996 campaign, and, in keeping with his agreeable nature, President Clinton gave the gang freedom to roam his Commerce Department and other territories of the federal government. John Huang, the Riady's man in America, was their chief agent.

Clinton's carelessness about the source of campaign funds is another trait whose roots reach back to his Arkansas days. So, too, is his seasonal panic as election day draws near. As discussed in Chapter 10, Clinton's first year in the presidency was made painful by ceaseless revelations in the press of the dubious loans that the Clintons had taken out in the 1980s, usually for last-minute electioneering. In Arkansas the Clintons hit up hayseed bankers. In Washington they hit up Asian bankers and apparently even the agents of foreign governments. No White House has ever appeared so unlovely to the world.

In the autumn of election year 1996, about the time this political biography began appearing on the nation's best-seller lists, one of the century's most listless presidential campaigns was twitching with welcome signs of life. Boy Clinton had been suavely stonewalling requests that he release his medical records, but now throughout our nation's capital tension was coiling up. Bob Dole's preparations for their first nationally televised debate were complete. War whoops could be heard from his training camp. Rumors spread that the challenger was about to ambush his opponent with the dreaded "character issue." His weapon would be those sealed and delicious medical records.

The only recent precedent available to Clinton for not releasing them, raw data and all, was that set by President John F. Kennedy. Now, however, every educated voter knew that during his 1960 campaign Kennedy had been hiding something. He had suffered from Addison's disease along with other ailments that had left him in frequent pain and subject to bouts of fatigue. Given the suffering that he had braved, his reticence was gallant. So what suffering might the gallant Clinton be braving?

Speculation was vigorous; at times, reckless. Some insisted that the Boy President's medical records might reveal cosmetic surgery. The artist John Springs, who had sketched him frequently, thought he perceived traces of a face lift. Others believed that the candidate's records would reveal treatment for sexually transmitted diseases. After all, Kennedy's biographer Richard Reeves had, among the hidden health problems suffered by Kennedy, chronicled "persistent venereal disease."

In researching this book I found no evidence of Clinton's suffering either condition. I did find some evidence that our forty-second president had become somewhat the cokehead while serving as governor of Arkansas, but by spring of 1996 when the book went to press I was unable to snare any witnesses. Then in late summer and early fall as the book began appearing in bookstores, my continuing investigations paid off. Working with two associates, I discovered people who had either observed Clinton using cocaine or who had used drugs with him. I also came upon leads indicating that Clinton may have been treated for a drug overdose at the University of Arkansas Medical Center, probably in 1980. If that is true, his reasons for keeping those medical records out of sight are understandable.

One witness to Clinton's drug use was Jane Parks, a middle-aged Arkansan hired in the mid-1980s as resident manager at an upscale Little Rock apartment complex, Vantage Point. Vantage Point was owned by Sidney Weniger, a New York developer. Using ample funds made available to him by the Arkansas Development Finance Authority—that being the brainchild of his friend Governor Clinton—Weniger did a lucrative development business in the 1980s. As we shall see in this book and as post-reelection news accounts reveal, the Clintons make very good political use of such financiers, whether they are American or foreign born.

This particular apartment complex, Vantage Point, consisted of three buildings. Mrs. Parks's office was in the middle building. It was apartment B107. The apartment had been subdivided by a flimsy partition, on one side of which Mrs. Parks worked with her assistant. On the other side was a temporary apartment referred to rather splendidly as Vantage Point's "corporate suite." In the summer of 1984 Governor Clinton's half brother Roger stayed in this room as a nonpaying guest. Mrs. Parks told us that she observed cocaine being brought into the apartment.

During this period she also says she had to relay complaints to Roger about noise from his parties. In an interview with one of my colleagues at Little Rock's Regas Bar and Grill, Mrs. Parks stated, "Once when I opened the door, Bill Clinton was sitting on the couch. He was staring straight ahead, looking stoned." She mimicked the governor sitting with arms stiff, looking straight ahead, glassy-eyed. She saw "lines of cocaine on the table in front of him." Mrs. Parks, a dark-haired, fine-featured woman, appearing surprisingly fit despite years spent fighting multiple sclerosis, had to overcome considerable fear to grant this interview. The people she had seen entering Vantage Point were powerful, and what they were up to revealed that they were already corrupt. Some of the girls she had seen there were very young. In the company of her assistant, Mrs. Parks had heard the governor, from the other side of the partition, enthuse over the high-quality cocaine that he was apparently using. Her son, Gary, told one of my associates that he had been ordered by management to "buy groceries. Leave the door open with the key.... He [says Gary Parks of brother Roger] had a lot of visitors. Lasater was there at least once."

Lasater is Dan Lasater, whom you will meet in this book's prologue. He was a major financial supporter of the governor. Under oath, Arkansas state troopers have testified to hustling then-Governor Clinton out of Lasater's famous Little Rock drug parties. The troopers never saw Clinton using drugs, but one said he recognized signs that indicated Clinton was under the influence of drugs at a Lasater party. Lasater later employed Roger. Eventually both were convicted on drug offenses. Clinton pardoned Lasater, and it speaks volumes about Clinton's moral sensibilities that when he became president he brought Lasater's top lieutenant, Patsy Thomasson, to the White House, where she is now deputy assistant to the president and deputy director of presidential personnel. Another witness to the Vantage Point revels, who wishes to remain anonymous, testifies that she saw Clinton at the apartment at least three times.

Eventually Roger Clinton checked out of Vantage Point. "When we went to clean out the apartment, we found marijuana," Mrs. Parks asserts. "We found barbiturates, sleeping pills. On the side of the tabletop, where a ridge went around, white power was wedged in the crack." She and her assistant found drug paraphernalia in the kitchen. Mrs. Parks's husband was an independent investigator. Alarmed by the drugs and licentiousness she witnessed at Vantage Point, Mrs. Parks had her husband Jerry monitor the place. "We had a video camera. We didn't get all of it." Her husband was shot dead in his car on an Arkansas road in September 1993. The murder has been described by police investigators as a "professional hit." The files Jerry Parks kept on these affairs were either hidden or stolen. After I published Mrs. Parks's interview in my syndicated column in October of 1996, she was threatened. It was the third threat against her in recent weeks. This time a man telephoned her to say, "You will be dead before the election."

I published all this information in my newspaper column the week before the Dole–Clinton debate. At the same time, Dennis Sculimbrene, an FBI agent who until April had conducted the bureau's background checks on White House employees, told the *Wall Street Journal* that "about 25 percent of the incoming administration... had a problem with illegal drugs. Not just casual experimentation, but a pattern of usage... not just marijuana but cocaine, amphetamines, amphetamine-derived 'designer' drugs such as Ecstasy, hashish, mushrooms." Some of those whom Sculimbrene was referring to were "senior aides and advisors to the president." Thus there was reason to believe that the "character issue" was about to explode in Boy Clinton's face. As the *Times* of London remarked just hours before the debate, "what intrigued Washington... was whether Mr. Dole would find an oblique way of raising" the allegations filed by Sculimbrene and me. Of course Dole never did, and most voters went to the polls unaware of these serious charges. You may decide for yourself why Dole remained mum. I believe the explanation resides in his own fatuous ignorance. In my conversations with him a year before the election I was never able to bestir any curiosity about Clinton's scandalous life. In fact, he dismissed Clinton's scandals as beyond the public's interest. To be sure, he knew more about the charges against Clinton than most voters, and he was unaware of how well documented they were. But Dole's insouciance was not unique. A cultural fact of the early 1990s was that many Americans in public life—journalists, politicians, and others—really did not want to know much about their president. Some shared his roguish background in 1960s counterculture. Others took his word for it that he was just an ordinary guy with a big heart. Both types were too intellectually indolent to recognize that this product of Arkansas machine politics was not really like either of them.

Yet these were not the first charges of drug use ever brought against Clinton. Sally Perdue, a Clinton girlfriend from the mid-1980s, made similar allegations. In Roger Morris's book *Partners in Power*, Morris quotes Roger Clinton on a 1983–1984 police surveillance film as saying, "[G]ot to get some [cocaine] for my brother. He's got a nose like a vacuum cleaner." And there is another woman who has admitted to using drugs with Clinton—Asharlene Wilson. She was an Arkansas drug informant who in 1990 testified before a federal grand jury that she sold her erstwhile boyfriend, Roger Clinton, cocaine sometime in 1979. She witnessed both Clintons snorting it. Though now residing in an Arkansas prison, Wilson has had her veracity attested to by Jean Duffey, a former Arkansas prosecutor who headed a local drug task force that used Wilson.

From all this evidence it is apparent that Clinton's medical records might well reveal a drug habit. They might also reveal a drug overdose. I have yet to uncover witnesses willing to admit that they saw Clinton suffering from the rumored overdose, but my colleagues have elicited some curious responses from suspected witnesses. As the rumor has it, Governor Clinton was admitted to the University of Arkansas Medical Center emergency room just after his defeat for reelection in 1980. He was suffering from a cocaine overdose. At some point, his wife arrived. My associates interviewed two nurses who supposedly had knowledge of the scene. Neither tendered a categorical "no" when asked if she knew about Clinton's arrival at the emergency room. One told my colleague that "I can't talk about that." The other stated that if she were to discuss that matter, her life would be in danger.

There is one Clinton scandal mentioned in this book that thus

far has not been duplicated in the Clintons' Washington—the Mena
Airport gun running and drug trafficking operations that are chronicled in the prologue. For years it was rumored that during Clinton's governorship, American intelligence operations supplied arms
to anti-Communist forces in Central America through Arkansas's
rural Mena Airport. In the prologue you will see that I have uncovered witnesses to that operation, as well as an Arkansas state trooper
who flew on two gun running flights over Nicaragua—only to discover that his flights were returning to Mena with cocaine and laundered money. When the trooper, L.D. Brown, notified Clinton of
his discovery, the governor shrugged off the warning, saying,
"That's Lasater's deal. That's Lasater's deal."

I identified Lasater a few paragraphs back. After you read the
book's prologue you can make your own judgment as to the cogency
of the adduced evidence. The reaction to my discovery that the CIA
was arming the contras and that the return flights were bringing
drugs back to Governor Clinton's financial supporters was bizarre.
The press for the most part ignored the revelations, though no one
in the press has ever disproved them. Rather, the national press
turned its attention away from charges made in a best-selling book
and for weeks recycled an inherently dubious story from the
obscure *San Jose Mercury News*. The story claimed that the CIA
profited from the sale of drugs to Los Angeles street gangs and used
the profits to arm Nicaragua's anti-Communist Contras. The
implausible tale was unsupported by documents or by witnesses.
Apparently the American press was willing to believe that despite
the billions of dollars appropriated by Congress for American intelligence, the CIA could not set aside a few million to arm the Contras. Instead it entered into the perilous area of drug trafficking.
This preposterosity eventually collapsed for want of evidence but
not until millions of Americans were exposed to reports of CIA
lawlessness and racism.

At Mena I found no evidence of CIA involvement in drug trafficking. Nonetheless in November of 1996, when it delivered to Congress its response to trooper Brown's Mena story, the CIA served up a feast of evasions, deceptions, and red-hot lies. It admitted its contacts with Brown, but claimed he was only a "candidate" for intelligence and that the CIA had ended its relationship with him in December 1984. That would be when Brown quit his flights to Nicaragua, but Brown has supplied evidence, which appears in Appendix A, that supports his claim that he ran further missions. He had every reason to conclude that they were CIA operations, and the CIA owes the taxpayer an explanation.

In its November report the CIA admitted that it had been engaged in activities at Mena Airport but diminished their importance, claiming to have maintained only a "two-week" operation "with another government agency." It admitted to only "limited contact" with the corrupt pilot, Barry Seal, who was flying cocaine back on the CIA flights. In its report the CIA admitted to having put cameras on his plane but insisted that there is "no evidence" that the CIA even knew Seal's "true identity." All that is lawyerly balderdash. Unfortunately for the CIA, I laid hands on the testimony of one Ernest Jacobsen before the House Subcommittee on Criminal Activities in 1988. During that testimony Jacobsen, a Drug Enforcement Administration (DEA) officer, testified that back in May of 1984 four CIA officials met with DEA officials regarding Seal's impending flights. They knew exactly Seal's identity. Later in his testimony Jacobsen described an actual meeting between Seal and CIA officials.

There is also the matter of the plane Seal flew both on those missions with Brown and at other times. It was a C-123K with a shadowy history and a tragic future. The facts are well established. It originated with Southern Air Transport, the well-known CIA front. After Seal was done with it the plane found its way back to Southern Air Transport, where it met a spectacular demise in Nicaragua after Sandinista fire brought it down, revealing one Eugene

Hasenfus. According to him he was on a CIA flight to supply the anti-Communist Contras. In its report the CIA was adamant that it had never engaged in drug trafficking, money laundering, or "arms smuggling" at Mena. Here again is lawyerly balderdash. No one has accused the CIA of secreting arms in to Nicaragua to avoid paying duties on them—that being what smuggling is. As for drugs and laundering money, neither Brown nor anyone I know of has evidence that the CIA was involved in either activity.

Doubtless in the years ahead more of the facts in this book will be verified. Thus far, the critics have only been able to hide—not always successfully.

PROLOGUE

ARKANSAS STATE TROOPER L. D. Brown had just returned from a mission flown to Central America from Arkansas's Mena Airport in late December 1984. The flight was commanded by pilot Barry Seal, an operative with the Drug Enforcement Administration (DEA) and a contract employee with the Central Intelligence Agency. Seal was also a legendary drug smuggler, known for having flown hundreds of drug-smuggling flights between 1977 and 1983 at low altitude and in complete darkness.[1] Now, supposedly, he had gone straight. After parachuting arms into the jungle, Seal landed at a sleepy Central American airport. He picked up two duffel bags and flew back to Arkansas. Brown, seated behind him throughout the flight, was moonlighting as a CIA contract employee [see Appendix A, items A, B, and C]. His boss, Governor Bill Clinton, had encouraged and assisted him in his employment at the CIA. Under the assumption that he was being trained for clandestine operations on this flight, Brown was following Seal's instructions. He was merely an observer, studying the activities of Seal and his crew.

But during this, his most recent flight, what Brown, a seasoned narcotics investigator, was to learn troubled him deeply. Seal was bringing drugs and money back in the duffel bags. Consequently, as soon as Brown returned to Little Rock he approached Clinton and asked, "Do you know what they're bringing back on those planes?" Clinton froze. "They're bringing back coke," Brown told him. In fact "they" were trafficking in cocaine, money, and arms. Clinton's response was blasé. He told Brown not to worry, adding "That's Lasater's deal. That's Lasater's deal."[2] At the time Dan Lasater, an Arkansas "bond daddy" known for his wide-open parties, was a major Clinton supporter. Clinton's occasional attendance at Lasater's parties had presented his bodyguard, Brown, with problems; in addition to young girls, the parties also included plenty of cocaine.

Brown is unclear as to the rest of Clinton's reply. It was either "And your buddy Bush knows all about it," or "And your hero Bush knows about it." Brown admired President George Bush, having met him in Portland, Maine, while traveling with the governor. After that meeting the two Arkansans visited with the president at his Kennebunkport compound.

Clinton's references to Bush and Lasater added confusion to Brown's anger. Brown was angry after this last flight when Seal showed him cocaine and money that he had just flown into the country. Brown feared that he, a member of the governor's security, was being set up to be blackmailed. Now upon finding out that Clinton knew about the operation, the trooper felt betrayed and a bit stupid. He says that the moment he saw the drugs Lasater's involvement should have "dawned" on him. "I'd never seen the governor around coke," Brown says, "unless he was around Lasater." At Lasater's parties Brown would hustle the governor away when the drugs came out. Though he had seen Clinton "stoned," he had never actually seen him using drugs. Others have, namely two of Clinton's lovers, Sally Perdue and Gennifer Flowers. Both have attested to Clinton's drug use during assignations.

Feeling angry, betrayed, and played for a fool, Brown left the governor and proceeded directly to a cottage on the mansion grounds where Becky McCoy, his future wife, lived. Listed on the mansion's payroll as a "courier," she was actually Chelsea's nanny. Eleven years after that day Becky remembers Brown's arriving in tears and complaining, "I've been betrayed."[3]

Over the next few months Brown would seek another assignment with the state troopers, but it would take him more than a decade to sort out his involvement and possible culpability as the governor's man on the Mena airport flights.

At the time, 1984, Brown was twenty-eight years old. He was not only Clinton's favorite bodyguard, but also a close friend. The other troopers called him Clinton's "fair-haired boy." He and Clinton shared an interest in books, ideas, and night life. Brown still has books that Clinton gave him, one being a bar exam study book in which the politician made some ironic underlinings. One passage discussed the deductibility of charitable donations, and another the length of residency required in Washington before tax liability is incurred. Like Clinton, Brown passed through a radical stage when he attended the University of Arkansas at Fayetteville. Indeed, when Clinton was a law professor in Fayetteville, Brown was working on an off-campus magazine, the radical *Grapevine*.

In the autumn of 1984, Brown made his first flight with Seal. It was on October 23 or very close to that date, and Brown found himself seated on a bench inside a cavernous C-123K cargo plane roaring over a Central American jungle. Seal, who piloted the plane, was one of the greatest daredevil flyers of the day.

His C-123K also had a history [see Appendix A, items H and I]. It was originally an Air Force transport plane. Seal dubbed it "the Fat Lady." He had purchased it from Doan Helicopter, Inc., of Daytona Beach, to which it would eventually be returned; both transactions appear suspicious. The plane would later be serviced and financed by Southern Air Transport, a CIA front company. It is the same C-123K that was eventually shot down over Nicaragua in a doomed supply effort to the Contras that left an American, Eugene Hasenfus, a prisoner of the Sandinistas and revealed the CIA link to the Contras. The plane's two pilots died.

On the morning of that first particular flight, Seal had told Brown to drive to Mena Intermountain Regional Airport in a remote area near the Oklahoma border. It is a tiny facility, infrequently used, and interesting only for an exceedingly long runway, the kind used by large planes with transcontinental ranges. Brown had expected to find, he says, a Baron or a King Air, small, twin-engined planes in which he had some training as a pilot. He had accompanied the governor on such planes throughout the state. Instead, he says, he found this "huge military plane" that was not actually a military plane. It was dark, almost black, and had only the minimal tail markings necessary for civilian operation. The C-123K is a military transport with twin engines, and Seal's had a tailgate at the end of its fuselage capable of loading such cargo as a small automobile.

Inside the plane, according to Brown, were another pilot and two "beaners"—common laborers who looked like Central American Indians. Later Brown would come to know them as "kickers," for they "kicked" cargo from the plane. All were wearing jeans,   t-shirts, and sneakers. Seal, Brown says, had prescribed the dress code and insisted that no one carry identification, not even keys or jewelry. To Brown's surprise Seal even asked about his shoes. They had to be untraceable. When Brown got on the plane, Seal's co-pilot was at its controls fiddling with gauges and making notes. Then Seal started the engines, and Brown remembers, "This fuckin', excuse me, I mean just thunderous noise. Scared the shit out of me just taking off." Brown says that when the plane took off, he was sitting on a bench behind the two pilots. The "kickers" were seated far to the back of "this shell of a plane" where there were pallets on casters. On the pallets were stacked crates, partially covered by a tarpaulin.

After it left Mena, the plane made a refueling stop—"Nobody got off," Brown says—and then resumed flight. The stop was at Stennis Airfield in Gulfport, Mississippi, an airfield frequently used by the DEA.[4] Once back in the air Brown recalls, Seal startled him by yelling, "Well, you all hang on." The plane dropped to what Brown calls "an altitude a hell of a lot lower than what you'd think you'd fly." He suspected Seal was trying to evade radar. Soon, he says, they regained altitude, but then they descended again and "that's when these two crazy bastards get these pallets and roll them on casters." Parachutes opened from the cargo on the pallets. Later Seal confirmed Brown's suspicions: the pallets carried M-16s for the Contras. It is unclear whether they ever got to the Contras. Seal seems to have had equally cordial relations with the Cali Cartel and the Sandinistas. He proved to be a very unreliable government employee.

Approximately thirty minutes later, Brown says, the C-123K landed in what he later thought was Tegucigalpa, Honduras, though my investigations leave me doubtful that this was their Central American landing site. After landing, the plane was refueled. While Seal and the kickers went to collect Seal's duffel bags, Brown and the co-pilot, who never exchanged more than a few words, remained on board. Then, Brown says, Seal and the kickers returned, carrying four bags. Brown says he never saw the bags again.

Once back on the ground at Mena, Brown says, he told Seal he had anticipated flying in a plane similar to those that he had been on with the governor. Seal, he says, laughed, and told Brown that all he had wanted him to do was "sit back for the ride." Then he paid Brown for the flight, handing him an envelope with $2,500 in cash—"not marked money, not banded money, just twenties, fifties, mostly twenties, used money, like you just went out and spent."

When Brown returned to the Governor's Mansion after this first flight he recalls, Clinton greeted him jovially, "You having any fun yet?" Clinton had been asking him variations of that question since the previous spring when he began encouraging Brown to apply for a job with the CIA. Indeed, Clinton had taken an active role in helping Brown. He told Brown he had acquaintances in the CIA who could expedite his application. As part of the application process, Brown had written an essay: "Marxist Influence in Central America." Three early drafts of the essay contain interpolations in Clinton's handwriting, the authenticity of which has been verified. Clinton also suggested that Brown study Russian, a suggestion Brown took seriously enough to begin attending night classes at the University of Arkansas at Little Rock. He began making entries in his daybook in Cyrillic. Clinton, Brown believed, was familiar with the CIA. He occasionally spoke of a college classmate who had ended up working there. The governor also talked as though he knew of ongoing operations nearby. "When I got back from that first trip he knew I had been out doing something," although Brown had not had a chance to tell Clinton "anything about it. That's when he said, 'You having any fun yet?'"

The CIA does not talk about these things, so we may never know whether Brown was actually a CIA employee or being deceived into thinking that he was. Whatever the case, he had good reason to believe that he was in the CIA's employ. It may also never be known for sure whether CIA officials approved or knew of Seal's activities.

Some facts, however, are indisputable. Entries in Brown's daybook indicate his flights. A month before his October flight the Southwest personnel representative for the CIA, Ken Cargile, in a letter to Brown, wrote that "I am pleased to nominate you for employment with the Central Intelligence Agency." Another entry in Brown's daybook indicates that he had met with another CIA representative only a few days before. Brown has identified him as Dan Magruder and says that he spoke admiringly of Clinton. Magruder, Brown says, asked him if he would be interested in "paramilitary, counterintelligence, and narcotics." Brown, who had worked in narcotics enforcement as a police officer, said he was interested. He then, he says, signed a secrecy agreement and was told he would be contacted further. Finally, there was a very suggestive call that Governor Clinton made to Becky (McCoy) Brown after she married Brown. It came a half year after Brown's last flight. It was summer, and Becky had announced that she was leaving the mansion staff. Clinton was livid. In this call he insisted that she stay, and then he reminded her of the help he had given Brown in "getting into the CIA."

In Dallas, Magruder told Brown that a contact would be made after he returned to Arkansas. Next Cargile sent him his letter of nomination. Then Seal called him at home and set up a meeting at Cajun's Wharf, a popular Little Rock watering hole. Bill McKuen, former secretaty of state of Arkansas, has told Danny Harkins, senior criminal investigator for the state of Arkansas, that he remembers seeing Seal and Brown together at Cajun's wharf in 1984. Seal, according to Brown, was familiar with the biographical information Brown had given the agency, thus reassuring Brown that he was the CIA contact Magruder had told him to expect. Seal was not, however, what Brown was expecting from the CIA. Magruder had been a "clean cut Ivy League-looking guy." Seal was "a very distinctive guy. I mean, a nut, big guy. And you never forget this kind of guy. Robust, devil-may-care, kind of, you know, dangerous."

If Seal's appearance and demeanor were not what Brown had come to expect from the "Ivy League" CIA, his conversation was reassuring. Brown says he talked knowledgeably about airplanes and spoke of an "operation" he was planning. He also referred to Clinton, familiarly, as "the guv." He talked as though "the guv" knew all about the CIA operation going on in Arkansas. Brown theorizes that Seal "needed all the help he could get." Trafficking in drugs, weapons, and currency often attracts unwanted attention. The more people around Clinton whom Seal might compromise, the less likely Clinton and other Arkansas authorities might be to sacrifice Seal in time of danger. Brown believes that this is why Seal eventually showed him that kilo of cocaine. Also, Brown would have made an excellent lieutenant for Seal who was always in need of competent hands. Brown adds that "the more people close to Clinton that he [Seal] could get working with him, the more comfortable he'd feel." When Seal was sentenced for drug dealing in 1985 and again in early 1986 his activities at Mena were never mentioned.

Brown's break with Clinton came after Brown made what he says was his second flight from Mena to Central America on or about

December 24, 1984. Becky Brown remembers the date of the flight vividly. Her brother, Read, was dying, and she was surprised Brown left town. He and her brother had been close. During that second flight two duffel bags were put on board the plane at what Seal identified as Tegucigalpa. Back at Mena, Brown says, he and Seal walked to Brown's car, a Datsun hatchback, and Seal put one of the duffel bags under the hatchback. Then both men got into the front seat of the car, and Seal reached back into the duffel bag and pulled out a manila envelope with $2,500 in it. He said the money had been brought back from Tegucigalpa. Brown considered this a currency violation. The next thing Seal pulled from his duffel bag was an even graver breach of the law, that kilo of cocaine.

That was it for Brown. He got upset. He says he feared he was being set up—made a conspirator in an operation he despised. He told Seal he wanted no part of what was happening; then he left. When he returned to Little Rock, he called his brother Dwayne. Dwayne Brown says his brother seemed "terribly upset." Dwayne immediately drove over to the Governor's Mansion to meet him. Like Becky, Dwayne Brown says he knew his brother had made some unexplained trips out of the country. He suspected a CIA involvement, although his brother did not confirm it. But when he asked, "Who's pushing this?" his brother, Dwayne Brown says, "nodded over toward the Governor's Mansion." From then on, until he left Clinton's security detail in June, Dwayne Brown says, his brother was in "a high level of despair." He says he feared his brother might be suicidal.[5]

Meanwhile, Brown confronted Clinton, asking him if he knew that Seal was dealing in drugs and unreported currency. That was when Clinton told him not to worry—"That's Lasater's deal. That's Lasater's deal." Lasater was well known to Brown. As early as 1982, his firm had been censured by Arkansas's security commissioner for cheating customers, which did not end or even impair his relationship with Clinton. By 1984—the time of the Seal flights—Lasater was contributing to Clinton's political campaigns. He was also providing Clinton with the use of a private airplane and entertaining him at various places, including his New Mexico resort, Angel Fire. He hired Clinton's brother, Roger, and helped him pay off a $20,000 cocaine debt. Later Roger was imprisoned for his dealings with a cocaine ring. As for Lasater, he was sentenced to two years in jail for dealings with the same ring and lost his state securities license. After six months in prison he got out on probation. Eventually Clinton pardoned him, claiming that the pardon was necessary to enable Lasater to renew his hunting license.[6]

Clinton's relationship with Lasater was obviously risky. It might still prove to be criminal. When Lasater went to prison his operations were taken over by an associate, Patsy Thomasson. She was a politically active Arkansan whose employment with Lasater was to last nearly a decade, despite his problems with the law and with drugs. DEA documents in my possession show her flying with him on one of his private planes to Belize on February 8, 1984, where he was interested in buying a ranch that was a known drug trafficking point [see Appendix A, item G]. In 1993 she joined the White House where she has served as White House director of the Office of Administration and later deputy director of Presidential Personnel. The night of Deputy White House Counsel Vince Foster's death, she was one of the trusted Clinton aides who entered Foster's office to spirit away documents. As for Lasater, by the mid-1980s he had become involved in several shaky savings and loans, at least one of which, First American Savings & Loan of Oak Brook, Illinois, had its difficulties with Lasater negotiated by the bank's legal team of Vince Foster, Webster Hubbell, and Hillary Rodham Clinton of Little Rock's Rose Law Firm, much to Lasater's satisfaction. Apparently the thrift was unaware of the relationship its own legal team enjoyed with Lasater. Though the thrift had sought millions, it ended up settling for $200,000.[7]

Drug trafficking was linked to Arkansas throughout the 1980s, occasionally to Clinton's friends and supporters. An investigator wrote in the minutes of a Resolution Trust Corporation meeting held on June 29, 1994, that Lasater "may have been establishing depository accounts at Madison and other financial institutions and laundering drug money through them via brokered deposits and bond issues."[8] Among the "other financial institutions" Lasater has been linked to is the Arkansas Development Finance Authority created by Governor Clinton. In 1994 when Secretary of Agriculture Mike Espy resigned owing to allegations that he was accepting gifts from the Arkansas poultry tycoon, Don Tyson, London's *Sunday Telegraph* published a story based on numerous state and federal police documents showing that Tyson was "under suspicion of drug dealing from the early 1970s until the late 1980s" by such diverse organizations as the Arkansas State Police and the DEA.[9] No charges were ever filed.

Still the most serious information on drug trafficking in Clinton's Arkansas has come from Brown. His revelations were first published in the *American Spectator* in the summer of 1995, and though objected to by President Clinton they have never been disproved. After splitting with Clinton, Brown spent the next few years investigating white-collar crime for the Arkansas State Police. He says that he became increasingly interested in going public with his knowledge of the Mena operation, but that he was mindful of the secrecy document that he had signed. Moreover, with officials at both the state and federal level involved, he did not know whom to tell. Eventually, it was the Clintons' heavy-handed incompetence in trying to control another damaging story involving Brown that led Brown to tell his story to me.

In the April-May 1994 issue of the *American Spectator*, Brown was quoted as saying that Lieutenant Governor Jim Guy Tucker had asked him and trooper Larry Patterson for compromising information on Clinton's private life in 1990. When Tucker became aware of Brown's revelation, he retaliated against Brown by demoting him from white-collar investigations to highway patrol. "I don't want to be getting any more reports from Brown" is the statement by Tucker that Colonel Tommy Goodwin, the former head of the Arkansas state police, quoted in explaining the demotion to me in an interview.[10]

Brown believed the demotion to be illegal because he was at the time working on a case that could have implicated Tucker. An indignant Brown began toying with the idea of exposing the corruption of Arkansas politics. About this time, the special prosecutor investigating Whitewater subpoenaed Brown to disclose what he knew about Clinton' connections to a Whitewater figure, David L. Hale. Clinton was supposed to have pressured Hale, the head of an Arkansas lending agency, into making illegal loans to Susan McDougal, the Clintons' Whitewater real estate partner. Brown's subpoena convinced him that "everything is going to come out." Nonetheless, he still seemed reluctant to disclose all he knew. The irony is that he might have remained silent about Mena had not Clinton's imprudent intervention provoked Brown into coming out into the open.

In the fall of 1994, ABC News interviewed Brown, principally about Hale. But the White House panicked, assuming that the interview was about Mena. And Clinton set out to malign Brown. White House officials, as well as Clinton's lawyer, David Kendall, who according to *Time* was "working very, very hard to keep Whitewater out of the headlines,"[11] approached ABC with numerous false allegations against Brown. Meanwhile, Betsey Wright, a Clinton political fixer and his former chief of staff, told ABC that Brown was a "pathological liar," even though his personnel file in Arkansas abounded with recommendations—some from Clinton and even one from Dr. Joycelyn Elders. ABC was also told that Brown had failed a psychological test. Goodwin assured me and ABC that Brown had passed it.[12] But of the charges leveled at Brown by the White House, the most unintentionally revealing was that Brown had flunked a CIA examination in the mid-1980s. That charge could only have come from the man—then–Governor Clinton—

who knew that his former bodyguard had had dealings with the CIA a decade before.

An ABC producer told me at the time that "Brown is telling the truth. You can trust him." Nonetheless the network apparently yielded to White House pressure. The interview with Brown, in which he had spoken mostly about Hale and not about Mena, was killed. Brown's patience was now strained beyond endurance. He decided to talk to me about Mena.

Clinton's position has always been that he knew nothing substantial about Mena and that the "state really had next to nothing to do with it.... We had nothing—zero—to do with it, and everybody who's ever looked into it knows that."[13] Brown says he is lying. His daybook records one visit to Mena by Clinton on May 21, 1984, and he says that he accompanied Clinton to Mena on several other occasions. Clinton claimed in a rare reference to Mena late in the 1980s that he was unaware of any problem at Mena until 1988. But a 1991 deposition by Betsey Wright reveals that the governor's office had in the early 1980s received repeated calls about drug trafficking there. In fact, in 1991 Governor Clinton revealed that a state police investigation had discovered drug "linkages to the federal government." He mentioned the CIA.[14]

Given the remoteness of Mena, it is curious that the governor would be showing up there so frequently in the mid-1980s. The airport is small and handles little traffic. The town itself is sleepy and extremely rural. Its voter turnout is, perhaps, the lowest in the state. Clinton could not have been stopping by the airport for political purposes. Since Clinton's election as president, moreover, others have come forward to implicate him in Mena. Arkansas State Trooper Bobby Walker has told me that "sometime in the mid-1980s" he was at Mena with Clinton. Walker said a "huge dark-green military plane" was parked there and that when he expressed surprise at seeing a military plane at Mena, Clinton said it was not military; it served another purpose.

In March 1995, in a legally binding deposition, Trooper Larry Patterson also said that Clinton knew about Mena. Patterson said he had overheard conversations about "large quantities of drugs being flown into Mena airport, large quantities of guns, that there was an ongoing operation training foreign people in the area." When asked, "Were any of these conversations in the presence of Governor Bill Clinton?" he replied: "Yes, sir."

Patterson was being deposed in a legal suit filed against Buddy Young, the former head of Clinton's security detail, by Terry Reed, who says he trained Contra pilots, under Seal's supervision, at Nella, Arkansas. In another deposition in the case, John Bender, a mechanic, says he saw Clinton at Mena three times in the summer of 1985. There were no local dignitaries present, Bender says, and Clinton did not seem to be taking part in any official function. Bender says that Clinton arrived in a Beech aircraft and was still there when Bender left for the day. Clinton's stays lasted for hours.

During his deposition Bender was shown a photograph of Buddy Young. He identified him as "Captain Buddy Young—that little beady-faced fellow," and said that Young was with Clinton at Mena. Young has since been made head of the Federal Emergency Management Administration in Denton, Texas. In another deposition in the Reed case, Russell Welch, an Arkansas state police investigator who has investigated Mena extensively, says that Young asked him in 1992 if Clinton's name had ever come up in connection with Mena. Welch said it had not, but Young's concern is intriguing.

At this juncture, no one, including Brown, can say precisely what Clinton was doing at Mena. Brown's role, after all, was quite limited. In early 1985, after Brown told Seal—and Clinton—that he would no longer take part in the drug flights, Seal contacted Brown again. Encouraging Brown to continue working with him, Seal said, "There's good money to be had." But Brown said he was out of that game for good. Brown was not going to have anything to do with drug shipments. He was not, however, done with the CIA.

In January 1985 while Brown was on duty at the Governor's Mansion he was paid a visit by a man he believed to be another contract employee of the CIA, Felix Rodriguez, alias Max Gomez. Before visiting Brown at the mansion, Rodriguez telephoned Brown while he was on duty there. Later he drove over, entering through the compound's back gate. His familiarity with the place surprised Brown. In the following months Brown concluded that Rodriguez must have known Clinton and was in continuing contact with him. Eventually Clinton made it clear to Brown that he knew Rodriguez. On the occasion of this first meeting with Brown it seems that Rodriguez's mission was to placate him. He wanted Brown to work with him on clandestine operations, but he wanted to reassure Brown that no more "monkeying around with Seal would be involved." At Rodriguez's mention of Seal, Brown explained, "I have had some bad experiences." Rodriguez responded, "Don't worry about Barry.... We're going to take care of that." He also told Brown he would "take care of things" with Clinton. Apparently he did. Clinton never talked to Brown about Mena or Lasater again.

Rodriguez said he was beginning a new operation and wanted Brown with him. Aware of how Seal's drug trafficking had compromised him, Brown was uneasy. Rodriguez attempted to propitiate him. He offered to get Brown another meeting with Magruder. Rodriguez talked of his friendship with two men Brown admired from his training days in narcotics work, Nick Navarro and Raul Diaz. The combination of Rodriguez's persuasiveness, Brown's continuing interest in a career in intelligence work, and the prospect of earning $1,000 for each mission convinced Brown to join Rodriguez in his new operation. It involved guarding the transshipment of weapons from the Caribbean to Central America. From what he saw on these missions Brown believed the shipments included AK-47s and explosives meant for the Contras.

The missions took place in 1985. During that year Brown's

contact with Rodriguez was sporadic and by telephone. But Brown was confident that Rodriguez was his CIA contact. His confidence was bolstered when Rodriguez suggested they enroll Brown in a medical school in Montserrat. The purpose, Brown thought, was to establish cover for his further intelligence operations. Rodriguez also talked with Brown about Seal, saying Seal had gotten "out of hand." On one occasion Brown expressed apprehensions to Rodriguez about Seal's co-pilot on their flights out of Mena. Brown feared exposure. Rodriguez responded, "Don't worry about it. We're going to take care of him. We're going to take care of all of it." Brown did not know the pilot's identity or his whereabouts, but in 1986, on February 19, Seal was shot dead as he entered a halfway house in Louisiana. Three Colombians eventually were arrested and convicted of the murder. The Louisiana attorney general has estimated to the Justice Department that Seal had "smuggled between $3 billion and $5 billion in drugs into the U.S."

In May of 1986, after Seal's death, Brown got another call from Rodriguez. "You hear about our man?" he asked. Brown had indeed heard of Seal's murder in Baton Rouge. "Well, we know who was flying in the second seat." Brown interpreted this remark to mean "It's like we're going to eliminate everybody." Brown went on to relate that Rodriguez "talked about Clinton... and gave me the impression they were going to do something to his ass." His impression from this conversation with Rodriguez was that Rodriguez's employer had been embarrassed by the drug trafficking that Seal and perhaps Clinton had mixed into the Mena resupply operations. Now they were going to kill "anybody that apparently had anything to do with what happened over at Mena." Brown began to fear for Clinton's life—though critical of Clinton's character and reckless improprieties, Brown obviously still harbored affection for his friend from the exciting days of the early 1980s.

After Rodriguez's May telephone call, he sent Brown a manual for a light automatic rifle, a Belgian-made F.A.L. Brown still has the manual. The official title of the gun as referred to in the manual is "FN Light Automatic Rifle, caliber 7.62mm. NATO." The gun is usually known as the "F.A.L." Rodriguez told Brown to fly to Puerto Vallarta, Mexico, where he would carry out a plan to kill the man he was led to believe was Seal's co-pilot. With his wife, Becky, to serve as cover, Brown flew to Puerto Vallarta on June 18, 1986, on American Airlines flights 537 and 535 [see Appendix A, item E]. A guard standing by the guard house of the port's naval installation gave Brown the F.A.L. It was in a straw bag, disassembled, which explains why Rodriguez sent Brown the manual.

Using the alias Michael Johnson, a name he had used in undercover work in Arkansas, Brown was to proceed to the Hotel Playa Conchas Chinas on the morning of June 21. There he was to identify himself as Johnson to the hotel clerk and give him $50. The clerk would direct him to his target. All went according to plan until the clerk pointed out Brown's prospective victim. The victim did not look at all like Seal's co-pilot. Brown left the hotel, ditched the gun, and flew back on American Airlines flights 292 and 512. The man he had been set up to kill was Terry Reed, the very same man Seal had been working with in training the Contras and the man who in 1991 was to file the aforementioned lawsuit against Buddy Young alleging that Young had "manufactured, altered, tampered with and/or removed evidence, all in the pursuit of advancing a wrongful criminal indictment." Reed believes that Young, the head of Governor Bill Clinton's security detail, set him up in 1987 to be killed. Young has admitted to authoring a national police profile saying that Reed was armed and dangerous and known to use a concealed weapon.

Brown did not know anything about Reed until 1995. Upon returning to Little Rock he received a call from Rodriguez who wanted to arrange an appointment. Rodriguez was en route to Washington but would fly down to Little Rock on his way home. Brown said no. He wanted nothing more to do with Rodriguez.

These last revelations of Brown's are now documented. His airplane tickets were purchased in late May. Photocopies of them are in my files. The date of purchase is May 27. I have seen the F.A.L. manual. Copies of Brown's map from Puerto Vallarta and copies of documents in which the Arkansas State Revenue Department lists Brown's alias, Michael Johnson, are also in my possession. Brown had used that alias in undercover police work and had an Arkansas driver's license under that name.

Reed too has inadvertently provided evidence supporting Brown's revelations. Without knowing anything about Brown, Reed wrote a book chronicling his misadventures with the CIA and with Arkansas officials while training Contras. The book implicates Clinton in Mena and places Reed in Puerto Vallarta. Oblivious of the fate that was awaiting him at the Hotel Playa Conchas Chinas, Reed reports that he was told to be at the hotel on June 21 to meet his new CIA handler. The man who ordered him there was Felix Rodriguez, known to Reed as Maximo Gomez.

Rodriguez somewhat imprudently has also written a book about his life, *Shadow Warrior*. In it he mentions Navarro and Diaz, saying he knew them as investigators in south Florida. He mentions traveling to Washington, at precisely the time Brown says he traveled there, June 1986. On June 25 he met with Ollie North. Of course, North was the National Security Council aide engaged in resupplying the Contras.[15, 16]

Brown has two more revelations. Though he left the governor's security detail in June 1985, he obviously continued to have numerous encounters with Clinton. Just before he went down to Puerto Vallarta, thinking he was being sent by the CIA to kill one of the last living figures associated with Mena, he told Clinton what their acquaintance Rodriguez had put him up to. According to Brown, he encountered Clinton, probably at the Capitol, and told him, "I'm going to take care of that problem in Mexico." Clinton acted as though he were aware of the mission, saying, "Oh, that's good, that's good, L.D." Looking back on that exchange, Brown believes Clinton also knew the identity of Brown's quarry, Reed. Brown's second revelation is that during the Iran-Contra hearings he discovered the real identity of Dan Magruder, the CIA official whom he met in Dallas on August 30, 1984, and whose name Rodriguez invoked in persuading Brown to undertake their Caribbean operation. Brown says he was actually Donald P. Gregg, at the time Vice President George Bush's national security adviser. Brown explains that he became aware of Magruder's real identity during the television coverage of Iran-Contra. The Donald Gregg appearing on screen and being accused of associating with one Felix Rodriguez in the Contra resupply operation looked and sounded to Brown like Dan Magruder.

Corroborating evidence that Gregg was involved with arming the Contras has been mounting for years. The stories began when Iran-Contra broke. They continued when Gregg's nomination as ambassador to South Korea came before the Senate early in the Bush presidency. Of particular interest during those hearings was Gregg's relationship with a CIA operative long famed for his daring anticommunist operations, Rodriguez. Gregg did not deny their friendship.[17] The Magruder whom Brown met in Dallas talked of his prior service in and extensive knowledge of Korea [see Appendix A, item D]. He told Brown that he was an "Asian expert." Gregg, it turns out, was CIA station chief in Seoul in the 1970s. Now two intelligence agents have come forward and confirmed that Gregg used the name Magruder while assisting in arming the Contras in the early 1980s in Florida and California.

Finally, remember Clinton's remark after Brown's last flight with Seal, "and your buddy Bush knows all about it." Were Clinton and Bush both politically exposed on Mena? This might explain one of the mysteries of the 1992 campaign, the mildness of the famously competitive George Bush and his refusal to attack Clinton where the challenger was most vulnerable—character. Some political observers have speculated that Bush's Graves' disease explains his listless campaign. Others have claimed that Bush lost his relish for political life. An alternative explanation might be that both men had a tacit agreement not to get personal, owing to their exposure on Mena. But there is no evidence that Bush or one of his financial supporters was involved in drug trafficking at Mena. Clearly Clinton had more to fear from Mena than Bush, which suggests a tantalizing detail: Might Clinton have hoodwinked Bush into a tacit agreement that lost Bush the election? Looking back on his years of service with Clinton, Brown recalls contacts between the two men that, given the Clintons' remoteness from Washington, were unusually frequent and cordial. Bush and Reagan were hated by Hillary, Brown says, but not by Clinton.

When Brown's revelations about Mena were published in the *American Spectator* in the summer of 1995 they met with mixed reaction. The *Wall Street Journal*'s lead editorial pronounced: "Mena cries out for investigation. A congressional committee with resources, subpoena power and the perseverance displayed by some past chairmen should look into this. If some chips fall on the Republican side, so be it. Important questions need to be answered."[18]

Other journalists for the most part ignored the story though they had previously vowed that if a Clinton bodyguard ever came forward with claims of serious wrongdoing by Clinton, as opposed to mere adultery and satyriasis, they would investigate to the utmost. Finally, there was a handful of journalists who set out to expose Brown as a fraud. I have in my files a cocky letter from one on the letterhead of a major news organization ridiculing Brown's assertions about flying with Seal and, incidentally, erroneously observing that Seal died in January rather than February.

That Brown's story stands unimpeached must give him great satisfaction. For over a decade he had lived in fear. He feared that his flights with Seal implicated him in a conspiracy to import cocaine. As people whom he had known at Mena disappeared or died violently he began to fear for his life. And as mentioned a few paragraphs back, he even feared for Clinton's life. While I was encouraging Brown to reveal his story to me and later while I was encouraging him to go public with it, I never quite understood the intensity of these fears—until he revealed to me his dealings with Rodriguez.

In my journalistic life I have not had to deal with many desperate men. Documents revealing drug dealing, gun running, intelligence-gathering cloak-and-dagger operations, and ultimately murder do not make amusing reading. As I have mentioned earlier, we might never know for sure what took place at Mena or who the principal players were. Yet there is a serious policy issue involved when government intelligence services link up with unsavory types and lose control of their operation. Further research into Mena leads me to believe that Seal's drug dealing might have been going on independent of and perhaps even unknown to the CIA. In fact it is possible that the CIA's dealings with him were not terribly close and that the guns he dropped were going to the Sandinistas rather than the Contras, or perhaps even to Colombian drug tycoons. Possibly Rodriguez was not even working that closely with the CIA but with others, for instance with North and Gregg, who had really lost control of their operation.

I have gathered information that sketches several agencies working with varying degrees of responsibility at Mena. In the early 1980s it appears that, to avoid prosecution for international drug trafficking, Seal approached the Drug Enforcement Administration, offering to serve as an informant. The DEA eventually used him on three counternarcotics operations. Through a government register, the National Source Register, our intelligence agencies became aware of him. They knew of his easy aerial access to Central and South America. By 1983 Washington had become concerned about the possible presence of Soviet-made missiles in Nicaragua and even the possibility that the Soviet Union might have nuclear weapons there.

The National Security Agency (NSA), which monitors such foreign activity, needed low-flying airborne platforms like Seal's drug
flights on which to place the sophisticated devices that would detect
nuclear weapons in a place such as Nicaragua. The CIA recruited
Seal to undertake these flights. The CIA provided the front for
dealing with Seal while the NSA equipped Seal's C-123K with the
required gadgetry. The plane was equipped with very sophisticated
Nuclear Detection Devices manufactured by EG&G in Las Vegas,
a highly classified Department of Defense contractor. The NSA
fabricated a TOP SECRET specially compartmented program for
all electronic collection directed against the Sandinista government.
The program was called "RAPPORT." When I filed a Freedom of
Information request to the Pentagon, it went immediately to NSA
without any urging from me.

Owing to Seal's status as a CIA asset, Customs and the Federal
Aviation Administration (FAA) could allow Seal to leave and enter
the country without inspection. For security reasons the NSA
barred Customs from inspecting Seal's plane. He was free to return
from his flights south with small duffel bags of drugs. All the NSA
wanted was its intelligence data tapes. Seal duped all these government agencies until someone put an end to his duplicity.

But to return to Brown's revelations about Clinton at Mena. One
might wonder why the governor of Arkansas would want one of his
top security guards on the Mena flights. The answer seems obvious
to anyone who has studied Clinton's behavior. Were the Mena operation exposed, Clinton could claim that he had a top state trooper
with experience in narcotics investigations flying surveillance.

When Brown's story was published in the August 1995 issue of
the *American Spectator*, I was unable to get an official White House
response. More surprising was the silence of all major news organizations except for the *Wall Street Journal* and the *Arkansas Democrat-Gazette*. For years journalists, most notably on the Left, had
been on to Mena. Now a conservative was validating at least some

of what the Left had suspected. As for Brown, major news organizations had been after him for months, suspecting that he knew something portentous about Mena. Once the story broke, their calls to him petered out. Unlike the aftermath of the troopers' revelations about Clinton's sex life, when he found himself peppered with journalists' inquiries day after day, the president never had to face similar inquiries from the press about this far more serious matter.

Thus one can imagine my delight on the evening of July 17, a week after publication of the August *Spectator*, when the president entered the dining room of Washington's Jockey Club. I was seated a few feet away with my fourteen-year-old daughter, Annie, and her young friend, Zaina Arafat. Finally I would get the official White House response to the L. D. Brown story and from the White House's top official—all in the comfort of Washington's finest eatery. The president proceeded to a table in the back of the restaurant where fifteen old friends greeted him. Upon meticulous reflection and with the principia of Miss Manners in mind, I asked the *maître d'* to tell the president that "Mr. Tyrrell of the *American Spectator*" would like to send over a bottle of champagne.

The Secret Service, of course, had to be consulted, but apparently the president was pleased. A beaming *maître d'* returned to tell me that "President Clinton" would like to thank me after my meal, but, she advised, there were fifteen people in the president's party. "Two bottles," I insisted. My generosity is the stuff of legends.

Frankly I was rather surprised by the president's response. Since late 1993 when the *American Spectator*'s Troopergate stories began detailing the scortatory side of Clinton's life, I had personally overseen an investigative team of journalists that both in Arkansas and Washington had turned up reports of conflicts of interest and abuse of power (for instance, David Brock's piece on Travelgate), and campaign irregularities, such as using "walking around money" to buy votes and filing false financial papers. We had reported real estate shenanigans, banking scams, and sharp tax filings that revealed the Clintons taking deductions on such piffles as the president's underwear. Yet I should not have been all that surprised. For over two years I had been doing research on the Clintons for this book. Clinton is a very reckless man, and he has many quirks, one of which makes him a tireless schmoozer. Down in Arkansas it was known that if there was one person at a party who, he felt, disliked him he would spend the entire party heaving himself at the skeptic. The evening of July 17, 1995 was my turn.

As we were almost finished with our meal when I sent over the champagne, I soon notified the *maître d'* that we were ready to accept the president's gratitude. Past a wall of security and through a corridor of flunkies we were led. The Clintons were seated at one long table with their guests and fifteen tiny servings of champagne. Large and amiable, the president rose from his chair to greet us. He was all smiles; Mrs. Clinton, seated across from him, was less joyous.

"And so we meet," I said. He joked, shook my hand, and immediately turned the charm on my daughter and Zaina. He asked the girls their ages. He spoke of Chelsea's summer camp. Out of the corner of my eye I espied an increasingly uneasy Hillary. Time might be running out. Her eyes put me in mind of a snake about to strike. Quickly I made my move for the White House's official response to the L. D. Brown-Mena story. Reminding the president of my respect for the Clintons' characteristically 1960s trait of "talking and talking" and debating every issue, I briskly addressed the issue of the moment. "What did you think of the L. D. Brown story?" I asked. He reddened. He ignited.

He denied that he had read the piece. He said I should be "ashamed" of publishing it. "Lies, lies," he intoned indignantly. The flunkies stiffened. The president's next charges were curiously familiar. He called Brown a "pathological liar" who had tried to destroy his own family. Those were precisely the lines that the White House's operatives had employed months before against Brown to kill ABC's interview with him.

I replied that the president's hometown paper, the *Arkansas Democrat-Gazette*, had just described Brown as a very credible witness who had never yet been caught in a lie. The president began reiterating his charges. I mentioned that it seemed to me he *had* read our piece. He continued with his charges and showed no sign of breaking off what was becoming an increasingly uncomfortable conversation. Surely, I thought, he will wheel on me and, as the sophisticates say, "cut" me. But, no, he continued to sputter and to whine. This too was what Arkansans had told me to expect. There stood this large man surrounded by bodyguards. His presence, however, was completely without force. The president was angry. His voice was labored. Yet this was anger without force. What came to mind was not the anger of a statesman, but rather Tinkerbell in a snit. I made my congés. Mrs. Clinton might join in, and I would be guilty of having placed young girls in harm's way.

The next day, when the press began inquiring about my presidential summit at the Jockey Club, I pooh-poohed the whole thing. Tim Watters, the leading impersonator of Bill Clinton, was a friend of mine. I insisted that it was Watters whom I had encountered the night before. Surely the president of the United States does not accept champagne in a restaurant. The man I had met was an impostor, but a pretty good one.

CHAPTER ONE

THE GLORIFICATION RITES
AND THE UNCOMMON
TROUBLES PRECEDING THEM

B OY CLINTON HAD PROMISED that upon being elected
president he would make history, and he did, almost immediately. On the morning of Inauguration Day, the president-elect
and Mrs. Hillary Clinton, who would soon rename herself Hillary
Rodham Clinton, in keeping with the family's propensity for creating discrepancies on the public record, forced President George
Bush and Mrs. Barbara Bush to wait thirty minutes before they
appeared for the traditional preinaugural coffee.[1] For thirty anxious
minutes White House stewards fidgeted and Secret Service agents
talked into their sleeves. When the Clintons did arrive at the Blue
Room, they trailed in their wake Harry Thomason and Linda
Bloodworth-Thomason, two Arkansas buddies who had become
Hollywood producers of prime-time entertainment. No president-
elect had ever arrived that late to take coffee with the outgoing
president on Inaugural Day, a ceremony that has come to symbol-
ize the irenic exchange of power that takes place in this great
democracy between two leaders who usually hold each other in
utter contempt. Nor had any of Mr. Clinton's predecessors thought

to bring the Thomasons along—or, for that matter, any other uninvited guests. The patrician Mr. Bush was left in wonderment and the White House staff beset with foreboding at this early spectacle of impudence. As he would so often, Clinton had rendered the first moment of his presidency unsatisfactory, mediocre, and disconcertingly shabby.

I

Bill Clinton keeps a lot of people waiting, and he has for many years. Back in Arkansas he repeatedly kept state troopers and government functionaries cooling their heels. Admiring audiences received the same treatment. Whether on long daises in the air-conditioned auditoriums of Little Rock or on dusty outdoor daises out in Dogpatch, Clinton has been known to keep audiences shifting in their seats for an hour or more while he hummed through his improvised schedule somewhere offstage. On the 1992 campaign trail there were always lapses—some decidedly mysterious—when the candidate simply could not be found. These mysterious disappearances continued even after his election. At his inauguration, some aides were certain their amiable, gregarious, unruly boss would be late. Clinton Time, the press began to call it, for he frequently has stood them up, too. Yet from Clinton's point of view, what is time? When is late, late? Or early, early? Reality is plastic. Truth is elastic. All things can be juggled.

At some dizzying instant during President-elect Clinton's incomparable glorification rites—perhaps when he descended the steps of the Lincoln Memorial, or when he sat on a common bar stool and pontificated to some children gathered at Monticello, or during his characteristically euphuistic acceptance speech—I saw a golden halo encircling the head of the gently smiling leader. It was not unlike the halo that the painter Fra Angelico used to confer on biblical notables back in the fifteenth century, and it remained with the new president for hours.

To this day I still do not know if it was a genuine manifestation of divine approval, or merely another of the technical marvels pulled off by Gary Smith, executive producer of the American Gala, as the rites were called. (They were also called "Reclaiming America" and "An American Reunion" in keeping with the incoming administration's penchant for having it all, not to mention the president's legendary indecisiveness.) Yet I am sure that if Clinton had but looked into one of the myriad of television monitors glowing nearby, he would have seen that halo and been pleased.

During Clinton's glorification rites the country heard some amazing testimonials to his character and to his astounding achievements. I have reviewed past inaugurations—those of Washington, whom some considered kingly, both Roosevelts and John F. Kennedy—and never in the Republic's history has personal glorification been so central a theme. It is difficult at this dismal point in the Clinton saga to recall the great gaudy euphoria of it all, but history has the facts down cold. His inaugural was a bash. Never has high tech been so exuberantly employed for what the Anointed One's Hollywood pals call "special effects." There was computerized lighting. Music seemed to come down from the clouds and up from the sewers. The streets were filled with delirious Clintonites. As I watched the majestic pageantry on my wide-screened television set, along with the halo I saw something else. At one point the president slowly turned toward his beaming co-president several inches below his chin, and there appeared not one, but two haloes radiating from the presidential couple. I expected the famous pair to sprout wings and levitate a few inches from terra firma, but good taste prevailed.

The proceedings were also stratospherically expensive. Never before had so much money been spilled on such ceremony—or, for that matter, so many tears. Yes, tears! Tears from the Clinton family; from the Hollywood stars; from yokels in the crowds; and tears from a mob of Clintonites, who, during the inauguration of earlier presidents, would have been called cronies. During inauguration week the mawkish sentiments expressed in any single twenty-four-hour period surpassed in range and intensity all the heavings witnessed by Oprah Winfrey in a year, perhaps two. In fact, so incontinent were the tears and the drivel that the casual onlooker might conclude that here, bawling on the screen, were life's victims, rather than the celebrants of a historic victory. The blubbering suggested catastrophe rather than Reunion! Reclamation! Gala! At the national convention the Democrats sang the old Rooseveltian hymn, "Happy Days Are Here Again," but one of their salient campaign issues was sadness, and no sadness was too rare or remote for them to exploit.

Perhaps the emotions were justified. Only eleven months before the beginning of the presidential primaries, God alone would have known that a Clinton presidency was in the cards. President Bush's approval rating stood at 91 percent, the highest presidential approval rating ever, higher even than President Harry Truman's immediately after nuking the Japanese.[2] At the time, Governor Bill Clinton was a comparative unknown in an obscure field of Democratic presidential candidates, half of whom were ex-politicians only recently roused from retirement. Some observers were anticipating Republican residency at 1600 Pennsylvania into the next century. Then Bush wilted; so did the other Democratic contenders, and Clinton triumphed. It was the esteemed Shep Gordon, manager of the singer Luther Vandross, who best captured the sudden sense of rebirth. To a reporter for the *New York Times* he said, "The inauguration has mobilized the whole entertainment community. We feel like we can be heard again after all these years."[3]

But the sense of Reunion! Reclamation! Gala! was sensed by eminences even beyond the "whole entertainment community." High culture, too, was liberated. The poet Maya Angelou finally could unburden herself without fear of further repression or possible federal prosecution. She had been tapped to compose a poem for the inauguration. Not since the Kennedys hauled in Robert Frost had such cultural daring been attempted, and a writer for the *Washington Post* "Style" section caught her in the very act of Creation: "In a bare hotel room, where she retreats to write with her Bible, her thesaurus, her bottle of sherry.... " Why this dreadful fake is so fearful I cannot imagine, though she might be fearful that people are actually reading her poetry. Without embarrassment she read from her poem "My Arkansas" to the *Post*'s writer: "Today is yet to come in Arkansas. It writhes. It writhes in awful waves of brooding.... The past is brighter yet."[4] Her life during the hellish Republican Ascendancy was apparently not easy, though through it all Wake Forest University was paying the former prostitute and stripper a six-figure salary for doing almost nothing.

This personal sense that a Democratic presidential victory represents National Salvation is not without precedent. Immediately after the inauguration of John F. Kennedy, another poet, Archibald MacLeish, wrote President Kennedy, telling him that his inaugural ceremony "left me proud and hopeful to be an American—something I have not felt for almost twenty years. I owe you and send you my deepest gratitude."[5] MacLeish was reacting to the authoritarian regime imposed on the nation by President Dwight David Eisenhower, a former general. MacLeish was forced to write from an infamous Caribbean hellhole, St. Lucia. Times had been tough on him, too.

It was, however, somewhat bold of the "whole entertainment community" to journey to Washington in such voluptuous numbers for these revels. Twelve years before, the Reagan inaugural ceremonies had been convicted in the public prints for "Hollywood glitz." Sidney Blumenthal bespoke the derision and contempt when, at the end of the last Reagan administration, he wrote, "The truest event of the Reagan presidency was the first inauguration. It was a celebration of wealth, by the wealthy, for those who wanted to be wealthy.... The line between fantasy and reality was constantly blurred, and the glitz of new money was presented as the heart of tradition." Blumenthal hissed that "tickets to the various inaugural events were priced up to $500. In 1977, at the Carter inaugural, all tickets were democratically priced at $25."[6]

Now, at the Clinton Glorification rites, Hollywoodians were everywhere, and not the sedate old stars that the septuagenarian Reagan brought to Washington. Barbra Streisand, Michael Jackson, Bette Midler, Michael Bolton, Diana Ross, and more, flew in to perform at eleven of the inaugural's glitzy galas.

As for the cost of tickets, a seat at the Clinton inaugurals went for as high as $1,500. Boxes at the Capital Centre gala cost $25,000. There was a plan for a Kennedy Center bash for erstwhile lobbyist Ron Brown, the incoming administration's nominee to head the Commerce Department. "The Friends of Ron Brown" bash was to be paid for by such friends as Sony, PepsiCo, Anheuser-Busch, J. C. Penney, and Textron before ethical jitters aborted the affair. And forget not the attempt by Hillary Clinton's brothers, Hugh and Tony, to put the arm on such corporate giants as Ford, Mobil, and Chevron. If only those corporations would cough up $10,000 apiece, the brothers would provide tables for a dinner dance where there was the promise of a handshake with the president.[7] All this was too much even in these gaudy days. The Ron Brown testimonial was canceled.

"There's so much more excitement about this president in Hollywood than we've seen in decades, maybe since Kennedy," enthused Patricia Medavoy, the amnesiac wife of former Tri-Star Pictures Chairman Mike Medavoy. And then Mrs. Medavoy intoned *affretando*: "His candidacy [Clinton's] was all about change, and he has enormous personal charisma. In some respects he's the ultimate star."[8]

Clinton is America's first president raised since birth in the television age. To an extent surpassing that of any prior generation, politicians of this generation have had to compete with and on the

boob tube. The first obligation of the modern politician is to seduce
the cold, unblinking eye of a television camera. Seduction, of
course, will get a man into scrapes, and a seducer unskilled at getting out of such scrapes will have a short career.

Mrs. Medavoy had taken a proper measurement of the new president. He *was* a star. On inauguration night he smiled to the cameras and shook hands promiscuously and brilliantly. He danced,
went from gala to gala, and danced some more. He sweated,
changed shirts, and sweated some more. As the week's ceremonies
continued, Hillary was often lost from sight, but her aggressively
amiable husband continued to put on a tremendous performance.
His characteristically rumpled suits took on whole mountain ranges
of rumples from shoulder to shoulder, and his baggy pants lost any
semblance of a crease. Even his well-pressed tuxedos soon erupted
in rumples. He stayed up late, got up early, doused his eyes with eye
wash, and frolicked, to the amazement not only of Barbra Streisand
and Bette Midler, but even to the amazement of such wilder stars in
attendance as LL Cool J, Boyz II Men, and En Vogue—all in all a
"younger, hipper, and more liberal" assemblage from the "entertainment community" than Ronald Reagan had ever imagined.[9]
Through all these fetes and carousals, I often wondered what this
émigré from Hope, Arkansas, might be thinking.

No other president in American history survived more scrapes en
route to glory, except, of course, Richard Nixon. Yet Nixon had
been exposed to danger on the national scene for decades in five
presidential campaigns, including his two runs as vice president.
Clinton's many brushes with death took place in but one presidential campaign, the first brush occurring precisely one year and four
days before his inauguration.

II

The peril commenced early in the New Hampshire primary, just

when Clinton was emerging as the bright hope in an otherwise
dismal field of presidential aspirants, half of whom were actually
retired politicians.[10] Then on January 16, 1992, the *Star*, a super-
market tabloid specializing in the sensational and the macabre,
reported that a former state employee down in Arkansas, Larry
Nichols, had alleged in a lawsuit against Clinton that as governor
Clinton had used state funds to pursue five adulterous affairs, one
with Gennifer Flowers, an ex-television reporter and night club
singer. At the time of this scabrous revelation, New Hampshire's
Democrats were giving Clinton a twelve-point lead over Tsongas,
who was campaigning valiantly from nearby Massachusetts, but
who was trailing far behind Clinton and even Jerry Brown nationally. Soon New York's tabloids were booming the story with such
flavorous headlines as the *New York Post*'s "Wild Bill" and the *New
York Daily News*'s "I'm No Gary Hart." The Clinton campaign
smartly filed denials, adding that these charges had been discredited
two years before and that all five women had denied any carnal
knowledge of the handsome young governor.

Insinuated into the struggling campaign's response was the notion
that the press was at fault for paying any attention to such ancient
and tasteless stories. The focus of the story had turned from the
embattled candidate to journalistic ethics and the sordid condition of
the tabloids. Relief flickered within the Clinton camp, but then during a New Hampshire debate, Cokie Roberts, an ABC News and
National Public Radio journalist, innocently brought the issue of
Clinton's libido into the august forums of mainstream journalism by
asking what he thought about the "concern on the part of members
of your party that these allegations of womanizing, that the Republicans will find somebody and that she will come forward late, and
that you would lose the all-important Democrat women's vote."
Clinton pounced on the reference to "Republicans" and slipped
away from the issues of his electability and infidelity to denounce
this "pack of lies" as "an example of what the Republicans have been

trying to do to me for years." Then he unveiled what turned out to be an enduring theme of his campaign, citing the charges as "the kind of rumor-mongering negative and totally irrelevant stuff that they [the Republicans] won on four years ago."[11] For an instant President Bush's 1988 campaign and not Clinton became the focal point of scandal. In the months ahead the embattled candidate would haul up Bush's 1988 campaign for reproach episodically, usually when the issue at hand was not Bush but Clinton's own questionable behavior. For now, at any rate, Clinton had earned a respite.

The scrapes that Clinton suffered throughout 1992 had a ghostly quality, making them all the more alarming to the candidate and to his hard-pressed aides. No sooner would Clinton and his people extinguish one charge than a different aspect of the charge would slink out of some hidden chamber, necessitating yet another declaration of innocence and a whole new set of villains to remonstrate against. On January 23, a week after its first revelations, the *Star* produced more news, an interview with Gennifer Flowers which vividly indicted the highlights of a twelve-year affair with the governor, an association that did not end until 1989. "They Made Love All Over Her Apartment," raved the *Star*, reporting that it had tapes of telephone conversations between the two, one of which was taped just before the candidate's announcement for the presidency. According to the *Star*, Flowers telephoned the governor seeking his advice on how to respond to reporters' mounting inquiries into the couple's intimacies. "If they ever hit you with it," came the avuncular reply, "just say no and go on. There's nothing they can do. I expected them to look into it and come interview you. But if everybody is on record denying it, no problem."[12]

This time Clinton and his aides refrained from blaming "the Republicans" and "the tabloids" and zeroed in on Flowers and the *Star*'s arrangement with her, which included a $150,000 guarantee for her shocking testimony. Clinton's slippage in the New Hampshire polls, however, was now genuinely disturbing. Putting out feel-

ers to the networks, the campaign's tacticians offered an intimate
interview with both Clintons, who now promised to answer questions about their marriage and about Flowers. CBS agreed to a special post-Super Bowl edition of *60 Minutes*. The taping occasioned
yet another painful scrape, poignant but mercifully unreported.
According to Clinton campaign aides, while the Clintons were sitting on the CBS set minutes before the interview, Governor Clinton
was approached by Don Hewitt, the *60 Minutes* producer who had
also produced the first 1960 debate between Senator John F.
Kennedy and Vice President Richard Nixon. Hewitt knelt beside
Clinton and whispered, "When he asks you if you committed adultery, say yes. It will be great television. I know. I know television.
The last time I did something like this, Bill, it was the Kennedy-
Nixon debates, and it produced a president. This will produce a
president, too."[13]

On January 26, after Super Bowl XXVI, 34 million viewers
watched Clinton, shaking off Hewitt's pitiless counsel and denying
any affair with Flowers. It was a brazen lie, as many Arkansans
knew, and a growing number of journalists must have suspected. Yet
Clinton betrayed no hint of the risk he had just taken. Nixon's eyes
would have betrayed him. Other politicos would have broken into a
sweat, but not the smartest young man ever to leave Hot Springs,
Arkansas. Bill Clinton lies like a man detached from conscience, or
perhaps born without one. The interview continued. The Clintons
admitted that Bill had committed "wrongdoing," the specifics of
which an unmindful interviewer failed to probe. Then the embattled couple affirmed their connubial happiness.

The day after the *60 Minutes* interview Flowers convened a press
conference at New York's Waldorf-Astoria. Fortunately for the campaign, she came off as an unlikable tart. The press's questions moved
from the amusing to the riotous when a puckish journalist inquired,
"Did the governor use a condom?" That ended the interview, but
not Clinton's anguish. Flowers had detailed a long-standing love

affair with the governor. Worse, a taped telephone conversation which she made public exposed him to peril from a new source, New York Governor Mario Cuomo, at the time a potential challenger.

In the taped conversation Clinton tells Flowers that Cuomo is a "mean son-of-a-bitch." Responding to Flowers's suggestion that Cuomo had "Mafia" ties, Clinton maligns an entire ethnic group by saying, "Well, he acts like one."[14] Cuomo's reaction was not magnanimous, and soon Clinton was pressed into explaining his true intent and offering a heartfelt apology to Italian-Americans. Again the candidate sought salvation in doubletalk. "If the remarks on the tape left anyone with the impression that I was disrespectful to either Governor Cuomo or Italian-Americans, then I deeply regret it." And, he skated on, "At the time that conversation was held, there had been some political give-and-take between myself and the governor, and I meant simply to imply that Governor Cuomo is a tough and worthy opponent."[15]

The public seemed to be out of sympathy with all this scavenging through the private life of a public figure. Moreover, Flowers had not come across as a wronged woman but as venal and vulgar. She was to make one more attempt on her ex-paramour's political life, just a few days before the election. Yet again she misfired, and this time her tawdriness made Clinton's licentiousness a nonissue for over a year. She granted an interview to *Penthouse* wherein she described her lover in terms that had never before been associated with any American president or even a vice president, putting Clinton and his Arkansas circle in a historic category familiar to students of Renaissance Italy and decadent Rome, but unknown to the American presidency even in Harding's lascivious days. In a pictorial spread featuring her flesh and lingerie she divulged such observations as, "He ate pussy like a champ."[16] Even in the heat of Campaign '92, that was unreportable. The story died.

The protean issue of marital infidelity injured Clinton's campaign, but he is a man of enormous persistence, and he mounted a spirited counterattack. He turned to the lifeless condition of the economy. In a state where the economy had been queasy for years he promised "change," a word that was to become his mantra. He seemed to recognize that in a country abundant with optimists the promise of "change" always suggests an even better tomorrow. The ever-hopeful lit up.

Unfortunately, just as his counterattack began, this child of the 1960s suffered what was to be the most costly and enduring scrape of his campaign. The hell began on February 6 when the *Wall Street Journal* published its report that Colonel Eugene Holmes, a retired army ROTC recruiter at the University of Arkansas, was complaining that in the summer of 1969 Clinton deceived him. Apparently Clinton promised to enter the University of Arkansas Law School, enrolling in the university's ROTC program, if Colonel Holmes would extend his draft deferment. Holmes reported to the *Journal* that subsequently Clinton "was able to manipulate things so that he didn't have to go in."[17] As with questions about his marriage, questions about his draft record had haunted Clinton's political life. But in past campaigns Holmes and other draft officials let his alibis stand. Now they were saying that he had gone to uncommon lengths to avoid military service. The candidate denied their charges. He insisted that he had gained Holmes's deferment in good faith. And he added that he had never received a draft induction notice. That last statement was to bring him grief later during the New York primary, but it was typical of the predicaments that Clinton was to find himself in even as president. Clinton's entire response to Holmes was false, but the reference to his induction notice was a bold-faced and, more important, gratuitous lie. Clinton is a child of the late 1960s, and this particular lie is characteristic of his cohorts in protest. Late 1960s student protesters were always eager to show their cleverness, a compulsion that has brought Clinton to the edge of self-destruction many times. He lies when he does not have to lie, and often he tells an extravagant lie when a modest fib would suffice.

For now his immediate task was to dispatch Holmes's charge that he had hoodwinked the colonel. Clinton responded by claiming that he passed up enrollment in the University of Arkansas Law School to "put myself into the draft when I thought it was a one hundred percent certainty that I would be called." Before an unruly crowd of journalists in the lobby of the Sheraton-Tara in Nashua, New Hampshire, he explained that "I just didn't feel right about having a four-year deferment."[18] His campaign released a chronology of his supposedly exculpatory dealings with the draft board.

Clinton was safe once again but only for a few days. Then the reporters were at his throat, forcing him to replace this temporary truth with yet another. What riled the reporters this time was the release of Clinton's famous December 1969 letter to Colonel Holmes. It seems that a hotel clerk in Myrtle Beach, South Carolina, stole a copy of the letter from another former Arkansas ROTC official, Lieutenant Colonel Clinton Jones, who had asked him to photocopy it. The clerk sent the letter to a friend in Washington. The friend then sent one copy to the Clinton campaign and another to an Iran-Contra schemer, former Air Force Major General Richard Secord. Secord sent it to ABC's *Nightline*.[19] In this extraordinary letter Clinton displayed all the 1960s student protesters' weakness for pontification, self-righteousness, and narcissism. He thanked Colonel Holmes for "saving me from the draft." He explained in vintage late-1960s grandiosity why he broke his promise to enter the Arkansas ROTC program. He boasted of his involvement in anti-war activities in Washington and in England. Then he reminded this World War II veteran, a survivor of the Bataan Death March who had languished in Japanese POW camps for over three years, of the student protesters' "loathing the military."[20]

The letter's contents stunned Clinton's aides. Theretofore he had denied active involvement in the antiwar movement. Never had he admitted to avoiding the draft. In this bleakest of hours it was his wife who came up with the requisite temporary truth to quell the uproar. She instructed the campaign to point to the embarrassing letter as proof that her husband had indeed voluntarily made himself available for the draft. What the campaign did not say, and what no one at the time noticed, was that Clinton had neglected to inform the draft board or Colonel Holmes that he was making himself available for the draft. On this he seems to have kept quiet until he had received a high draft lottery number that made it virtually impossible for him to be drafted. The confused reporters settled down, and now both Clintons began campaigning through New Hampshire, at times hoofing it from door to door. They carried with them a videotape of Clinton holding forth on the issues. A thousand Arkansan volunteers swarmed into New Hampshire, supplied with the same videotape. It was another of the campaign's death-defying feats. To the charges raised against him, Boy Clinton alternately roared, "I'm going to fight like hell," and whined, "All I've been asked about by the press are a woman I didn't sleep with and a draft I didn't dodge."[21] He blamed his problems on the "Republican attack machine" and "the tabloids."

In New Hampshire Clinton finished second behind Tsongas. Accepting this defeat jubilantly, he referred to himself as the "Comeback Kid" and was able to sell the implication though he had repossessed only a few percentage points after glissading twenty points following the publication of the *Wall Street Journal*'s revelations. His actual achievement was to finish in front of two undeclared candidates, Ralph Nader and Mario Cuomo; two corpses, Bob Kerrey and Tom Harkin; and the quixotic Jerry Brown, who would campaign without benefit of much staff or money right onto the convention floor. Perhaps even now, somewhere in America's outback, the Mullah from the Golden State is still campaigning for the 1992 presidential nomination, attired in his trademark soiled trench coat, scowling about other people's low ethics, and accompanied by his mysterious campaign advisor, Jacques Barzhagi, a Frenchman encased in black leather clothing and not given to small talk.

Nationally, Clinton remained comfortably ahead of this undistinguished field. His organization had the money, and it was now too late for any of the more seasoned Democrats to mount a campaign, though the original obstacle that had dissuaded them from running—namely, President Bush's soaring approval rating—had turned to dust. Soon, fortified by a "bridge loan" from Arkansas's Worthen Bank and attendant federal matching grants, Clinton was corralling delegates in the border states, the South, and the West, bankrupting his opponents, and leaving only the defiant Brown taunting him as the "scandal-a-week candidate."[22] Brown was hardly exaggerating; the scrapes continued.

Reflecting back on the future president's many brushes with death, one might well ask why only he suffered so many scandals involving deceit, womanizing, petty corruption, and blatant lies. The scandals trailed back through all the years of his public life and into his earliest college days. They seemed to be immortal. No pundit or journalist on the campaign trail seemed to notice how different candidate Clinton was from his opponents, and the press has been slow to notice how different Clinton's presidency has been from past presidencies. Many of the scandals that surfaced during the campaign reemerged months later, along with new scandals, deceits, and mishaps that were downright grotesque. Surely some of Clinton's scrapes were the consequence of the singular political mores of Arkansas. Others, however, were the consequence of a very odd set of traits developed in the 1960s' protest movement. In due course you will see them stuffed and mounted and put on display for the edification of mankind.

For now let us stick to the campaign. Clinton's scrapes followed him right into the July Democratic National Convention. In March he was harried not only by questions of draft evasion and philandering but also by questions regarding possible graft. Reports appeared in the *New York Times* suggesting that during the 1980s the Clintons had engaged in sharp practices with James B. McDougal, a developer and majority owner of Madison Guaranty Savings and Loan, by 1992 defunct and in the hands of U.S. Treasury undertakers. Then there were reports suggesting that Governor Clinton had allowed fecal coliform bacteria to pollute Arkansas streams rather than properly police such giant chicken producers as Tyson Foods, owned by a longtime political supporter, Don Tyson. Equally embarrassing were the news reports of unwholesome contacts between Hillary Clinton's Rose Law Firm and various agencies regulated by her husband's government.

Mrs. Clinton was drawn deeper into these revelations when, during the New York primary, she attempted to deflect Brown's charge that Governor Clinton had been "funneling money to his wife's law firm." Clinton's response was petulance and threats. Hillary's was an insulting pout: "I suppose I could have stayed home, baked cookies and had teas. But what I decided was to fulfill my profession...."[23] The country's cookie bakers and tea servers assailed her for again depreciating traditional women. Less noted was the sanctimonious blush: "to fulfill my profession"—as though a member of the governor's family accepting a retainer from a government-regulated concern were an act of noblesse oblige. The grandiosity and self-righteousness of the 1960s protest era still throbbed in Hillary's bosom.

Despite the enlarging controversies around Hillary, it was her husband's errancies that remained the major source of the campaign's scrapes. He had to apologize for playing golf at the Little Rock Country Club, after the press reported its all-white membership. The *Los Angeles Times* reported that in 1985 Governor Clinton directed a questionable bond deal to Dan R. Lasater, a political supporter who later did time on cocaine charges. In a *Vanity Fair* interview Hillary suggested that the press was remiss for not investigating charges that President Bush had a mistress. Then columnists Rowland Evans and Robert Novak revealed how Clinton had dissembled in claiming to have supported the 1991 Gulf War and in topping his con job with another brazen lie.

As Evans and Novak pieced it together, this deception had begun about the time Clinton declared his candidacy in the fall of 1991. At a September 16 Godfrey Sperling breakfast in Washington, Clinton described himself as a supporter of the war. That stand helped him raise money from pro-Israel contributors. No one thought to question his claim until the Evans and Novak column the following March, in which they reported on an Associated Press (AP) story published in Arkansas two days after Congress authorized hostilities against Iraq. According to the AP, Governor Clinton then said, "I would agree with the arguments of the people in the minority on the resolution that we should give sanctions more time and maybe even explore a full embargo... before we go to war." Responding to Evans and Novak, Clinton's campaign claimed the AP story was "inaccurate." For the true Clinton position on the Gulf War, a campaign spokesman suggested that readers turn to the January 15, 1991, *Arkansas Democrat-Gazette*. Unfortunately Evans and Novak did; there they found Clinton saying that he "agreed" with his state's two Democratic senators. Both had voted against the war! So Clinton had actually lied when he said he was for the war. No, he insisted, reaching for the doubletalk that was to become his rhetorical Vaseline, "I guess I would have voted with the majority if it was a close vote, but I agree with the arguments the minority made."[24]

As he moved on to late May and the New York primary, Clinton found himself in a new scrape when WCBS's political reporter, Marcia Kramer, questioned him with sufficient specificity to elicit an admission that he had avoided making for years. "When I was in England, I experimented with marijuana a time or two and I didn't like it. I didn't inhale, and I never tried it again." Reporters asked him why he had not made this admission on earlier occasions when he had been asked about drug use. He replied that he had never been asked so specifically. But he had! In 1990 an *Arkansas Democrat-Gazette* reporter asked him if he had used marijuana "as a col-

lege student," and he answered "no."[25] Again, the candidate had
lied recklessly, averring a big lie when a little one might have served
his purpose.

In May the question of Clinton's draft record reemerged. Cliff
Jackson, a fellow Arkansan who had been at Oxford with Clinton,
released a letter he had received from Clinton in 1969. Since their
Oxford days Jackson had developed an abiding hostility toward
Clinton, but in the late 1960s they must have been on friendly
terms, for Clinton then wrote Jackson seeking assistance in avoiding the draft. Contrary to Clinton's February denial, the letter
revealed that he had, indeed, received a draft induction notice in
1969. Obviously, the candidate had been an energetic draft dodger.
Fortunately, by the New York primary, no serious challenger
remained on the field, and the electorate was either bored or thoroughly confused by his lies. Many voters had no idea what an induction notice was. Others were trying to weigh Clinton's conflicting
explanations. Clinton said he, too, was confused. Was an induction
notice a call for a physical or what?

Ultimately his campaign acknowledged that he had in fact
received an induction notice while at Oxford in the spring of 1969,
before his shenanigans with Colonel Holmes commenced. What
makes all his conjurings with draft boards, with ROTC programs,
with universities, and with influential Arkansans slightly idiotic is
that, given Clinton's very serious allergy condition, it is almost
inconceivable that he would have passed an army physical.[26] The
will to scheme overcame the instinct for self-preservation. Clinton
is not courageous, but he seems always to have been a daredevil.

Irony is one of Clinton's constant companions. Having begun his
campaign as the candidate of youth, optimism, and change, he left
New Hampshire as the candidate of gloom and grievance. Battered
by suggestions of scandal, he portrayed himself as the sad victim of
Republican conspirators and low-down journalists. Perhaps reflecting his own mood, Clinton's campaign began focusing on the pes-

simistic, the fearful, the unemployed, and the angry, and he reverted to the usual class-warfare rhetoric long favored by Democrats of a demagogic disposition. Having begun his campaign emulating the glamour and dash of JFK, Clinton found himself adopting the oratory of a grim Bobby Kennedy haunting the hovels of the Mississippi Delta. The voter being cultivated by Clinton through the spring was that ever-reliable staple of the modern Democratic party, the American with a grievance. Clinton's pollster, Stan Greenberg, provided the game plan when he wrote, "The key to Democratic success is becoming a middle-class centered, bottom-up coalition— a mass party, encompassing the needs of the have-nots and working Americans." With Greenberg as his guide Clinton returned to class war, encouraged resentment, and mocked Tsongas for preaching a "refined version of 1980-style trickle-down economics." Bitterly he mocked Tsongas: "Let's cut capital-gains tax across the board; let's make corporate executives less accountable and they'll do what's best for us, create jobs. Don't worry about economic fairness; we'll deal with that later. That candidate is not me."[27]

The middle class that Clinton and Greenberg envisaged was a middle class of losers and victims. In *The Liberal Mind*, a historic study of modern liberalism and that which motivates it, Kenneth Minogue depicts liberalism as St. George. "St. George," Minogue tells us, "needed his dragons. He could live only by fighting for causes—the people, the poor, the exploited, the colonially oppressed, the underprivileged and the underdeveloped. As an ageing warrior, he grew breathless in his pursuit of smaller and smaller dragons—for with the spread of liberation, tolerance, equality, and prosperity, the big dragons were now harder to come by and they were increasingly fanciful."[28] Clinton in 1992 was making the most prosperous middle class in the world out to be a casualty of a decade-long recession and was referring to 1991's shallow recession as a "Depression." As he approached the Democratic convention his oratory darkened. He murmured about "the people who have lost faith" in our country, "the people who have lost faith" in material improvement, "the quiet, troubled voices of forgotten middle-class Americans," the lost souls "in your home towns and mine." And he inveighed against "people who have power," who make "backroom deals," and worse, the "people who keep them there."[29]

III

The 1992 Democratic National Convention in New York City was the best organized in over two decades. Those Democratic youths who in 1968 protested the Democratic Convention from the streets were now middle-aged and all over the convention floor. Still, the Democratic insiders who choreographed the convention were apprehensive. Polls showed Clinton running behind both George Bush and Ross Perot. A *Washington Post*/ABC poll showed Bush with 42 percent, Perot with 30 percent, and Clinton with 20 percent. Even his 20 percent was fragile, for his negative ratings were high. As for the nominee himself, he arrived at the convention in the dumps. His many buffetings along the campaign trail had taken a toll, as had that dolorous game plan prepared for him by his strategist Greenberg. In fact, despite his many primary victories, no presidential nominee of either political party had ever arrived at a national convention suffering such a case of the blues, not even George McGovern or the woeful Coolidge. Senator Al Gore, Clinton's hand-picked running mate, made it clear in his acceptance speech that he, too, was rather sad.

All this sadness is understandable. With so few real dragons left to slay, by 1992 these misery mongers had developed a very sensitive hot button for moral indignation. It is a heavy burden to bear. One can hardly be in buoyant spirits after a day of empathizing with the down and out.

The Germans have a word for people who take pleasure in the troubles of others: *schadenfreude*. For those American liberals who cultivate misfortune and sadness, who win elections by building coalitions from "the quiet, troubled voices of the forgotten middle class," who earn livelihoods by exploiting grief, we Americans should coin a word. How about *schadenfarming*? With plow and oxen the Clintons and Gores of this world walk the furrows of human suffering. For whole seasons these *schadenfarmers* water and fertilize every gripe, calamity, and paranoia. Ultimately they harvest misery and take it to market, where there are many buyers. Senator Gore is a veteran *schadenfarmer*, as is Boy Clinton, and let us not forget Zell Miller. He was governor of Georgia during the 1992 Democratic Convention. He was also one of the convention's three keynote speakers. This trinity of orators poured a pall over the assembled Democrats, but Miller's speech was best. It evoked more heartfelt grief than the death of Little Nell.

Miller railed at the Republicans for their "cynicism and skepticism." He bawled that Ronald Reagan and George Bush had "robbed us of our hope." Then he wandered deeper into despond as he hymned a young messiah's up-from-the-log-cabin struggle: "I'm for Bill Clinton because he is a Democrat who does not have to read a book or be briefed about the struggles of single-parent families, or what it means to work hard for everything he's ever received in life. There was no silver spoon in sight when he was born three months after his father died. No one ever gave Bill Clinton a free ride as he worked his way through college and law school"[30]—though it did help to be on scholarship. (And that swell convertible Bill Clinton used during his early political campaigns at Georgetown—who paid for it?)[31]

This was just the beginning of several nights of Democratic grief. On came the women disillusioned by the Republican party's stand on abortion. Then came the unfortunate victims of AIDS. According to each evening's misery merchants, the environment had become a deadly pestilence. The economy was in ruins. Nothing outside this great convention hall was satisfactory. And it could all

get worse if the Republicans remained in power. On the third day
of the convention Mario Cuomo nominated Clinton in a speech of
staccato whoops and sobs. Governor Cuomo also included many
uncomplimentary remarks about the Loyal Opposition. The vote
was 3,372 delegates for Clinton, 596 for Brown, 209 for Tsongas,
and 74 on a higher philosophical plane. Then the nominee broke
another of the party's traditions. (Since the time of Franklin Roosevelt, all Democratic nominees have been assiduous tradition
breakers, leaving few traditions left to break. The years ahead could
prove tough.) Rather than delay entering the convention hall until
the following night, as custom would have it, Clinton entered the
hall immediately, from a party that happened to be a mere block
away, a block happily lined with television cameras.[32]

The next night Clinton duly delivered an acceptance plaint that
proved to be the convention's saddest, a speech that journalists Germond and Witcover esteemed "longer than might have been prudent,"[33] though tremendously admirable. Network television
cameras caught children in the audience fast asleep and adults nod-
ding off or repairing to the restrooms with unnatural frequency.
Nonetheless, for fifty-four minutes the Democratic challenger
expatiated upon "... my hope for the future, my faith in the American people, and my vision of the kind of country we can build,
together.... I have news for the forces of greed and the defenders of
the status quo: your time has come... and gone.... Tens of millions
more work harder for less pay... putting power back in your
hands... I've shared these thoughts with people all across America.... And don't let anyone ever tell you you can't become whatever
you want to be.... Those who play by the rules and keep the faith
have gotten the shaft. And those who cut corners and cut deals have
been rewarded.... Housing, health care and education are going
through the roof... falling into poverty.... Our country is falling
behind... thirteenth in the world.... He has raised taxes on the people who drive pick-up trucks... lowered taxes on people who ride in

limousines.... They are the work of my life.... Trickle down economics... failed... into the twenty-first century.... Sons and daughters of stenographers and steelworkers.... Those making over $200,000.... It's time to heal our country.... Them, the minorities. Them, the liberals. Them, them, them.... The incumbent president... took the richest country in the world and brought it down.... We are unstoppable.... Seize this moment.... My life.... A blessing my own father never knew... Hold my child in my arms.... Our cause... a hopeful future.... Our cause... God-given abilities.... Our cause... never struggling alone.... Our cause... moving ahead.... Our cause... New Covenant.... I end tonight where it all began for me: I still believe in a place called Hope."[34]

The speech was a mad jumble of cant and poesy, of inaccurate ideas and real problems, of lofty promise and faulty analysis. In other words, it could have been written by almost any old Democratic demagogue and delivered by almost any trained parrot, but it did include one especially lachrymose riff that revealed something fundamental about Boy Clinton. He abruptly swung into an autobiographical largo: "my mother.... So I lived with my grandparents.... I can still see her through the eyes of a three-year-old.... My mother taught me.... steady through tragedy after tragedy... through tough times... at a time when it wasn't very easy to be a working mother.... I watched her fight off breast cancer.... Always, always she taught me to fight."[35] Even into middle-age, Bill had remained a mama's boy. He saw the world on that historic night, as he said, "through the eyes of a three-year-old." And then there was grandpa: "He ran a country store in our little town of Hope.... No food stamps back then... whether white or black... he'd give them food anyway.... I learned from him to look up to people other folks looked down on....

"Grandfather had a grade-school education.... He taught me more... than all my professors at Georgetown... than all the philosophers at Oxford... than all the jurists at Yale Law School."[36] In his youth it appears that Billy Clinton never saw sunshine or happiness, and then he started in on Hillary, on her "teachings."

Egad! No misery was left unexploited. Tragedy after tragedy! Tough times! Grandpa, the barefoot sage! Then Hillary's teachings! Did I hear him close this gawdawful melodrama with the ensuing finale or did I make it up? *"Listen folks. The winters were cold. The summers were hot. We all had bad breath, no money for mouthwash.... There was body odor. Grandpa had plantar's warts and bunions. Mother got yeast infection. For six months ah lived in a garbage can. But ah never et the garbage. Grandpa wouldn't let me. He distributed it to the really poor, to people who couldn't afford the rent on the garbage can. There were people in Hope who considered my garbage can a mansion. Of course, ah'm not really sure ah had legal title to that garbage. Ah've asked Hillary about it. Some day we plan to do a scholarly paper on who owned the garbage and on its nutritional value. At Yale we called this sort of paper a cross-disciplinary study."*

What an acceptance speech! Dirt poor and miserable, *yet* exalted among the elites of Georgetown! Oxford! And Yale! Always just folks, *yet* the tone of moral and intellectual superiority is rampant. He is the victim of negative campaigning, *yet* he reviles the character and motives of his opponents. He raises his own character and personal experiences atop Corinthian columns, *yet* scolds those who make character an issue. It was a speech destined to amaze the unamazeable.

Earlier Senator Gore had warmed up the crowd. He sounded the alarm for the fate of the nation. He rebuked the rich and the powerful. He blubbered about the poverty of the middle class, and he lamented that the sitting administration had "ignored the suffering of those who are victims, of AIDS, of crime, of poverty, of hatred and harassment." He accused them of having "nourished and appeased tyrannies." There was also this historic line, averring that "the task of saving the earth's environment must and will become the central organizing principle of the post-Cold War world."[37] Does anyone with any knowledge of history or society believe that?

And there was his dubious attempt to portray his prosperous family from Tennessee's high society as noble dirt farmers. Then he made one of *schadenfarming*'s most colossal and tasteless efforts, asserting that "I know what it's like to lose a sister and almost lose a son." About his sister's loss we were told nothing, but about his son's accident we were given gruesome details. A fair amount of mediocrities have preceded him to the vice presidency, a fair amount of cads and dopes, but not one has been so bereft of dignity as to exploit a son's suffering. Still, the sheer ignominy of the revelation swept the audience; Gore, too, had a heart!

The day after Clinton's nomination, dour portents were again shadowing him. Gory as his acceptance speech had been, it was obliterated by the morning's headlines announcing H. Ross Perot's unanticipated retirement from the presidential race. As a news story Clinton's arrival had been swamped by a freak's departure. Then a miracle took place that has yet to be explained. National polls suddenly showed that the Clinton-Gore ticket was receiving the largest postconvention boost in half a century, a twenty-four-point turbo-boost that put it well ahead of Bush-Quayle. Off Clinton and Gore went on a campaign bus tour from New York to St. Louis. It was a stupendous success. And as the two joyous candidates rode through towns large and small, shouting their slogans and delivering their promises of economic rebirth and "change," they were "experiencing a bonding that became obvious to their fellow bus travelers." The words are those of Germond and Witcover, but the whole press corps shared their enthusiasm. "After the longest of days, they would sit on the bus talking, talking, talking," observed Germond and Witcover benignly, "while the rest of the entourage groaned for them to get off and go to bed."[38] Talking and talking. For now they talked about a middle-class tax break, building "infrastructure," reforming welfare, revitalizing education, health-care reform, and other grand policy shifts. Their anthem became Fleetwood Mac's "Don't Stop Thinking About Tomorrow." They played it on the bus, at rallies, day and night. The song's lyrics might hail the future, but it was a song out of the past. So was Clinton. In the months ahead, in debates, in rhetoric, in policies propounded, in presidential appointments made, Boy Clinton was to reveal himself as quick–witted, generally amiable, but dated. He had a good brain. It was not, however, his brain that governed his politics. It was his heart, and that heart was shaped decades back in the late 1960s.

CHAPTER TWO

FROM STUDENT POLITICIAN TO COAT AND TIE RADICAL

B OY CLINTON IS a charming vagabond from a spoiled sub-group of 1960s youth who, since college days, has been given to discarding society's conventions and—as the phrase has it—doing its own thing. Here is the cultural semen that accounts for President Bill Clinton; its egg is Arkansas. With an understanding of Clinton's classmates and Arkansas's politics, one is well on one's way to understanding the singularity of the Clinton administration and the terminal condition it found itself in after but two years.

But Clinton was not a normal 1960s undergraduate. He was a student government goody-goody, and at an epochal moment in American history, the late 1960s. As all who have researched the subject have discovered, the student government goody-goody is in every era a sycophant. Generally of prosaic mind, the student government goody-goody rushes through four years of college, living a delusory life usually in frequent and unwholesome proximity to precisely those professors judged by serious scholars and discerning students to be decidedly flaky. Always, the student government goody-goody imagines himself cast in the role of a famous leader.

In the early 1960s it might have been Winston S. Churchill or John F. Kennedy, whom the goody-goody glimpsed in the mirror whilst brushing perfectly aligned and gleaming teeth. By the late 1960s, the list of historic exemplars would be expanded to include such giants as Gloria Steinem and possibly Che Guevara, the latter being a revolutionary communist executed by Bolivian authorities and not to be confused with the Spanish vegetable of the same name.

At any rate, during the years most crucial to a young person's intellectual development, our forty-second president's experiences were almost wholly vicarious. The goody-goody campus pol may look a professor or a fellow student directly in the eye, but it is never clear what he imagines himself to be seeing. Quite possibly from his delusional world he sees standing in front of him Adolph Hitler, Eleanor Roosevelt, Henry V, Charlemagne, or a cow.

Many of Clinton's most historic bungles become instantly comprehensible and occasionally even poignant if we bear in mind that Clinton is living in a fantasy begun long ago. While most of his fellow students were reading Plato or shooting baskets or chewing gum, young Clinton was preparing to take an oath of office that was not really an oath of office. Or perhaps he was delivering an address to a student senate that was not really a senate. Or was he organizing a political party that was *only* a party? I am sure that there were times when he summoned the masses and no one showed up aside from the bored and the deranged.

As a college student in the 1960s, I saw many delusional young men like this among my peers. My memory is vivid. The campus politico was a hoot, frequently very personable but really a bit daft, and Clinton would be his campus's most energetic. At Georgetown he was freshman class president, 1964-1965; Sophomore class president, 1965-1966; and Senior class president, 1967-1968. On and on his campaigns went until 1993, when he became president of the United States. Obviously the democratic process has some problems, yet a campus pol can escape reality only so long; Clinton's last elective office brought with it the burden of real political power, inescapable political responsibility, and eventually the unwanted scrutiny of Robert Fiske and Kenneth Starr.[1]

During the campus upheavals of the 1960s many student government goody-goodies were transformed from the harmless joke figures of the early 1960s into real pests. Eventually they were almost as instrumental in the destruction of what had been centers of learning as their radical professors and craven administrators. Through much of the 1960s, first as an undergraduate and then as a graduate student, I witnessed the whole catastrophe. At first, as a varsity athlete, I snickered at the phony competitions of the student government campaigners. Later, in 1967 and 1968, when I was working for my doctorate in history, I became active in the growing movement of student conservatives who opposed Clinton and his fellow campus Machiavells. The radicalization that these student government apple-polishers underwent was another of their delusions, another puppy-like attempt to please the real radicals who seduced them effortlessly.

The student government goody-goodies of the early 1960s had been the despair of progressive sociologists who since the 1950s had been railing against American "conformity." They had a point. Our campus Machiavells were mostly ambitious grade grabbers with no deep appreciation for anything they studied. They possessed facile minds. They had neither the will nor the capacity for serious thought. They were pert and boring.

As I remember it, they dressed according to the fashion of the times in blue: blue slacks, blue button-down shirts, and, in springtime, blue Windbreakers. They wore penny loafers with blue socks, and they had haircuts. They were almost always young men, feminism having yet to make its mark. The fatuousness at the base of their conformity quite understandably troubled progressives. Then, between 1965 and 1967 the student government goody-goodies began exchanging their blue slacks for bell-bottoms, work shirts, and "love" beads. Clinton made

this wardrobe change late; London's *Sunday Times* sets the date as
1969, which was *the* critical year in the student revolution (the revolution then being clearly the wrong side and already widely approved by
grown-ups) for goody-goodies to go Marxist-Leninist-Conformist.[2]
At any rate, once the campus goody-goodies had tiptoed into radicalism, the progressives's critique of conformity shut down. Once students began conforming to a New Orthodoxy, progressive critics
appraised conformity differently, as Youthful Idealism and, incidentally, the beginning of Political Correctness.

The New Orthodoxy that was making its way from the outer
fringes of intellectual life into the heart of student government was
an orthodoxy of radicalism and humbug, drawing, in the main, from
ideas excogitated by German and French writers of the 1930s. Most
of these writers were charlatans who had woven calico philosophies
with theories of "authenticity," "alienation," "false consciousness,"
urban woe, and rural bliss. When they were not completely incom-
prehensible, their cerebrations vulgarized Freud and Marx. Their
ideas always had to be discussed in jargon-laden language capable of
inducing sleep in normal readers and nausea in competent writers.
Unfortunately, this New Orthodoxy survived in one form or
another on college campuses for decades, eventually even elbowing
aside the humanities and replacing them with the straitjacket of
Political Correctness. By the 1970s this New Orthodoxy was even
seeping into society at large in the form of those quack therapies
and personal help strategies that make certain Americans a laughing
stock: the personal growth guru, consciousness-raising propagandists, members of the chicken pox support group, the bald peoples'
rights movement, multiculturalists.

Clinton eventually brought it all into his government at the
highest level. Among his earliest acts as president-elect was a Little
Rock "Economic Summit" where serious economists sat alongside
Indian chiefs, Arkansas cronies, and New Age charlatans. Presently
he was inviting his cabinet appointees to Camp David to engage in

personal growth therapy with "facilitators." Mrs. Clinton, another of his generational cohorts, began boasting of her admiration for Michael Lerner, the pseudo philosopher. Lerner was the editor of *Tikkun*, an irregularly published magazine incorporating ground-up Marx, finely-minced Freud, and herbs and spices from every bunko artist since the great days of Robespierre.

Do not be surprised if some day historians report that, during breaks in the proceedings of Clinton's National Security Council, "therapeutic massages" were administered. The origins of all this hocus-pocus reach back to the campus ferment of the late 1960s and even beyond, to the 1930s and some hopelessly confused Kraut prof, cerebrating in the shadow of Hitler at the University of Berlin over the possibilities of extracting humane values from one's own waste products.

In social science courses students of Clinton's type went agog over such concepts as "alienation," "anomie," and similar rationales of the malcontent. Young profs, too, were frequently enraptured by the passing enthusiasms of the New Orthodoxy. They urged their students to challenge "the system" and "the war" and people "over thirty," though to challenge the New Orthodoxy was as unthinkable as entering a lecture hall in blackface or a three-piece suit. Classrooms became bull sessions on such *outre* topics as Yoga, eastern mysticism, and hallucinatory drugs (though drugs prescribed by certified physicians for actual illnesses were increasingly frowned upon in deference to herbs and tree barks). Professors led seminars on what to do about the university's ban on shoelessness and shirtlessness. Seminars on breast-feeding in the main library would not be unthinkable, and surely there was discussion, at least on California campuses, of those positions of the Kama Sutra least likely to occasion lower back pain and a trip to the chiropractor. Twenty-five years later many of the juvenile ideas and sentiments that had reverberated through late 1960s classroom bull sessions were reverberating within the heart of the president of the United States. Sometimes they slipped into the endless White House meetings recognized by the press as not unlike bull sessions.

The majority of students even in the late 1960s was not in sympathy with this new species of conformity. Instead they stuck to the original variety, anchored as it was to the American Dream and a proper job. Studies now indicate that the majority of students from this era of youthful idealism eschewed drugs and even sexual liberation.[3] In fact, even the Vietnam War had the support of the era's youth, as was clear in the 1972 presidential campaign, where President Richard Nixon shanghaied the majority of the youth vote. Clinton's cohorts worked for McGovern. Clinton helped run McGovern's campaign in Texas, as did the future Mrs. Clinton. It was in that campaign that he met Betsey Wright, who was to become one of his political operatives in Arkansas brief years down the pike.

The progressive profs doted on Clinton and his peers. No longer did they bawl for diversity. Now that the campuses' mix of radicals and moderates provided diversity, the progressive profs simply ignored the moderates, acting as though all students shared the sentiments of the vociferous radicals. The progressives put all their mythopoeic powers into creating legends about the conforming radicals' genius, their idealism, and their vast potential for saving America from itself. The youthful idealists too had a mythopoeic knack and a megalomania that inspired them to advance the myth that all late 1960s youth shared their urge to revolt. Together the profs and the idealistic radicals simply faked the present and assumed the future to be theirs.

The Reagan years must have been inscrutable to them, for, as the world was to discover in Clinton's first calamitous year in the White House, their intellectual development never progressed much past 1968. It is as though their brains had been hard-wired and could apprehend nothing new. When the Clintons took residence at the White House, 1968's enthusiasms were dusted off and dressed up as policy. To be sure, the Clintons had adjusted their rhetoric to the

1990s, but their goal seemed to be about the same as in 1968—to transform America into the Sweden of Gunnar Myrdal, but with bureaucrats who would be more laid back.

There are social scientists and psychiatrists who have come to the conclusion that the 1960s radicals' peculiar inability to revise their ideas in light of experience stems from their youthful indulgence in drugs. Some medicated themselves with drugs on a daily basis. Others doped up only at parties. On weekends a certain kind of 1960s college student would go bohemian, turning some off-campus apartment into a Berlin or a Paris of the imagination. All-nighters would be convened to guitar accompaniment. The weed would be passed, jugs of Rhine wine consumed, and e.e. cummings might be scrawled on a wall. Someone would throw up. A car might be run off a road. Most of these revelers sprang from the nests of 1950s Babbitts. On Monday morning all the weekend hippies would be back in class intoning the boilerplate of the New Orthodoxy. Later in the week they would sign up for their law school interviews and—rather self-consciously, I should think—their interviews with the agents of the Giant Corporations.

To those 1960s youth who had seen through the allure of radicalism or the romance of bohemianism and opted eventually for individualism, these poseurs were known as Coat and Tie Radicals—Radical in the lecture halls of their accommodating profs or on those exotic weekends or on the day the reporters arrived and the big demonstration was scheduled; but Coat and Tie when the time came for job interviews or meetings with distinguished alumni. By the late 1960s most were, as Clinton was, semiradical student government goody-goodies. Most did as Bill did; they partook of the Old Conformity and the New Conformity, depending on the opportunities presented. They were—again—having it all, enjoying the narcissistic ambivalence of their peers. Few of their professors objected. Within "the system," they were going to be antisystem; for all agreed that the system was profoundly corrupt, though none seemed pained by the obvious fact that within this "system" they were flourishing. They wanted to keep their options open. As a grateful young Clinton explained in that historic letter to an ROTC officer who probably thought he had seen everything, it was important "to maintain my political viability within the system"[4] while dodging the draft.

The Coat and Tie Radicals were distinguished from the rest of us and from all prior generations of Americanos by a congeries of unusual traits that we thought petered out in the 1970s and 1980s, only to make their unanticipated reappearance in Washington at the end of 1992, when Boy Clinton began populating his government with his old schoolmates. These traits (along with Arkansan political mores soon to be discussed) brought the administration almost immediately to ignominious foozle.

To begin with, most Coat and Tie Radicals were colossal megalomaniacs. More specifically, they were stupendous narcissists, often solipsists, who, despite all the bosh about their idealism, were coolly amoral in their ambitions and in their goatish pursuits. Nor did this amorality in any way put a damper on a self-righteousness that even Woodrow Wilson would have deemed unseemly. So closely have they identified with all the good causes they have espoused that at some point in their development they assumed that they themselves *were* good causes.

This coexistence of amorality and self-righteousness within each Coat and Tie Radical was to have historic consequences. It explains how Clinton, despite all the corruption he had presided over in Arkansas, could launch his presidential campaign as a moral crusade or how he could repeatedly declaim on behalf of those "who play by the rules" and continue to intone this tired line repeatedly during the very days when his friend and number three official at the Justice Department, Webster Hubbell, was copping a plea on two felonies in late 1994. It is the amorality of the Coat and Tie Radicals that got Clinton into the scrapes that enlivened his campaign, and it is their self-righteousness that explains his intense indignation when questions arise over his probity, character, and fidelity.

Most people, even when very stupid, learn at least something from experience. When Cro-Magnon man saw his wife fall into a lake and disappear, he avoided the lake; it looked like no other fierce animal he had seen, but he knew that it had eaten his wife. By the first month of the Clinton administration it was clear that the Clintonites had through twenty-five years of experience learned nothing at all. They still believed government was the answer to most problems. They still believed they could have it all. Practically everything they attempted was amateurish and unsatisfactory. They, however, were satisfied. Their megalomania, narcissism, and grandiosity left them hugely arrogant. Though they were perpetrating perhaps the most corrupt and incompetent presidency in American history, it was not until early 1996 that the Clintonites sensed the catastrophe.

Was it their arrogance or their hard-wired brains that accounts for one other trait that the Coat and Tie Radicals brought from the late 1960s to Washington in the 1990s—that incomparable capacity for double-talk, for being on all sides of every issue? On the campaign trail in 1992 Bill and Hillary claimed to be New Democrats, populists, progressives, even as Hillary said three months after the election, "conservative in the true sense of the word."[5] Since the 1960s these megalomaniacs have had a stupefying propensity for declaring themselves any incongruous thing that catches their fancy. And so in the Clinton administration policy has repeatedly been concocted without any attention whatsoever to the real conditions of society. Thanks to the Coat and Tie Radicals' megalomania, narcissism, and grandiosity, they are, of a sudden, capable of an Ascent from Reality that to me seems almost miraculous. Others, less familiar with 1960s youth, witness this Ascent from Reality and suspect they are being lied to.

At some point in the 1970s these idealistic youths from 1968 slipped from sight. With the rest of their generation they joined the rat race. Yet as their hair grayed and thinned, and as they fattened and acquired that agglutination of contradictions that so frequently compose the mindset of the middle-aged liberal, they apparently kept in touch. During the dark days of Reaganism all their peculiar traits and infantile ideas were sedulously maintained in the melancholy of a cloistered world of graduate schools, college faculties, think tanks, select law firms, and corporate bureaucracies. During class reunions the Coat and Tie Radicals would congregate to reminisce, to solemnize some New Age epiphany, to condole over the unanticipated expiry of a classmate to a drug overdose or, perhaps, to a suicide. In 1983 some of the most gifted of their number concocted *The Big Chill*, that poignant Hollywood depiction of one of these somber reunions, the Coat and Tie Radicals stranded at middle age, brought together by the suicide of a college pal, once the group's most idealistic and promising revolutionary. At their reunion they confront the chilling question, "Have we sold out?" Perhaps, but at least their narcissism remained, along with their self-righteousness, their abundant contradictions, and their amorality. It is a sad movie, and I wonder how its dialogue compares with what was said in late July of 1993 when all the Clintonites went back to Arkansas to bury Vince Foster.

CHAPTER THREE

OXFORD AND PRAGUE:
A COAT AND TIE RADICAL
ABROAD IN THE 1960S

I N THE LAST days of the 1992 campaign Boy Clinton faced one final scrape. It must have caused him more alarm than any other. It revealed the lengths that Clinton had gone to to evade the draft. It also revealed the grave compromises a Coat and Tie Radical might make geopolitically during the height of the Cold War when his country was up against the era's equivalent of the German Nazi, namely the Soviet Bloc Communist. The origins of Clinton's last campaign scrape reach back to Clinton's graduate school days at Oxford. It was then that his heart was stocked with all the progressive sentiments that were to reappear in his presidency. At Oxford Clinton began playing both sides in the great political matchup of the Cold War. Ostensibly he was merely trying to cultivate the *good* Communists among the *bad* Communists, the moderates among the hardliners, in the parlance of Western liberals. But here was another example of Clinton writing his own rules and recklessly pursuing his own ambiguous objectives.[1]

Today the Cold War seems to have left history's stage without a trace, not a drop of blood, not even a final peace rally. The slogans once painted on campus walls by the so-called peace demonstrators have faded: "Give Peace a Chance," "Better Red than Dead," "Ban the Bomb." Nor is there talk today of monuments, victors, or even of losers. America's military-industrial complex slowly contracts with no generally held explanation of why it grew in the first place. The Red Army, a military machine that for over four decades threatened world peace and from its first engagement in 1917 butchered more than 50 million people, abruptly withdrew from conquered territories. Suddenly in the early 1990s its uniforms with their historic red stars were being hawked in the back alleys of Prague and Budapest. I bought one in Prague in April of 1992. Redolent of the Red Army's condition, my back-alley haberdasher advised me to treat the garment for lice. While a student at Oxford in the 1960s Clinton would never have envisaged this debacle, nor would his progressive profs. Now this last scrape of Clinton's presidential campaign revealed why. At Oxford in the late 1960s Clinton fully participated in the anti-American revels of the counterculture.

I

The Oxford of the late 1960s was a hive buzzing with moral superiority. Its dons and left-wing students were fixated on the sordid past of Western civilization and the colossal future awaiting mankind if only the dons and their students were put in charge. Clinton was a Rhodes Scholar. Yet at Oxford in those days anti-Americanism was as much a force as were sentiments of left-wing superiority. Ever the striver, ever the apple-polisher, Clinton adapted to it. His mentors were many: left-wing British dons, visiting Americans such as Keynesian Robert Solow and leftist linguist Noam Chomsky. Undoubtedly there were also the usual gimcrack luminaries of 1960s youth culture: the quack guru in the smelly tunic, the socially conscious rock singer believed to be a poet, the vegetarian disc jockey, the salesgirl at the organic food shop who always left the top two buttons of her blouse undone. All might be numbered among what in the late 1960s were called the Voices of Protest. All helped shape the Coat and Tie Radical's *Weltanschauung* and resume.

At Oxford Clinton and those Rhodes Scholars who would be his life-long co-conspirators became confirmed collectivists. Later, at Yale Law School, the future president fell in with still more advocates of the Nanny State. It has been from these two staging grounds that the Clinton administration acquired much of its supporting cast and futile ideas. Oxford University and Yale Law School—the friends that Clinton made there calcified his faith in government and his leeriness of markets. While studying at Oxford Clinton often departed for pilgrimages to all the European shrines. During Campaign '92 it was revealed that one such pilgrimage was to Spain to blubber at the historic markers to the Spanish Civil War. He went to Oslo to consult the International Peace Research Institute. He journeyed to Moscow and to Prague. This last trip was a problem. It constituted the last scrape of Campaign '92, and for a brief but bright moment the Republicans thought it would finish him off.

On October 25 the *Washington Times* published a news story reporting that, contrary to Clinton's prior claims to being just another red-blooded American boy while at Oxford, he was in truth a counterculture protester of admirable industry. He had cashiered his preppy look for the black and olive drab of protest. The *Times* printed pictures of him grinning from beneath a disheveled mop of hair and behind a shaggy beard. He wore rumpled fatigue jackets and granny glasses. Parties in a house he and his friends rented on Leckford Road—a "hippie commune," said some—became legendary.

But the most damaging revelation made by the *Times* was that at the height of the Cold War Clinton had engaged in continuous antiwar activities. Amid all the anti-American propaganda and international espionage of 1969 the Democrats' 1992 presidential

nominee sided with the anti-Americans. Our soldiers were facing
death in Vietnam while the war protesters shouted such verses as
"Ho, Ho, Ho Chi Minh/The NLF Are Gonna Win." The *Times*'s
revelations appeared to be devastating. The report even refuted
Clinton's gratuitous lie of the previous spring—his claim that he
had never received an induction notice. According to the *Times*'s, he
had received two and set out to beat the draft by calling his uncle,
"Ray Clinton, an automobile dealer in Hot Springs, and Mr. Fulbright's office [that being Senator J. William Fulbright, Arkansas's
antiwar senator for whom Clinton had interned] in Washington,
seeking the application of political pressure on his draft board to
avoid induction."[2]

Unmasked as a counterculture stalwart, an antiwar protester, and
a draft dodger, Clinton was even denied the defense of high principle. Apparently he was as unprincipled in protest as he would be in
politics. The *Times* quoted Lincoln Allison, a politics lecturer at
Oxford's University College, who recalled that Clinton's antiwar
activity was "purely selfish," arising upon no serious ethical pedestals
at all, just cowardice or, perhaps, impatience over the inconvenience
a stretch in the military would impose on his well-planned political
career. Of all the *Times*'s revelations, the one that appeared most portentous was news that late in 1969 Clinton had embarked on a "40-
day train trip through Sweden, Finland, the Soviet Union and
Czechoslovakia." Though a student on a modest budget (his Rhodes
scholarship provided only $2,760 annually for tuition, room, and
board) he had journeyed to Moscow and "stayed in one of Moscow's
more expensive hotels—the National, much favored at the time by
the Soviet elite," then he visited Prague, the capital of one of the
Soviet Bloc's most repressive regimes.[3] The trip to Moscow alone in
those days could have cost as much as $5,000.

There was more. On the day the *Washington Times* came out,
London's *Sunday Times* filed a similar report, detailing still more of
Clinton's counterculture activity. He had attended meetings of

Group 68, an organization of American peace activists supported by the pro-Soviet British Peace Council. While in Oslo he had met with a leading international antiwar activist. His stay in Moscow was booked through Intourist, the state travel agency.[4]

Where did the money come from? How did an American student acquire such clout with the Soviets? Surely the KGB or some propaganda arm of the Soviet government was involved. Cold Warriors had always suspected that the international peace movement was somehow controlled by Moscow. For a day or so after the appearance of these two reports Washington was resonant with rumors. State Department files supposedly contained evidence that Clinton had given up his citizenship to avoid the draft, that he had committed treason, and that while in Moscow he had slipped away for a clandestine trip to Hanoi similar to the highly publicized trips to Hanoi made by more renowned antiwar activists such as Jane Fonda.

Clinton's election prospects flickered and dimmed. Then, as his staff pondered how to salvage the campaign, something amazing happened. The stories simply died. Reporters were not offended by the lies Clinton had been laying on them for years. Citizens' groups did not demand an honest account of his draft record, his antiwar activities, his visits to Communist countries at the height of the Cold War, visits that seemed to have the support of Communist governments. The stories had absolutely no effect on the election; few news organizations even picked them up. Perhaps that was because in debate Clinton had already excoriated George Bush for questioning his patriotism. He had called Bush a "McCarthyite." Soon he had the Bush administration in panicky retreat from charges that its agents were rifling State Department files. According to the Clinton campaign, the Bush administration was even investigating Clinton's mother. Perhaps the journalists feared being called "McCarthyite" too. At any rate, the stories of Clinton's travels behind the Iron Curtain and of his antiwar protests made no mark. Even a year after the two stories broke in the London and Washington newspapers, no American journalist had bothered to look into them, as I was to discover.

II

Months after the election, when I decided to turn my attention to Clinton's life, I reread the stories in the *Washington Times* and the London *Sunday Times*. My curiosity aroused, I decided to look into Clinton's trip behind the Iron Curtain. Inquiries I made about his trip to Moscow turned up little that was new. People were still wondering where he had gotten sufficient funding for the trip. Some still suspected a KGB front. Others suggested the CIA, recollecting that Coat and Tie Radicals and liberal college students had accepted CIA funds in the 1960s, for instance Gloria Steinem and the National Student Association.[5]

When I looked into Clinton's trip to Prague, however, I made an interesting discovery. Clinton had stayed at the home of Bedrich Kopold. My contacts in Prague, all former dissidents, tipped me off that the Kopolds had been members of what they called the Communist party's "ruling class." Some had actually helped found the Czech Communist party. I laid immediate plans to interview them, arriving precisely a year after publication of the fall 1992 revelations about Clinton's 1969 pilgrimage. To my amazement I was the first Western journalist to interview the Kopolds since that *Sunday Times* reporter. It would be fifteen more months before the press showed any interest in the Kopolds, and then only because, en route to a summit with Russian President Boris Yeltsin, Clinton stopped off in Prague and invited the Kopolds to have a beer with him and Czech President Vaclav Havel.[6] The press had missed another fascinating Clinton story. A poignant tale awaited the Western journalist in Prague, a story full of insights into Clinton, his generational cohorts, the politics of the Cold War, and the unchanging mentality of the utopian Left, some of which he brought from Oxford to Washington in a journey taking a quarter of a century.

III

Prague is the little Paris of what has been known to history as Central Europe, though during the Cold War we knew it as Eastern Europe. Kings and emperors, cardinals and monks, burghers and craftsmen have for centuries garnished its hills and slopes with a glorious salad of architectural delights: palaces, churches, public buildings, a castle here, a bell tower there, all in a melange of architecture from the baroque to the classical and the neo-classical. During the late Marxist-Leninist period, the commissars put down just enough steel and glass monstrosities to demonstrate that history's most feeble-minded Hapsburg or lunk-headed cardinal was a Christopher Wren by comparison with Dr. Marx's politically correct designers of multistoried file cabinets. Wandering through the ancient city is the swift-flowing Vltava, crossed by one of the handsomest bridges in Europe, the fourteenth-century Charles Bridge. Prague is a city of artists and musicians. They say Mozart loved Prague, but recent history has not. When I first visited, shortly after communism's collapse, the city's many charms were hidden beneath the drabness of Communist life. Improvident Communist economics had left the city dilapidated and grimy. Its recent history had left its people somber. Communist Czechoslovakia had long been associated with worldwide Communist intrigue: secret police, international espionage, munitions running, and the production of semtex—the plastique explosive favored by terrorists. In fact, Communist Czechoslovakia had been a training area for international terrorists.

The so-called Prague Spring, meant to liberate Czechoslovakia from hard-line Communists, had been crushed by Soviet tanks in 1968. Before that, Communists of various degrees had ruled. Preceding the Communists had been the Nazis, who had been free to overrun Czechoslovakia after the British and French sold out the Czechs at Munich. By the time I returned to Prague to see the Kopolds in October of 1993 the city was reviving. The grime was being scrubbed away. The Czechs were regaining their feel for commerce and artistic expression, relearning the role that free citizens play under limited government. They could speak without fear of the *polizei* lurking in hallways. Prague's new intelligentsia favored the free market and democracy. The Austrian economist, Friedrich Hayek, was a god. The Czech interpretation of his work brought in a heavy dose of Catholic morality. The mix startled me, though perhaps it should have been anticipated. Nazi and Communist lawlessness had shown the Czechs the brutal side of man's nature during long years that must have stretched out into an eternity for the ordinary citizen. In this elegant old city the confiscations, murders, jailings, and beatings had continued right up until the end of the 1980s. I approached my interview with the Kopolds apprehensively; even in 1993 the dangers of Prague's totalitarian past still seemed to lurk in every dark passageway.

Given my politics, I decided that a request to interview members of communism's "ruling class" would best be cloaked in strictest perfidy. Who knows? The old Communist might even admire me for it. I telephoned Mr. Kopold to set up the interview, palming myself off as a 1960s idealist engaged in writing a book testifying to that era's noble protests. He was obviously pleased. His naiveté should have tipped me off that this member of communism's "ruling class" was unlike the other Communists whom I had known. Zoologically speaking, I could recall two types, neither of which was very pleasant. One was the suave, clever charmer with a lewd delight in capitalism's abundance. The other was the thick-necked bully, always peremptory and accustomed to sycophants at his side. He was obviously brutal and a little stupid.

Kopold was neither. He lived in a large contemporary flat that would have been brilliantly out of character with the blocks of gray to olive-drab prewar apartment buildings in the neighborhood, except that it too was now drab. Its design was modern with a white stone facade that after years of neglect had become dingy. After my battered Skoda taxi dumped me on the sidewalk and coughed back up Czech Army Boulevard, a weathered old man in a threadbare black suit with a white shirt open at the wattle of his throat approached me and weakly offered his hand while his insouciant dog waved its stupendous, flowing tail back and forth in lordly hauteur. This was the Communist Kopold? His overbearing hound conformed more with my idea of a proper Communist.

Kopold had been waiting for me on the sidewalk because the elevator to his top floor apartment was 1990s Communist unreliable. The interior of his building was as tired as its exterior, the functional stainless steel railings all inexplicably stained, the once-contemporary wood veneer now torn and peeling. Dust was everywhere, and the concrete stairs were bowed like those of an old European palace. For members of communism's elite, this place had been the Ritz. In his flat Kopold introduced me to his wife and daughter. Both were soft-spoken and rather sweet. They offered me coffee in their sitting room and fruit from a large bowl. The dog barked and thumped his incomparable tail. The Kopolds were a diffident trio. It had been a long time since much interest had been shown in them.

Their sitting room held a wealth of pictures featuring the Kopolds with former Communist party celebrities, among them Alexander Dubcek. Dubcek had been the hero of the Prague Spring. Having mellowed from the Stalinism of his youth, Dubcek by the late 1960s was leading moderate Communists in efforts to render their regime as humane as their revolutionary forebears had promised. The enterprise was hopeless, in fact, dangerous—and after Soviet tanks rolled in, Dubcek was hustled into obscurity. Demoted from general secretary of the Czechoslovakian Communist party, he was sent to a Slovakian boondocks and made a forester. The hard-liners thought it a good joke: the idealist Dubcek suddenly reduced to the sylvan pursuits of a Boy Scout—the insult, so typical of the Communists, laid bare their essential barbarism with its contempt for something as decent and harmless as the Boy Scouts.

The Kopolds suffered similarly, though less dramatically. Obviously, those who hosted Clinton back in 1969 were Communists neither of the suave roué variety nor of the brutish sort. He had been housed by another of the improbable creations of left-wing theorizing, a Stalinist evolving into a Noam Chomsky. At precisely this point in history, as these Stalinists evolved toward the religion of Progress, Western progressives were evolving toward a vaguely Marxist worldview. It was a convergence of political nitwits! Both would have done the world a good deed had they left politics in the hands of Richard Nixon or Lyndon Johnson and culture to *Reader's Digest*. When Clinton bounced into the Kopolds' flat, the Bedrich Kopold whom he met might have put him in mind of one of his Oxford lecturers, though Kopold would have been better mannered. The ultimate masters of Communist regimes enforced a grim etiquette even on the idealists who had been their naive heralds. It would have vastly improved the manners of the American left if, during the Cold War, they had been forced to live under the regimes they espoused.

In the late 1960s and early 1970s there were a lot of progressive profs like Kopold on both sides of the Iron Curtain. As to precisely what he was a professor of, I wasn't sure; his family's erratic translation of his scholarly line of work often defeated me. In one context it sounded very academic; in another it sounded as though he might have run the local high school's driver's education program. Communism had a way of conferring bogus academic degrees on true believers whose chief talent was merely to intone the party line. It also had a habit of depositing the truly learned into menial labor for some ideological lapse. The Kopolds were of the true believer variety, but Kopold had been deposited into many dull jobs. From 1950 to 1956 he landed in the dullest job of all, a cell in a Communist prison. Yet, apparently, no unpleasant experience was sufficiently unpleasant to awaken him from his dreams of a state-run utopia— not even the fact that here in 1993, after living his entire adult life in his family's Communist state, he could recall only two "good times," 1945 to 1946 and 1964 to 1968. "What about the present," I asked, "What about since the fall of communism in 1989?" "Not so good," a weary Kopold replied.

He was the sort of Marxist who, during the Cold War, might be trotted out by Eastern European regimes to reassure the Western intelligentsia, gathered at international conferences in support of one visionary endeavor or another, that behind the Iron Curtain were dreamy intellectuals just like them—visionaries eager to attend international symposia on international brotherhood, on the peaceful uses of the moon, on the bicycle's role in the metropolis of the future, on preventing the CIA from spreading the AIDS virus. They would sip cappuccino and eat yogurt, possibly in the cafeteria at Oxford or the Yale Law School. On those blessed occasions the academic Kopolds would trumpet socialism's superiority, say, in treating tooth decay or designing mass transportation. Meanwhile, back home in Prague, tanks and semtex were rolling off the production line, and back in the Socialist motherland an archipelago of concentration camps held millions of Kopolds, many with firmer backbones than my host.

That was the Cold War, and during much of it the Marxist profs behind the Iron Curtain shared a supreme cocksureness with their Western counterparts. Surely as a student Clinton was familiar with the professoriate's confidence that the state could cure all manner of human misery and inconvenience. About the time Clinton visited the Kopolds, *Cherwell*, Oxford's student newspaper, reported that 10 percent of the Oxford faculty claimed to be either Marxist-Leninist, or Trotskyist, or some other variation of communist. The majority of the profs were Socialists. Faced with the ubiquity of left-wing thought among the university faculty, it is not surprising that this congenital apple-polisher would become a sentimental acolyte of Progress. That he never was to change his essential faith in government is more surprising, though admittedly there is something about the Left's criticism of normal life and its promise of a better future that is enduringly alluring. The thought occurred to me as I listened to the Kopolds rumble on about their last years under communism and their memories of Clinton's visit. Now the progressive's old cocksureness had dimmed; but gleams still sparkled in Kopold's watery old eyes when such words as "modern" or "idealism" danced across his tongue. Or "Rational!" "Progressive!" "Education!" "Art!"—all very good things, these. One of the Left's conceits is that it has a special handle on the good. Then too the leftist always expects more good on the morrow. It is a trait he shares with the patrons of the gaming tables.

The cosmopolitan Kopolds had been consumed by politics their entire lives, yet in 1993 they remained political idiots. When I told Kopold that my most recent books were *The Liberal Crack-Up* and *The Conservative Crack-Up*, he sighed, "Ah you too believe in the Third Way." After our interview he escorted me to the metro, accompanied by his dog. His mind seemed elsewhere; perhaps it was recalling the Youth of 1968 and that far-off Prague Spring. He pointed to some monstrous space-age tower way off on one of Prague's tree-lined hills and offered to take me there the next day— "the highest point in Prague," he asserted. It would be, he vowed, the same walk that he had arranged for Bill Clinton twenty-three years earlier! I liked old Kopold. In fact, I was beginning to like Boy Clinton. They had an enthusiasm for ideas and culture that was appealing back in the 1960s. But I took a rain check on his proffered walk. I was feeling melancholy. Sweet as he was, his values had doomed this historic city. If he had his way, they would again.

I never brought up the name of Clinton. The Kopolds did. Clinton had been an Oxford acquaintance of their only son, Jan, and a guest in this sparsely furnished apartment in January 1970. Looking around at the fading pictures of communist grandees, it occurred to me that nothing had changed here in this apartment, not for twenty-three years! The pictures of the apartment contained the very same contemporary furniture that now was so worn and faded. The pictures showed the Kopolds looking younger, and none of the grandees looked as out-at-the-elbows as all Prague did now. When had all the brag and bounce vanished? When did the trained intelligentsia of Eastern Europe cease to cut such cocky figures at the international conferences?

As college students in the 1960s, Clinton and I had heard our profs sing of statist-planned societies. They were forever holding up East Germany, Hungary, or Czechoslovakia as a paragon of economic and social promise, civil rights aside. Through the 1970s and 1980s Western progressives remained convinced of collectivism's superior qualities. Characteristic was Paul Samuelson's 1976 pronunciamento. He had been the author of my era's most popular college economics text, and in 1976 he wrote that it was "a vulgar mistake to think that most people in Eastern Europe are miserable."[7] A decade later John Kenneth Galbraith, the media's most popular economist, opined that the Soviet Union was making great economic strides: "One sees it in the appearance of solid well-being of the people on the streets, the close-to-murderous traffic, the incredible exfoliation of apartment houses, and the general aspect of restaurants, theaters, and shops.... Partly, the Russian system succeeds because, in contrast with the Western industrial economies, it makes full use of its manpower."[8]

In fact it had consumed that manpower. Now, even after communism's fall, the blank faces of Eastern Europe's older citizens betrayed no joy. Their children might anticipate more prosperous lives; but life was over for the sixty-five-year-old citizens of Prague or Budapest, leaving them spent and mournful. When World War II ended they had been young. In Prague, educated Czechs had harbored the same hopes as their counterparts in those territories held by the armies of Britain, France, and the United States. Yet whereas youthful Western Europeans were to pursue their ambitions in free societies, the Czechs remained in suspended animation, treated like children by their government. Here in Prague at the end of their productive lives, the senior citizens of the Marxist experiment had no time left to realize freedom's promise. In the quiet streets of Prague these old men and women shuffled along with their sad faces. Perhaps the saddest place of all was the Kopolds' sitting room.

In the late 1960s the Kopolds' flat had been a hopeful place. When Clinton plopped himself down, probably on the very couch where I now sat, enlightened people throughout the West shared the Kopolds' enthusiasm for collectivism, believing, of course, that they could dispense with the secret police. Many of the best minds believed social engineering an essential tool toward justice. Western capitalism and liberal democracy were on the defensive. A new left-wing critique was the fashion at the universities. Student demonstrations were threatening Charles de Gaulle's Fifth Republic. Such demonstrations—often with Communist party support—were a staple of the evening news all over Western Europe and North America. Mick Jagger sang "Street Fighting Man," with the oracular exclamation: "Everywhere I hear the sound of marching, charging feet." In the West the Left was shaking the foundations of liberal capitalism. In Prague Dubcek's "soft left" was shaking the foundations of Stalinism. In the Kopolds' flat I glanced over the fading pictures of those great days. The flat had become their own private museum to 1960s protest. It even contained Clinton's letters from 1970, neatly filed away in scrapbooks. After the *Sunday Times*'s reporter visited them, the Kopolds reread them with renewed respect. Until the reporter knocked on their door they had not realized that their American guest of so many years past had become that fall's leading presidential contender.

Clinton had arrived from Moscow on January 5, 1970. It had been but two years since Soviet tanks led five Warsaw Pact armies in suppressing Dubcek's reformist government. At gunpoint Dubcek had been abducted and flown to Moscow where he was forced to capitulate to Soviet demands. By the time Clinton visited Prague, however, things had quieted down. The city was comparatively open. He stayed through January 12. Only after he was back in Oxford did those whom the Kopolds called the "hard Left" or the "Sovietika" clamp down. There is no evidence that Clinton's trip was arranged by Soviet intelligence. What is clear is that young Clinton was not just another red-blooded American collegian. He was very much a part of the sentimental Left. Such was his network of acquaintances that even behind the Iron Curtain he found himself in the company of the sentimental advocates of utopia. The Kopolds might have had admirable intentions, as did their friend Dubcek, but they had no appreciation of history even though history had landed them in Communist jails. Experience meant nothing to them. When Dubcek died in 1993 his posthumously published memoir revealed him a Socialist still. His youth spent in Stalin's Russia never registered in his conscience. Exiled in Slovakia with time to think, he merely dreamed. The dream never changed.

Prague, 1970: Boy Clinton was a long way from home. He was even a long way from Oxford. Yet here in the Kopolds' flat he found himself with Progress's closed minds. During the Cold War Kopold had been locked up and denied advancement. Possibly his son, Clinton's campus friend, was murdered, as we shall see. Even at the end of the Cold War Kopold, like Dubcek, remained a Marxist. The Kopolds I met in 1993 did not even have a good word for Vaclav Havel, the dissident playwright who became the Czech Republic's first president. How do we account for the shared conclusions of a Czech Communist, an Oxford Socialist, and an Arkansas applepolisher in 1970?

At University College Clinton was studying politics, philosophy, and economics—PPE, as it was called. It was a series of soft courses notably devoid of history's hard messages and free from the more rigorous versions of economics. The Keynesian ideas of the visiting American, Robert Solow, were to re-echo for years in the writings of Ira Magaziner and Robert Reich, Clinton's fellow Rhodes Scholars. So would the envy and essential nihilism of Chomsky, who then called himself an "anarcho-Marxist." Some of Clinton's instructors interviewed in the 1990s, for instance Zbigniew Pelczynski, who taught Clinton politics, insist that he was a conscientious and promising student.[9] Others demur and describe him as a sheer opportunist. The irrefutable fact is that while at Oxford Clinton was deeply involved with the counterculture—contrary to years of campaign propaganda. Of the thirty-two Rhodes Scholars in his class, he was one of only six who failed to complete their prescribed course. The Clinton who emerges from these years is a personable young hustler with few fixed ideas. Observers who knew him at Oxford report that he would argue on either side of the great issues of the day—even on either side of the race issue and the Vietnam War. Philip Hodson, now a London psychologist, testifies that at social gatherings Clinton's eyes would be scanning the room for bigger fish to charm.[10] Still, it was out of character for him to fail to finish his degree. For a clever student, Clinton could have gotten by with ease. Something had disturbed him deeply. It was the draft.

Clinton had grown panicky about being drafted. It radicalized him temporarily. Even after the threat of the draft passed he could not settle down, and so the pilgrimages to Europe's shrines to Progress. In an Oxford lecture hall he hears a left-wing prof rhapsodize on the class struggle against Franco, and off he goes. He has read, or claims he has read, thirty books on the Spanish Civil War and so he knows the sacred spots. That journey took place in the spring of 1969. Then in the winter he takes off for Oslo, Moscow, and Prague. God knows what provoked that wintry undertaking, but obviously in 1969 Clinton was restless.

The arrival of the big, likable Yank at the Kopolds' door was about what we have come to expect of him. He was late. His papers were in gay disorder. He did not bother to register with the local police as the law then required. Naturally he wanted to see everything and to talk and talk. "He was very interested in politics," Mrs. Kopold assured me. Her mother, Marie Svermova, a founder of the Czechoslovakian Communist party and once a member of the Party's Central Committee, took a liking to him. "He was typical American student... open and friendly... high spirits, simpatico," Mrs. Kopold went on, her dog alternately yowling and barking from the sitting-room carpet. Her husband walked the quiet streets of Prague with "our Bill," as the Kopolds now called him. Naturally, they, too, "talked and talked." One evening they passed the American Embassy, and a happy Mr. Kopold remarked, "Bill, it would be nice since you are so much interested in Czechoslovakia that you will in a few years come back to us as a cultural attaché." "Why not" Clinton replied; Mr. Kopold adds that he underestimated "Bill's political talents."[11]

On Clinton's final walk in Prague he and Mrs. Svermova visited the twelfth-century Strahov Monastery now housing the Memorial of National Literature. On that walk the young American confided to the old Red that upon returning to the United States he intended to "sacrifice" his life for politics. Sacrifice his *life* for politics? To a woman whose politics almost cost her her life and who thought the United States a fascist stronghold, this must have come as a courageous statement of solidarity. I can see them now, two defiant idealists sweeping down St. Wenceslaus Square, the secret police discreetly shadowing them. Did either have any idea that another Communist clampdown was in the works, and would Czechoslovakia have been worse off had Mrs. Svermova and her progressives never been born? The pleasant land of Mozart and pilsner that they transformed into a police state held promise after World War II. But Mrs. Svermova's flawed political principles led to four more decades of repression and the bankruptcy of an energetic, civilized people.

There is something touching about Clinton's stay with the

Kopolds. His enthusiasm and charm had sozzled them, as it would later sozzle America's true believers. They worried about his departure, fearing that his unsigned travel documents would cause him problems at the border. A hand-written letter at the end of January relieved their anxiety. He had not been arrested. After twenty-three years they still had his letter; the friendly voice of the boy who would in eight years be elected governor of Arkansas and, in twenty-two, president of the United States, was there even then.

Dated Friday, 23 January, it read: "Dear Mr. and Mrs. Kopold: I returned to Oxford four days ago and delivered all the things you gave me for Jan. Then one day we went and met for dinner and talked for a long time. He looks well and was glad to get news from you. Thank you so much for having me into your home and for taking the time to talk with me and show me around Prague. I am very grateful for the opportunity to have spent a few days with you, days which gave me vivid memories that will last for years. Sincerely, Bill Clinton." There were other letters, one promising to get Mr. Kopold sociology books, others from Clinton's mother thanking the Kopolds for their hospitality and expressing worry about her son's safety behind the Iron Curtain. And there was that very sad letter from Clinton after he had enrolled in Yale Law School. From Milford, Connecticut, on October 14, 1970, he wrote, "Dear Mr. and Mrs. Kopold: Only yesterday did I receive the sad news of Jan's death. Your notification was sent from England and it took a long time to reach me. In the past 24 hours I have relived many moments of my brief friendship with your son. I have recalled his smile and the distinctive charming way he moved his head up and down in conversation. But most clearly I have remembered the persistent way of searching for the truth of a matter that he had. For that quality I admired him very much. He had in him the best promises of man. All of us at Oxford who were close to him recognized that and we were proud to be his friends. I join you in your sorrow. My deepest sympathies to your family. Sincerely, Bill Clinton."

After I read the letter aloud into my tape recorder, Mr. Kopold said wistfully, "You see. They were *really* friends."[12] The sentence lilted from the hopeful to the melancholy in what the poets call a "dying fall." Many of the Kopolds' sentences did that, no matter what they might be discussing. They had dwelt in melancholy. After Clinton returned to Oxford and to the Kopolds' son, Jan, the Kopolds were again in hot water with the newly repressive regime. Kopold was banished to another obscure job. Jan's parents advised their son not to return, fearing for his safety. By the summer Jan had been "expelled" from the Czech Communist party. Yet here the Kopolds' reminiscences lapsed into the barely believable. Jan, despite his expulsion from the party, hoped his father would secure funds from the Czech government so that he could travel; and do you know where he planned to travel? Moscow! How does one get "expelled" from the party and still assume that funds can be procured for a trip to Moscow? And why would one go there when one's security from the secret police could not be ensured even in Prague?

Was Clinton's friend, Jan, entangled in international intrigues beyond the ken of the naive Kopold *père*? Certainly life under communism was riddled with compromise and intrigue. Whatever the case, Jan Kopold had little time left. That summer, accompanied by two American girls and a European friend, he went to Turkey to see the ruins of Troy. In Turkey he suffered a mysterious "accident." While walking on the roof or the upper floors of a building, he fell to his death. I asked the Kopolds if possibly Czech secret police had a hand in this. "Oh, no," the Kopolds said in choric response. "It was dark," explained Mr. Kopold, "he don't see good in the dark." In the late 1960s the Kopolds were devoted adherents to the same religion of Progress that had fetched Clinton. They had long ago invested total trust in the state, though in life the state had imposed on Mr. Kopold many "complications." That was the euphemism he reflexively employed in alluding to the many occasions when an individual came into conflict with the Czech state. (When he discussed young Clinton's departure from Prague, Mr. Kopold mentioned "complications" at the border.)[13]

True to the religion of Progress, Mr. Kopold was spooked by all the bugaboos his religion decried: the rich, the clergy, the aristocrats. Yet here we were seated in his apartment decades later: the Berlin Wall but rubble, the dissidents freed from jails, the barbed wire gone from the border—no more "complications." Nonetheless, the Kopolds remained stubbornly opposed to Havel, to my Czech friends who had tipped me off to Kopold's background, and to all the other democrats governing the Czech Republic. Like the Coat and Tie Radicals, the Kopolds were hard-wired.

The sad old man put me in mind of another Marxist from the 1960s whom Clinton and the Coat and Tie Radicals esteemed, T. W. Adorno. Adorno was one of the intellectual fathers of the German student rebellion. In 1968, when his students began to bomb and to burgle on behalf of their fondly envisaged utopia, the old quack accidentally turned them against himself by exclaiming in the German newspaper *Der Spiegel*: "How could I know that people would try to translate my theories into action by means of Molotov Cocktails?" Alas, in the spring of 1969 during a lecture at Frankfurt University, "Introduction to Dialectics," he was interrupted by a student demonstration of "planned tenderness." The radicals distributed a leaflet entitled *"Adorno Als Institution Ist Tot,"* ("Adorno as an institution is dead,") after which revolutionary females circled the old boy. They heaved bouquets at him, kissed him, disrobed, and assailed the astonished prof with "an erotic pantomime." After attempting to protect himself with his briefcase, Professor Adorno fled the lecture hall. He canceled further lectures indefinitely; soon he was lying horizontal at room temperature. Yet before this last dialectic transformed him into ether, he told an interviewer, "In my writings I have never set up any kind of model for practical action. I am a man of theory and feel theoretical thought to be extremely close to the purposes of the artist."[14]

In the 1960s Adornos were on every elite campus including Oxford. Years after Clinton and his fellow Rhodes Scholars returned to America, Ambrose Evans-Pritchard in London's *Sunday Telegraph* described their Oxford staging ground on March 21, 1993. With his usual precision he assessed the influence Oxford had on the future president: "... the bond Mr. Clinton formed with his Class of '68 was akin to brotherhood.

"They were a group of young men who had started their American colleges in the heady days of 1964, brimming with optimism about the civil rights revolution and the Great Society of Lyndon Johnson, only to see their ideals shattered four years later by the race riots, the assassination of Martin Luther King and Robert Kennedy, and, the Vietnam War.

"From the moment they boarded the *USS United States* in New York for Southampton, they began 'The Conversation' that has been going on ever since about the destiny of their country. For most of them Oxford was one long elaboration of the theme.

"Bill Clinton and Robert Reich would linger after dinner at University College, sometimes joined by Strobe Talbott (Magdalen, '68)... and talk for hours about how they would change the world." And Evans-Pritchard concludes that their views were essentially unchanged right up to 1993: "Their view of the world seems to be a refinement, updated but not substantially altered, of the prevailing orthodoxies at Oxford in the late 1960s." To Evans-Pritchard, himself a Cambridge graduate, these Rhodes Scholars have remained "charming dreamers," much like those other charming dreamers whose views remained frozen in the late 1960s, the Kopolds.

CHAPTER FOUR

THE MAKING OF THE CLINTON CABAL

I T HAS NOW been over a quarter of a century since Clinton and his Rhodies set about to improve humankind. They ministered to their universities, to our cities, and to giant corporations. In 1992 they returned Greatness to Washington. Now with all those years of hubbub behind us I think we can duly conclude that the Rhodes Scholars who joined Clinton at Oxford constituted the silliest group of Americans to go abroad since the last world tour of Ringling Bros. and Barnum & Bailey Circus. At Oxford they became even sillier, if arrogance can beget silliness—and surely these insufferable marplots have demonstrated that it can. Their arrogance was first acquired in America, where they were dubbed "the brightest, most idealistic generation in America's history."[1] Yet it was at Oxford, amongst the Marxists and Marxists manqué, that Clinton and his chums were confirmed in the belief that intellectually and morally they towered above their countrymen.

Their delusion is not only that they are superior in mind and spirit. They are superior joggers, Frisbee heavers, cyclists, designers of sandals, cooks of haute cuisine, singers of arias, and players of

Trivial Pursuit. They quickly came to believe that they comprised a momentous generation. More accurately what they comprised was only a subgroup of a generation. My peers in that generation shared almost none of their conceits. As an undergraduate I avoided politics and student government. So apparently did Newt Gingrich, Tom DeLay, and Robert Livingston. Those last three went on to comprise the Republican Revolution in the House of Representatives and to bring great mischief to Clinton's reign. Like most students in the 1960s generation, they were normal, conservative, and protesters only of the protesters.[2] The 1960s generation that has passed into history books as being bohemian and in protest was only the left-wing subgroup of the 1960s generation. Frequently the members of this subgroup were the progeny of an earlier left-wing generation. Most of the rest of us were pretty much like earlier generations of Americans.[3]

It was always preposterous to refer to them as comprising America's "brightest, most idealistic generation." Yet they had pleased the left-wing intelligentsia who in turn exaggerated their numbers and inflated their importance. Such intellectual energy! The brightest generation would draw amazing comparisons between Nazi Germany and the administrations of Lyndon Johnson or Richard Nixon. *Applause from the professoriate!* They would argue passionately that the North Vietnamese communists were the bearers of "peace and freedom" in Indo-China. *More applause!* They would gain self-awareness through hallucinogenic drugs, "love-ins," and Frisbee bacchanalia. *Still more applause!* They turned their student unions into instruments of class warfare and fine marketers of tie-dyed T-shirts at reasonable prices. The junior faculty bought the shirts and wore them to class on demonstration day. The adult members of the intelligentsia adulated the left-wing youths for all this and left them feeling very self-important. But the Rhodies who shipped off to England gained an arrogance that set them even above their pompous pimply faced peers back home.

They returned to America exalted even above the colonized, the feminists, the neurotics.

Clinton and the Rhodies whom he inflicted upon Washington during his incomparable presidency were all remarkably similar. Hillary Rodham, Robert Reich, and Ira Magaziner came from the same mold. Doubtless scores of lesser officials had the same stamp upon them. All had gone to prestigious schools. All had been student government Machiavells even in high school, except for their diplomatist, Strobe Talbott. As a Yale undergraduate he took a pass on make-believe statecraft and worked on the *Yale Daily News*. Yet Talbott shared his classmates' enthusiasm for the peace movement, for perceiving "moral equivalence" between the United States and the Soviet Union, for goading the United States to get on—as the phrase had it—"the right side of history." All had a fling with the counterculture.

Even the Rhodies' resumes were similar, and they kept them that way throughout the 1970s and 1980s. Reich had headed student government as an undergraduate at Dartmouth. He spent summers working with inner-city youth. He interned for Senator Robert Kennedy, worked in the left-wing presidential campaign of Senator Eugene McCarthy, and rejoined Clinton at Yale Law School. Then he served in the federal government briefly under Jimmy Carter.

Magaziner's early resume features more of the same. As a teenager he volunteered as labor organizer at a summer camp in the Adirondacks. While a student at Brown University he was elected class president all four years. At graduation he organized a demonstration against the Nixon administration's national security advisor, Henry Kissinger. Magaziner's valedictory speech, interlarding all the trendy left-wing pontifications of the day with the usual Rotary Club truisms was, characteristically, on both sides of the issues of the day. Not surprisingly, when it was printed in *Life* magazine it appeared opposite the equally oleaginous valedictory speech of... mirabile dictu, Wellesley's Miss Hillary Rodham. Her resume looked very

much like his, though without the Oxford interlude. Upon graduating and shipping off to Britain, Magaziner joined Rodham's future
husband in anti-war protests and other idealistic projects.

For the next two decades these creatures of 1968 kept the era's
ideals and deceptions alive in their hearts. Rarely did the lessons of
the ever-altering present teach them anything. From the perspective
of a quarter of a century it is apparent that they were clearly wrong
about all the major issues of their time, Vietnam not excepted. Yet
they have never smartened up. They assured America that South
Vietnam's capitulation would result in "peace and freedom" for the
Vietnamese. In 1996 Vietnam remains one of the world's last communist dictatorships along with another of the 1960s left-wing
enthusiasms, Cuba. Drugs? Sex? Human rights? The good society?
They got it all wrong. About all they can truly brag about is that
their 1960s upheaval was responsible for a slight increase in petty
crime, VD, and drug abuse, yet about this they do not brag.

The years during which Clinton and his fellow world-savers were
student government politicos, student government ceased to be the
powerless, harmless retreat of the student nerd. University faculties
actually ceded some power over student life to these campus busybodies. They were even given a voice in setting curricula. It might
have made some sense to give students more say over their personal
lives; many were young adults. However, as all came to college in
search of an education, or at least the certification of an education,
it made no sense to allow them to prescribe its elements. On each
campus there were different infamies to erase—a beauty pageant
here, an ROTC ball there. But one reform all the radicalized youth
agreed upon was curriculum reform, which meant lowering standards, lowering workloads, and gutting the curriculum of difficult
courses. As a consequence of the reforms devised a generation ago
by the Clintons, the Reichs, and the Magaziners, many universities
in the 1990s demand of their undergraduates little more than what
high schools once demanded.

There was a logic to the Coat and Tie Radicals' curriculum reform. It allowed them to arrogate the fiery sloganeering of the radical along with the all-embracing uplift of the university progressive. Once again they were having it all, being on both sides of the issue, being everything to everyone—or almost everyone. The non-protesting majority had little interest in this sham. There is no record of Newt Gingrich instructing his teachers at Emory University as to how they might better educate him and his fellow students.

At Dartmouth, Reich's reforming endeavors involved developing something called "an experimental college." In accord with contemporary intellectual fashions the "experimental college" offered its students opportunities for self-realization, self-esteem, personal identity, and other such approved objectives. As we shall see, Magaziner's efforts were even more ambitious. The Clintons themselves were tireless nuisances for both the faculty and administration, though neither seems to have been as importunate as their future colleagues Reich and Magaziner. Incidentally, not one of these busybodies has yet to contribute to the intellectual patrimony of the country anything comparable to that of their antecedents in earlier generations. By middle age Woodrow Wilson and Theodore Roosevelt were accomplished writers; even Calvin Coolidge could turn a phrase. But Clinton's Rhodies turn out only second-rate tracts, and Clinton is the rare president with not one book, not even a pot-boiler to his name.

He was, nevertheless, an active reformer of his university even as an undergraduate. A communiqué, preserved from the pages of his college's news sheet, the *Georgetown Courier*, conveys the childish urgency and self-importance of the Coat and Tie Radical playing at campus statecraft. This is what Boy Clinton wrote:

> Freshman elections are coming soon, football season is almost here and interest is running high in all those diverse activities which fall under the direction of what we call

"student government." Before this enthusiasm ebbs—and if history provides any indication, it will—I think, for the benefit of freshmen and all those who care about the direction of student activity, we ought to examine the accomplishments, the failures and the future of the cumbersome, curious group of organizations by which we attempt to govern ourselves....

My greatest fear is that student government... is going to be rejected unless it takes the lead in trying to stop the kind of failure exemplified by the following instances, all of which might not have been failures except for a lack of leadership initiative, or purposeful power and a grim determination:

> (1) We ought to have pushed harder for a five game football schedule. We could have gotten it.

> (2) We ought to throw out, or at least boycott, the cafeteria's meal ticket system for men, which requires a deposit by parents on which Georgetown draws the interest....

If elected representative government is to have any meaning at all, it must make a deep commitment to meet head-on issues like these above. We cannot adopt a policy of isolation or inaction, or our politics will be without substance. We, as student body, must urge our representatives to enter and support them in those fields where they are most needed—to plant the seeds of improvement, to reap the harvest of beneficial change. The times demand it.[4]

If Reich and Clinton were campus pests, their fellow Rhodes Scholar, Magaziner, was a Superpest. In the summer of 1967, after his sophomore year at Brown, he wrote a 425-page report titled "Draft of a Working Paper for Education at Brown University." Not unlike his 1994 masterwork, the Health Security Act, which would have consigned another 14 percent of the gross national product to the federal government's general incompetence,

Magaziner's "Working Paper" was the product of his truly maniacal energies. Fortunately America in 1994 got off easier than Brown in 1967. Magaziner's "Working Paper" included a review of the entire curriculum from the point of view of an adolescent and prescribed remedies written from the point of view of a truant. "Working Paper" found the curriculum relevant only to adults— and learned adults at that. To resolve the troubling situation, "Working Paper" prescribed longer vacations, the relaxation of course requirements, and the elimination of grades. Magaziner spent much of his remaining undergraduate career marshaling student support. By graduation most of his reforms were adopted. Ever since, Brown has been the country club of the Ivy League, albeit enveloped in an atmosphere of intellectual arrogance. "A paradise for airheads and idlers," is how the *Economist* described the place after having reviewed Magaziner's handiwork. Most of his reforms endure, and not surprisingly a poll of university presidents and deans, taken for *U.S. News and World Report*'s annual ranking of colleges, deposited Brown in the academic cellar of the Ivy League in its 1994 report.[5] Here is more evidence, if more be needed, of the baleful influence this silly subgroup of 1960s youth had on the institutions that fetched their genius. Yet they joined the Clinton administration unbowed and unenlightened.

The credulous intellectuals of the 1960s fell for all of it and on campus accepted all sorts of educational experiments. Profs in the 1960s could not bring themselves to tell upstart dilettantes such as Magaziner and Reich the truth, namely, that they were as ill-prepared to define a college curriculum as they were—well—to devise a national health care policy. As with other institutions, the universities were losing the ability to distinguish intelligence from unintelligence, a just complaint from malice or mischief, the workings of a fine mind from the blazing angers of a malcontent or the con job of a fraud. The universities became blowzy and disorganized after engorging themselves with bogus departments and quack studies:

Afro-American studies, women's studies, peace studies. Even so venerable a university as Harvard was losing its definition and sense of purpose. Faculties of learned professors found themselves taking a back seat to humbugs claiming equal rank as scholars of womanhood and negritude and peace. Despite the existence of a fine Department of Government, Harvard set up a spurious center for governmental studies, the John F. Kennedy School of Government, where has-been public figures pulled on their chins and sipped sherry. At the Kennedy School a relatively new species of hustler was allowed to write tendentious tracts and to agitate on behalf of those tracts. This was the policy hustler, and in 1992 Reich was named "America's premier policy hustler" by no less an authority than the *New Republic*.[6]

At the Kennedy School Reich had been plying his trade since the early 1980s. His appointment there was the culmination of the vulgar process that he and his student government goody-goodies had been part of since the 1960s. The very erosion of standards that they had been abetting since writing their first "working papers" on curriculum reform allowed Reich to set up shop at Harvard and palm himself off as a sage on business, economics, and government, though his only advanced degree was in law. As a "Lecturer on Public Policy" at the Kennedy School Reich never had to submit his writings to the professional rigors of economists or of business professors who would have reviewed them if he had pursued a real academic discipline. Since his college days all Reich has ever been is a pamphleteer and activist. But with his bogus position at Harvard, he could claim the mantle of the scholar; and throughout the 1980s with characteristic hustle he wrote or cowrote a string of books on business and economics and government, most of which were flawed by repeated errors and by insights that he frequently had to revise. The best of his work is interesting journalism, the worst mere propaganda for himself. Who will be surprised to read that Reich's coauthor on a couple of these books was Magaziner? Magaziner is himself but a pamphleteer and activist.

After Oxford, Magaziner refined the techniques he had applied to the reform of Brown's curriculum and entered upon a well-paid career of advising governments and corporations. As with Reich's ambiguous role, so too with Magaziner's; they had attained eminence solely because of the erosion of authorities throughout American society. Magaziner's preeminent talent was to sell himself as a fix-it man to institutions that were not really sure of their purpose but suspected that they were in need of repair. He could not really be considered a reformer as reformers have been known in the past, for he stood for no recognized set of reforms. He could not be considered a successful businessman, for he had never been in business. He came to reform government, unbidden by voters. He came to advise corporations, having neither produced successful products nor marketed anything save himself. That, I suppose, is what both men essentially were, marketers of themselves. This was also Clinton's basic talent and Hillary Rodham's too.

And so through the years Clinton, his Rhodies, and those kindred spirits whom he met at Yale repeatedly revised themselves. They had a keen ear for society's buzzwords and momentary enthusiasms: Compassion! Community! Infrastructure! Rarely, if ever, however, did they revise their essential ideas or even attempt to understand the buzzwords or enthusiasms they mouthed. By the early 1980s almost all ideas, institutions, and even language had become so drained of authority that few critics ever thought to apply the word hypocrisy to the liberals as they come down foursquare on both sides of every issue. The very word hypocrite almost disappeared. Liberals were now in favor of business and growth while insisting on consumer and environmental regulation. They would boast of their advocacy of a forceful foreign policy while expressing righteous indignation over the Reagan military buildup, the Strategic Defense Initiative, and the president's depiction of the Soviet Union as an "Evil Empire." With phony candor throughout the decade many soi-disant progressives claimed to be growing, learning, adjusting their views to New Realities. In truth, they were stunted. A pervasive collapse of accountability in American cultural life allowed their vast hypocrisy. The dull, gray sameness of America's political culture closed out genuine criticism. Woe to the public figure who challenged the sameness. The sameness polluted public discourse.

Strobe Talbott was Clinton's third fellow Rhodes Scholar to take a high-profile job in the Clinton administration, first as the State Department's ambassador-at-large for Russia, later as deputy secretary of state. Though a Coat and Tie Radical in the 1960s, Talbott later followed a more conventional course than Reich and Magaziner. Having been a summer intern for *Time* magazine in 1969, he went on to translate and edit for Time Inc. two volumes of Nikita Khrushchev's recollections and reflections. He climbed steadily up through the ranks at *Time*. Yet his career too betrayed the Coat and Tie Radical's propensity for being on both sides of major issues. Throughout the 1980s he followed the liberal's fashion of decrying Soviet expansionism while piously disdaining Reagan's resolute policy toward the Soviets. It was too "provocative."

As with his other Coat and Tie Radicals, Talbott had learned little through all his years of adulthood. In 1990, after the Reagan administration arms buildup had bankrupted the Soviet Union and allowed reform to begin in the land of Stalin and Brezhnev, Talbott popped up from a trap door on history's stage to utter pronouncements perfectly echoing pronouncements he had heard at Oxford from Professor Chomsky, the visiting "anarcho-Marxist" of 1968. Citing George Kennan's 1947 *Foreign Affairs* essay arguing that the West must resist Soviet aggression until Soviet power "decayed," Talbott sneered at "the $4.3 trillion ($9.3 trillion adjusted for inflation) that it has cost the U.S. to wage peace since 1951." "The doves," he wrote in *Time*, "in the Great Debate of the past 40 years were right all along."[7] Where had Talbott been these past forty years? His hard-wired brain was perhaps even more resistant to experience than old Mr. Kopold's. Even Mikhail Gorbachev had learned more.

The Coat and Tie Radicals' peculiar trait of "having it all" or "being on both sides of the issue" became increasingly remarked upon once they came to Washington. Their ambivalence was observable in Clinton's budgets and in his huge, unwieldy health care plan. In an early examination of incoming Labor Secretary Reich, Mickey Kaus reflected on Reich's lifetime propensity for "trying to have it both ways." With insight and prescience, Kaus anticipated the policy confusions that lay ahead.[8] A year later, in a piece on the scandals of the Whitewater Development Company and the Madison Guaranty Savings and Loan, another journalist, Jonathan Alter of *Newsweek*, noted both the Clintons' "habitual desire to have it every which way." He pointed out that, starting with Clinton's governorship, the Clintons "wanted to be selfless public servants *and* comfortable 1980s Yuppies; crusading reformers *and* cozy courthouse politicians; careful about appearances... *and* capable of exploiting the connections that came with their positions."[9]

When Reich became secretary of labor he took a strong hand in Clinton's first budget, a budget that clearly had it "both ways." It would cut the federal deficit *and* pass on a $30 billion fiscal stimulus program. (Reich originally favored a vast spending package on what he called "investments" until he ran up against Treasury Secretary Lloyd Bentsen and his more conventional aides.)[10] It would raise taxes on "the rich" (those making $200,000 annually, according to candidate Clinton; those making $100,000 annually, according to President Clinton; those making $30,000 annually, according to White House aide George Stephanopoulos on February 16, 1993).[11] Such tax increases notwithstanding, Clinton's budget would "grow" the economy. It was at once Keynesian *and* budget-balancing. Actually it followed no single economic theory known to man. If Clinton's first budget were a Rhodes scholar reposing on the couch of a qualified psychiatrist, it would be diagnosed schizophrenic and put on thorazine. Actually, Clinton's policymakers could have used vast quantities of thorazine. The health

care plan eventually unveiled by Hillary Rodham Clinton and
Magaziner was schizophrenic too. Again the Clintons were "having it all." This plan would guarantee universal health care *and*
expand individual benefits. Costs would be controlled or even cut,
and there would be no price controls—conventionally understood.
The system would be more expensive *but*, over the long run,
cheaper. The economist Herbert Stein on the op-ed page of the
Wall Street Journal skewered Magaziner's numbers, calculating that
the Clintons' health care package would be adding $120 billion to
the deficit annually by the middle of the 1990s.

Those who were college students with the Clintons when they
were auspicating their early campaigns for dormitory mayor or
chewing gum rights recognized the narcissistic ambiguity of their
health care legislation when it was finally unveiled late in 1993. It was
a throwback to the self-indulgent late 1960s. These spoiled brats
were not the first Americans to want to "have it all," but they were
peculiarly flagrant and infantile in flaunting their excesses. The mentality of Magaziner, Rodham, and Reich et al. was perhaps first displayed to the nation back in 1968 in *The Strawberry Statement: Notes
of a College Revolutionary*. In that memorable tome nineteen-year-old
James Simon Kunen chronicled his role as an activist at Columbia
University during the student takeover of several campus buildings.
He overcame police barricades, climbed through windows, and
joined his fellows in occupying the offices of President Grayson Kirk.
Then in the company of his olive-drab colleagues he urinated in
Kirk's wastepaper basket and read his mail. Reviewers esteemed the
book highly and pronounced the youthful urinater an authentic
Voice of Protest. Eventually he made literary and political history,
becoming a staff writer for *People* magazine, another Voice of Protest.

Those wondering how the Clintons, Reich, and Magaziner
sounded back in those days might pick up an old copy of *Strawberry*.
Early in the book, and by way of introducing his revolutionary
chums to the world of fuddy-duddies, Kunen wrote:

"I, for one, strongly support trees (and, in the larger sense, forests), flowers, mountains and hills, also valleys, the ocean, wiliness (when used for good), good, little children, people [classic 1992 Clinton campaign oratory, no?], tremendous record-setting snowstorms, hurricanes, swimming underwater, nice policemen, unicorns, extra-inning ball games up to twelve innings, pneumatic jackhammers (when they're not too close), the dunes in North Truro on Cape Cod, liberalized abortion laws, and Raggedy Ann dolls, among other things. I do not like Texas, people who go to the zoo to be arty, the Defense Department, the name 'Defense Department,' the fly buzzing around me as I write this, protective tariffs, little snowstorms that turn to slush, the short days of winter, extra-inning ball games over twelve innings, calling people consumers, pneumatic jackhammers immediately next to the window, and G.I. Joe dolls. Also racism, poverty and war. The latter three I'm trying to do something about."

Then he tells us what he and his fellow revolutionaries did at Columbia to rectify the situation. He also demands amnesty in the event that he is jailed for civil or even uncivil disobedience.[12]

Why the Clintons did not find a place for this soul mate on their White House speechwriting staff I have not been able to ascertain. Possibly the Clintons were saving him for a seat on the Supreme Court, or they wanted to make him their first astronaut. In keeping with the Coat and Tie Radicals' easy departure from reality, Kunen might qualify for almost any role.

Kunen's demand for amnesty for his fellow protesters was characteristic. Compare it with the example set by the old Irish radical and friend of the poet Yeats, John O'Leary. He never whined about his British captors, though they had treated him so badly during his imprisonment that for the rest of his life he could not digest a normal diet—"Why should I complain?" he would say, "I was in the hands of my enemies." The 1960s protesters made amnesty a "non-negotiable demand." Consider O'Leary's response when asked about an Irish politician who was bemoaning his plight while on hunger strike. Said O'Leary, "There are some things a man should not do to save a country, one is to cry in public."[13] The 1960s protesters cried frequently, though saving their country was rarely the cause. When one of their own became president, he became the greatest presidential bawler in history.

As the 1970s passed, those of us who were the Coat and Tie Radicals' contemporaries assumed that they, like us, were living normal lives: a job, a family, a mortgage. We were wrong. *The Big Chill* was the window into their lives. After their march of destruction through the universities they graduated to counsel local communities and gullible corporations. All were left the worse for wear. The Arkansas that the Clintons first inflicted themselves on was a backwater. The Arkansas they left was a backwater still, but with higher taxes and various government programs mired in debt. And despite the Clintons' boasts along the presidential campaign trail (Arkansas Education, IMPROVED! Arkansas Health Care, IMPROVED! Arkansas Criminal Justice, IMPROVED!), the average Arkansan remained only marginally healthier and better educated than the average Eskimo. Moreover, this rural state continued to have one of the highest homicide rates in the nation.

CHAPTER FIVE

A SON OF OLD ARKANSAS

A ND THEN THERE is Arkansas. President Bill Clinton
brought many of his administration's most memorable per-
sonages from home. As a consequence of these Arkansan importa-
tions, the earliest chroniclers of the Clinton administration have
not been historians or even journalists, but bank examiners and an
unprecedented procession of Senate investigators, House investigators, Justice Department lawyers, officials from the Drug Enforcement Administration, the FBI, and several independent counsels,
some famous, some not. Admittedly there have been a handful of
independent-minded writers, but most of them have only picked up
where the criminal investigators left off.

Later waves of historians will not grasp the historic dimensions
of the Clinton presidency until they understand that singular rec-
tangle of piney woods and alluvial soils that is the great state of
Arkansas. It is a state rich in resources. Along with the 53,187
square miles, mostly of stately timber, Arkansas abounds with
petroleum, minerals, natural gas, and cheap labor. That cheap labor,
alas, bespeaks another, darker truth. Arkansas's masses remain poor,

save for a rich elite of political prestidigitators and titans of commerce. Understanding Arkansas is essential to understanding the Clinton administration and to understanding Clinton himself. He may have traveled the world and been educated on two continents, but stamped on his soul are the crudities of a country politico cutting deals back in Ouachita County, Arkansas. I can think of no other twentieth-century president so profoundly imprinted by the folkways and mores of home.

Jimmy Carter is fully comprehensible, absent Georgia. Gerald Ford is a recognizable American type, notwithstanding his larval period on the football fields and the golf courses of Michigan. Warren Gamaliel Harding's legend owed nothing to Marion, Ohio, per se, or even to the Midwest; fellows like Warren hail from every purlieu. But in the waxworks of twentieth-century presidents, the figure of William Jefferson Blythe Clinton will remain confused and slightly enigmatic, his professional practices and ultimate rise being as mysterious as an early morning Sicilian automobile mishap, until Arkansas is factored in. The state's political practices are unusual even by the esoteric standards of the Deep South. The Clintons and their home-grown cronies brought as many of those political practices to Washington as they could pack into the back of Air Force One. Washington's press corps had witnessed the likes of Lyndon Johnson and Richard Nixon; its members thought that there was no infamy or misdemeanor that they had not seen. Then up the road came the Clintons, bringing with them in the rumble seat David Watkins, Patsy Thomasson, Bruce Lindsey, Webster Hubbell, Vince Foster, and their very own Kennedy, all with skeletons in their closets and some with indictments in their futures. In the fullness of time Americans were agog with Whitewatergate, Travelgate, Troopergate, the Waco inferno, and the miracle of Hillary's cattle futures. It was not solely Oxford University and the Yale Law School that shaped the policy and peopled the bureaucracies of the Clinton administration; forget not Arkansas.

Years ago, public relations-conscious Arkansans began packaging their state as "The Land of Opportunity." The term was not without merit, but it would have gained in precision had it read "The *Government* of Opportunity." Government, not land, is the chief source of opportunity in Arkansas. Certainly that is true for the elite circle of politicians and businessmen that has been in place there since the founding of the Rose Law Firm in 1820, well before Arkansas became a state. The opportunities alluded to are the very same that New York's turn-of-the-century Tammany Hall politico George Washington Plunkitt had in mind when he averred, "I seen my opportunities and I took 'em." So have generations of prehensile Arkansans—some being life-long politicians, others being *incorruptible* government commissioners or regulators, while others have been businessmen, pleading total innocence of the political process whose levers they so artfully tickle.

Newsweek's Howard Fineman conveyed a fine thumbnail sketch of Arkansas's capital at the end of President Clinton's first year in office. Fineman described Little Rock as "the capital of a poor state, but with a large number of wealthy people. They all know each other, and most went to school together at the University of Arkansas. Many fortunes were built on politically influenced deals at the intersection of private markets and government: regulated utilities, municipal bonds, state banks. In Little Rock, as elsewhere, those businesses got out of hand [in the 1980s]. Out of the way, with a small population—and essentially controlled by one party, the Democrats, since the Civil War—Arkansas produced an elite that generally dealt only with itself and that viewed conflicts of interest as business as usual."[1]

Actually, when Fineman depicts Arkansas as a "poor state," he fails to do justice to that poverty, for it is of a special sort. Arkansas's poverty is more like that of a developing country. Like Jakarta, Little Rock's skyline is bejeweled with a few towering skyscrapers built by the state's handful of growing economic concerns—Stephens,

Inc.; TCBY; Worthen Bank (now Boatmen's Bank). Meanwhile, out on the countryside, economic torpor persists. In the *New Republic*, L. J. Davis conveyed this unhappy aspect of the state when he wrote, "It bears a close resemblance to a Third World country, with a ruling oligarchy, a small and relatively powerless middle class, and a disfranchised, leaderless populace admired for its colorful folkways, deplored for its propensity to violence (on a per capita basis, Little Rock has one of the highest murder rates in the nation), and appreciated for its willingness to do just about any kind of work for just about any kind of wage."[2] And the Peruvian novelist Mario Vargas Llosa, himself a former candidate for the Peruvian presidency, conveys the political and economic significance of the Arkansas condition when he writes: "In an underdeveloped country, exactly as in a totalitarian one, the government *is* the state and those in power oversee it as though it were their private property, or, rather, their spoils."[3]

If life has been stagnant and pinched for most Arkansans, it has been bountiful for the oligarchy and their political allies. Three of the defining characteristics of the state explain their opulence and ease. To begin with, there is the modus operandi at what Fineman calls "the intersection of private markets and government." In Arkansas over the decades there has developed a symbiosis of politics and commerce: the entrepreneur assists the politico, and the politico reciprocates. Only rarely does one or the other end up behind bars. The other two defining characteristics prevent such eventualities and further explain the politics and the wealth of the oligarchy: the state's one-party political system and an historic lawlessness that frequently turns to violence. All the scandals that have entoiled the Clintons, first in the Governor's Mansion and later in the White House, can be traced to these defining characteristics. To be sure, the peculiar traits of the Coat and Tie Radical have contributed to the Clintons' arrogant reaction to their scandals, but the scandals themselves are indigenous to Arkansas.

In Arkansas it is not considered unseemly for the owner of Anthony Forest Products, Beryl Anthony, Sr., to be chairing the state forestry commission; and so much the better that Beryl Anthony, Jr., has served in the United States Congress and that his wife was the sister of an influential partner at the Rose Law Firm— Vince Foster, now deceased. The Arkansas Poultry Federation recently had on its payroll the chairman of the state's Senate agriculture committee. In fact, lobbyists for the state's chicken producers are regularly members of the state legislature. Don Tyson, chairman of Tyson Foods, Inc. (and architect of the Rock Cornish hen), has bragged publicly that he contributed to Bill Clinton's first gubernatorial campaign in 1978 in return for Clinton's promise to raise the ceiling on the weight that a poultry truck may bear in lugging its feathery products over state roads. Tyson is equally boastful of how he shifted his campaign contributions from Clinton to his 1980 Republican challenger after Clinton failed to make good on that promise. Arguably, Clinton's failure to return Tyson's favor cost him the 1980 election. Arguably, too, the favor was a bribe, at least as the term is understood in jurisdictions beyond Arkansas.

How Clinton and Tyson, one of the richest members of the Arkansas oligarchy, responded to that defeat sheds light both on Clinton's essentially adaptable politics and on the Arkansas symbiosis. At first Clinton went into a tailspin. Some testify that he became a heavy user of cocaine. His marriage suffered another of its recurring crises. A friend reports seeing the defeated governor singing to his baby daughter, "I want a div-or-or-or-orce" while Hillary busied herself in the nearby kitchen.[4] But soon he recovered. He hired a political operative from his days in the McGovern campaign, Betsey Wright, adjusted his politics to attract Tyson and the rest of the oligarchy, and by 1982 had persuaded them that he would never again obstruct their economic schemes. From then on the Boy Governor's populist rhetoric rarely deterred him from accommodating the commercial exigencies of his well-heeled supporters.

Tyson did pretty well too. At the end of the 1980s Tyson Foods, Inc., was the world's largest producer of chickens; its climb to the top had been neatly facilitated by Tyson's ability to flout Arkansas law. Throughout the 1980s Tyson Foods, Inc., was polluting Arkansas rivers with fecal bacteria in blatant disregard of Arkansas's environmental regulations; Tyson had a friend in the governor's office. Objections were filed, but the chicken excreta kept coming. Tyson continued supporting Clinton throughout the 1980s. When Clinton ran for the presidency, Tyson and his business associates were there, checkbooks open. He, his family, and his corporate executives contributed at least $29,000 to Clinton's presidential campaign. His rewards were almost immediate, as was the ensuing scandal. Don Tyson was tapped to speak at the president-elect's "Economic Summit." Soon Tyson was schmoozing with the Clinton administration's secretary of agriculture, Mike Espy. Then both were dodging indictments for practicing Arkansan politics outside Arkansas.

Tyson had kept his eye on the Clintons for years. Tyson's lawyer, Jim Blair, a Democratic apparatchik with years of experience in Senator William Fulbright's campaigns, had been friends with the Clintons since their days on the law faculty at Fayetteville. It was Blair who handled Hillary Clinton's historic magnification of a $1,000 investment in cattle futures into a $99,537 fortune within nine months. The miracle began on October 11, 1978, less than a month before her husband's shoo-in election to the governorship and continued unbothered by margin calls through July 1979. Skeptics have called it a bribe. "The Arkansas system had always been to find some good young people and encourage them to work on the local level," Don Tyson has injudiciously blurted out. "The system kind of weeds them out, and out of that comes a United States senator or a governor.... It's like a horse race. You back three or four, so you always got a winner."[5]

Another fortune created by the symbiosis of politics and commerce is that of the Stephens family. Like Tyson Foods, Inc.,

Stephens, Inc., predates the governorship of Clinton, but it has been even more dependent on political clout, its growth revealing the emergence of the Arkansas elite on the national and even world stage. By 1990 and after accumulating capital comparable to that of Morgan Stanley & Company, Stephens, Inc., became the largest private American investment bank headquartered outside Wall Street. It is housed in downtown Little Rock, and at noon scores of eager young Stephens deal-makers in white shirts and rep ties rush from it to lunch at the tony restaurants nearby—Wall Street, on the River Arkansas.

In the late 1920s Wilton R. Stephens, founder of the Stephens dynasty, departed his father's cotton farm to sell Bibles (and belt buckles) up and down the rutted roads of rural Arkansas. He was a big, hearty, likable man and, like many Arkansans, a born salesman. His days of mongering Holy Scripture behind him, he borrowed $15,000 in 1933 to establish his Little Rock brokerage house. From there he loaded up his leather satchels with municipal bonds badly depreciated by the Depression and returned to the life of a dusty-foot; only now his targets were rural bankers, not impoverished hicks. Naturally he encountered many pols. His father was a two-term state representative. Stephens bought depreciated highway bonds recommended by his father at ten cents on the dollar. Later his father prevailed on the state legislature to guarantee the bonds, thus returning them practically to face value and setting the cornerstone of the family fortune.

The Depression waned and the rest of the bond market recovered. The bonds that Witt (as he was coming to be known) had acquired produced their profits, doubling and tripling in value. At the end of the war, he hired his brother, Jackson Stephens. Though sixteen years Witt's junior, Jackson was given management of the natural gas and oil holdings that Witt had astutely purchased with his bond profits. Now the brothers extended their underwriting activities to local governments outside the state and eventually to other state governments. To win these contracts the Stephenses spread their campaign contributions ever wider. Always they and their lieutenants mixed politics with business, frequently state business. In time they became the preeminent force in the Arkansas symbiosis. By the 1990s Stephens, Inc. employees were carrying on where the brothers left off, occasionally with unhappy consequences. The case of Preston C. Bynum popped into the news in 1995. A Stephens banker, he was convicted of bribing a Florida politician $28,200 to give Stephens, Inc., two bond issues totaling $36 million.[6]

The Stephenses also entered into corporate underwriting after World War II, eventually assisting such Arkansas companies as Wal-Mart, TCBY, and Tyson Foods, Inc. Then in the late 1970s they entered international banking and brushed up against the perpetrators of the Bank of Credit and Commerce International (BCCI) scandal. It is speculated that the encounter was more sustained and less innocent than the Stephenses care to acknowledge.

A BCCI-engendered brush with one global wheeler-dealer, Mochtar Riady, raised their ambitions to become global wheeler-dealers themselves. The story starts with Jackson Stephens's days at the U.S. Naval Academy, where Jimmy Carter was a classmate. During the 1976 campaign Bert Lance, soon to be President Carter's head of the Office of Management and Budget (OMB), rekindled the friendship between Carter and Stephens. Lance knew Stephens from political fund-raising in the South. Stephens in turn brokered the sale of Lance's National Bank of Georgia. Selling it had become a requirement if Lance were to head the OMB. The requirement grew in urgency as Lance fell into political difficulties and then financial problems. The main buyers who approached Stephens were foreigners. One was Agha Hasan Abedi, the shadowy Pakistani who founded BCCI. The other was Riady, a very rich Indonesian banker. Eventually Stephens sold off Lance's bank to Abedi, thus allowing BCCI entry into American banking. In 1984

Stephens became Riady's partner in banking closer to home. They put large sums of capital into a statewide chain of Arkansas banks named First Arkansas Bankcorp and merged it with a group of banks owned by C. Joseph Giroir, Jr., chairman of Arkansas's Rose Law Firm, thereby creating the Worthen Banking Corporation, Arkansas's largest bank holding company.

With its new partner, Riady, a central member of the ethnic Chinese clique that controls much of Indonesia's economy, Stephens, Inc. broadened its horizons to the entire Pacific Rim. It opened an office in Hong Kong and plunged into the island's banking whirlpool. Jack Stephens's banking allies back home began to regale civic groups with visions of a financial axis linking Hong Kong, Jakarta, and Little Rock. Some of these dreams withered in 1985 when the Stephens financial vehicle, Worthen Banking Corporation, nearly collapsed in a bond market fiasco, but Arkansas companies are now well positioned for the coming Indonesian boom. A presidential visit to Jakarta in November 1994 produced $40 billion in business deals. Razorback stalwarts like Entergy, which owns Arkansas Power and Light Co., and Wal-Mart, whose board was once graced by Hillary Rodham Clinton, are bursting into the Asian market in deals brokered by Little Rock attorney Giroir, the former chairman of the Rose Law Firm and still Jack Stephens's personal lawyer.[7]

"I worked the state of Arkansas, and I worked it pretty close and good," Witt declared to a *Fortune* magazine reporter at the outset of the 1990s. "My brother Jack comes along, and he works the United States and does an excellent job. Now my nephew Warren comes along, and he's working the world,"[8] helped by the Arkansas symbiosis which along the way acquired a president.

Like Don Tyson, the Stephenses had spotted Clinton for the political prodigy that he undoubtedly was—pliant, winsome on the campaign trail, always in need of money owing to his reckless ways. The Stephenses helped the Clintons, and except for an early-1980s break in their friendship, the Clintons responded with millions of dollars in state bond-underwriting contracts. The Coat and Tie Radicals, never fans of exile or martyrdom, had announced repeatedly in terms of rich self-congratulation their condescending willingness to "work within the system." For the Clintons and their supporters, the system worked! As the Stephens's income from state bond issues increased they brought in the Rose Law Firm to handle attendant legal matters, causing Rose to expand its activities into banking and the bond business. Sometime in 1980 the Clintons and Stephens, Inc. had a falling out similar to the falling out that Clinton had with Tyson—though it lasted longer, well into 1985. By the late 1980s the Stephenses and the Clintons were back together, allowing the Arkansas symbiosis of politics and commerce to achieve a greatness never envisaged before: an opportunity to do politics and business from 1600 Pennsylvania Avenue. The prelude to the 1992 election is interesting.

The reconciliation between the Stephenses and Clinton was secure enough by 1990 that the Stephenses were again playing a prominent role among his financial backers. Clinton went into a panic during the last stages of that final gubernatorial campaign. Always insecure, he suddenly feared a Republican surge capable of knocking him off or at least so diminishing his margin of victory that it would dim his luster en route to the 1992 Democratic presidential nomination. Abruptly Clinton turned to the Arkansas oligarchy for hastily conceived loans, enabling a last-minute media blitz. In a move that was to bedevil Clinton's presidency, the Stephenses and their associates personally stood behind a $50,000 loan to Clinton from the Bank of Perry County.[9] Loans like that have a malodorous fragrance outside the "underdeveloped country" of Arkansas, and little more than a year into the Clinton presidency the air was full of it.

The Arkansan oligarchy emerged on the national scene at a grim moment for presidential candidate Clinton, and only years later did the country recognize how important the intervention was. Clinton was thought to be the poor-boy candidate of a poor state. He was actually the Democratic field's best-heeled contender. The moment of reckoning came in January 1992. Repeated public revelations during the New Hampshire primary regarding Clinton's philandering, draft dodging, and lying had left the campaign tottering. The Stephens-influenced Worthen Bank and Trust (the family denies that they controlled Worthen) had to be called upon for a $2 million line of credit to allow Clinton to survive. The assistance not only saved Clinton's candidacy but put him well ahead of the Democratic field financially. As in Clinton's initial race for Congress in 1974, so too in his presidential bid, the Boy Candidate had a knack for last-minute fund-raising. It is a talent that attracted the first chroniclers of his presidency, the bank examiners. Arkansas's generosity continued beyond the New Hampshire primary. Approaching the crucial 1992 Super Tuesday races, the Worthen Bank increased Clinton's line of credit to $3.5 million, virtually ensuring victory. By the Democratic National Convention the Clinton campaign owed $4 million, much of it to Worthen. By the end of President Clinton's first year in office the Federal Reserve had begun examining the legality of a security firm directing bank funds to a presidential campaign.[10] After exhaustive investigation the Federal Reserve Bank concluded that no supervisory action was needed. By that time, March 1995, Worthen had passed from Arkansas hands into a merger with Boatmen's Bank of St. Louis.

Other members of the Arkansas elite also contributed to the Clintons' political well-being. Wal-Mart and TCBY were steady supporters of the Clintons and even had Mrs. Clinton on their boards. But sometime in the early 1980s the Clintons found themselves in decidedly more dubious company when the Arkansas symbiosis introduced them to another rich Arkansan, Dan Lasater.

Lasater made his first fortune in the 1960s while quite young. He established the Ponderosa Steak House chain in Indiana. He then began breeding race horses in Kentucky and Florida. He met Clinton's mother, Virginia Kelley (who was then Virginia Dwire), at Oak Lawn Park race track in Hot Springs, where both gambled avidly on the horses, and where his horses were frequent winners. In 1979 she introduced Lasater to her son, Roger Clinton. Precisely when Lasater met brother Bill is unclear to me, but by 1982 Lasater had become a major contributor to Clinton's political war chest and one of Little Rock's infamous "bond daddies." His firm became well known for its libertine soirées featuring pretty young things and cocaine. After Clinton's 1982 reelection the governor gave his new supporter access to underwriting the state's tax-exempt bonds. From 1983 to 1985, Lasater's firm figured in fourteen state bond issues worth about $1.6 million, though Lasater was under investigation in a drug conspiracy. In all fourteen issues Clinton's old law firm, Wright, Lindsey & Jennings, did the legal work.

Lasater hired Clinton's shiftless brother Roger as a factotum and continued to prosper. It seems Clinton envisaged Lasater as an alternative to the Stephenses, upon whom Clinton did not want to be too dependent. When Clinton established the Arkansas Development Finance Authority as a bond-issuing agency to assist economic growth in Arkansas, Lasater was a major underwriter. Even when law enforcement agencies began investigating Lasater's drug habits, his lucrative dealings with the state continued. In early 1985 Lasater's stable hand and driver, Roger Clinton, made a deal with U.S. Attorney George Proctor, pled guilty on two counts of cocaine distribution, testified against Lasater before a grand jury, and went to the calaboose for two years. Despite it all, in May Lasater won permission to underwrite a $30 million bond issue for a new communications system for the Arkansas state police that Governor Clinton had strongly supported. The communications system was a notable failure, but Lasater walked off with $750,000. He was soon indicted for drug distribution and served six months. Clinton later pardoned Lasater, the official explanation being that without the pardon

Lasater could not get his hunting license back. Well, a man has to feed his family. While he was in jail, Patsy Thomasson ran his company. She eventually found a job with President Clinton in the White House (and was one of the White House aides that would come under scrutiny for entering Vince Foster's White House office the night of his death and making off with his papers). Proctor, the U.S. attorney who handled both the Roger Clinton and Lasater cocaine indictments, was rewarded for his ardent pursuit of justice with a slot at the Department of Justice once Clinton won the presidency.

Two more lurid story lines follow Clinton's relations with Lasater. In 1985 Lasater was sued by an Illinois savings and loan for losses in unauthorized T-bond trades. Mrs. Clinton and the Rose Law Firm negotiated a confidential settlement for Lasater that cost him $200,000, far below the $3.3 million that the savings and loan sued for originally.[11] The second luridity comes from trooper L. D. Brown and the Dow Jones News Service. Brown reported that after he discovered cocaine being flown into Mena airport by convicted drug trafficker Barry Seal in 1984, Governor Clinton told him not to worry. "That's Lasater's deal," he said.[12] A decade later, in another of the arresting news stories that should have attracted attention from the general press, the Dow Jones News Service reported that "A rogue Whitewater investigation by a senior federal official produced allegations that a one-time associate of President Clinton used Madison Guaranty Savings and Loan to launder illegal drug profits." The "one-time associate of President Clinton" was Lasater. The news report quoted from the minutes of a 1994 "high-level RTC meeting," concluding that Lasater "may have been establishing depository accounts at Madison and other financial institutions and laundering drug money through them via brokered deposits and bond issues."[13]

With the possible exception of Louisiana, no other state in the Union would allow such blatant corruption within its government and among its public figures. This is the consequence of Arkansas's second defining characteristic—more than a century of one-party government. In no other state of the Union does the Democratic party dominate as thoroughly and repressively as it does in Arkansas. More so than in any other state, Arkansas's laws and customs are designed to perpetuate—and occasionally to expand—the party's suzerainty. Only two Republicans have won state-wide elections in Arkansas in the past quarter of a century. Of the 135 campaigns for the state legislature in 1992 only fifteen were won by Republicans. Seventy-five percent of the races had only one candidate on the November ballot.[14]

In 1993, when Republican Mike Huckabee was elected lieutenant governor in a popular rebuke to Clinton, the Democratic majority in the state capital sealed the doors of the lieutenant governor's office. For weeks Huckabee was without an office. He wandered the halls of the state capital like an Untouchable. Colleagues shunned him. Even office workers stepped out of the elevator when the forlorn Republican stepped in. It has been years since any other state had such a high percentage of uncontested elections. One would have to leave the country completely and journey to Vargas Llosa's Peru to find such a phenomenon or such backwardness at the polls. In Arkansas paper ballots are hand-counted in a third of the state's seventy-five counties; the comparisons with Peru proliferate.

Arkansas's political elites have demonstrated a genius for excluding undesirables from the political process. In a trenchant discussion of Arkansas's singular political system, the *Wall Street Journal*'s John Fund has observed that "Arkansas is the only state where the political parties, and not the state, operate and pay for primary elections. The costs are covered by steep filing fees that serve as the equivalent of a poll tax on candidates."[15] The filing fee for a place on the ballot in a U.S. senatorial primary is $9,000, the highest in the nation. To contest a judgeship the filing fee runs from $2,500 to $5,000. Until 1994 the Arkansas Democratic party required loyalty oaths from its candidates in which they vowed "to vote for and actively support all the nominees of the Democratic party." Such practices have militated against reform-minded candidates and have even affected the administration of justice. In his aptly titled book on Arkansas politics, *Conflict of Interests*, Gene Wirges explains: "Everyone knew the judge on their case would be, more or less, part of the Democratic machine."[16]

Given the Democratic Party's enormous presence within Arkansas, the party can avail itself of vastly deeper financial reservoirs than can the Republicans, whose presence in the state is at best skeletal. Very few Republicans have any stature, and those who do are usually Democrats who have seen better days. As the state's courts and police agencies are almost all in cahoots with the Democrats, the Democratic Party can spread money around like catnip and engage in ballot box tampering with impunity. State Auditor Julia Hughes Jones tells the story of how, after losing the Democratic nomination for secretary of state, she was visited by a union leader: "He was dying," she explains, "and said he had to calm his conscience. He told me how they [Democratic Party apparatchiks] switched enough votes to guarantee I would lose."[17] For whatever reason, the Democratic leadership was not confident that Mrs. Jones would go along with the traditional combination of vote-buying, job-selling, and government boodling that is the Arkansas way of doing business.

The Civil Rights movement of the 1960s actually made vote buying easier. Vowing to involve more blacks in the electoral process, the party publicly spends "street money" to "get out the vote" in black neighborhoods. In 1992 the *Arkansas Democrat-Gazette* reported that the Democratic Party spent at least $89,000 in "street money," usually to black preachers and funeral parlor owners who then paid their clientele to vote for the appropriate candidate. The black mortician, of course, is a man of lofty political estate in Arkansas. He is to poor blacks what the small-town automobile dealer is to rural whites, a kind of political Mullah. In Arkansas blacks go to their morticians and whites to their car dealers for political wisdom, political power, and election eve money. As early as his sixth year Billy Clinton was recognizable as the possessor of a bright political future. That was when his mother moved the family to Hot Springs, where Uncle Raymond presided over the local Buick dealership. Only Billy's boyish charm and lack of principles did more to ensure his political future. As Virginia Kelley confides in her chilling memoir, *Leading with My Heart*, Uncle Raymond's showroom was "a gathering place for powerful, politically savvy men in Hot Springs."

Beyond having ample funds to get out the vote, Arkansas's Democrats have devised safeguards to keep uncooperative voters at home. During his twelve years in the Governor's Mansion, Clinton was particularly gifted at devising electoral prophylactics against competition, despite all his swanking as a herald of reform. In 1987 he signed a bill making it almost impossible for third-party candidates to run for state-wide offices, though to envisage such candidates as a menace to Democratic dominion over Arkansas is to see such frail entities as the Prohibition party becoming a thousand times more powerful overnight. Clinton's bold stroke had previously been ruled unconstitutional by federal courts, but the governor proceeded unperturbed by judicial robes. In the one-party bliss of Arkansas, every Democratic governor knows that there is no individual or agency capable of challenging a Democratic Party bull.

Even the state's ostensibly nonpartisan institutions have been brought to heel by the dominant party. For instance, the public television system owned by the state has a long record of barring non-Democrats from televised debates. Even the supposedly nonpartisan League of Women Voters has a Democratic ring to its ultimata.[18] Usually the one-party state's laws are sufficient to suppress dissent, but occasionally even violence is applied. After publishing exposés of ballot box fraud, reformist newspaperman Gene Wirges was indicted seven times on charges of conspiracy, perjury, and slander. He was convicted and sentenced to three years imprisonment, a sentence that was overturned only after it was found that his main accuser lied under oath. Wirges asserts that there have been nine attempts on his life.[19]

And this is where Arkansas's third defining characteristic comes in—violence. In his history of the state, Harry S. Ashmore writes of "the extraordinary psychological isolationism that has colored the relationship of Arkansans with the outside world. In part a product of the inherited trauma of a lost war and its aftermath, the attitude is somewhat different from the defensive parochialism that characterized all the Confederate states for a century after Reconstruction." Ashmore explains this "psychological isolationism" in terms of geography. He writes that "the frontier did in fact survive in Arkansas long after the main body of settlers had pushed on across the great plains." The Indian territory to its west blocked further western expansion to Arkansans who settled along the state's western border and established communities that in Ashmore's words "provided a sanctuary for desperadoes of all descriptions, and many of these became familiars, and sometimes heroes, to the farmers who filled in the valleys and clung to the slopes of the Ozarks and Ouachitas. The remnants of Quantrill's raiders rode through those parts, followed by Jesse and Frank James, the Youngers, Belle Starr, and the Dalton boys."[20] Law enforcement became rough, uneven, corrupt, and frequently violent. With adjustments for our modern sensibilities it has remained so.

As Tyson has attested, he and the other members of the oligarchy keep a sharp eye out for every rising Clinton in the state. To Tyson and the other members of the oligarchy, Tyson's "Arkansas system" may be "like a horse race," but to the aspiring politician it is a ladder. The first rung is a place on the local school board. The next rung might be the county sanitation commission, and then the state legislature, perchance a judgeship. In time the clever deal maker might reach the governorship and after that, what every Razorback

Boss Tweed must see as his Eternal Reward, a seat on the Arkansas Highway Commission or the Arkansas Game and Fish Commission. There is real money up there. As historian Ashmore writes, Arkansans "have, from the founding of the first government at Arkansas Post, displayed a pronounced tolerance for boodling by public officials."[21]

The school district is the basic element in the Arkansas political system. There are three hundred school districts. Each has its own school board. Candidates about to campaign for the school board stand at the entry level of Arkansas politics. It is on the school board that the political neophyte learns to cut deals with those commercial interests that supply the local schools with textbooks (each district chooses its own), school buses (per capita, Arkansas has more school buses than any state in the Union despite its poverty and a low level of educational attainment), and fuel for the buses and for classrooms (supplying fuel to government facilities has for years been a boodler's ideal scam). Supplying the expensive and comparatively ineffectual Arkansas educational system is as lucrative as supplying the Arkansas State Highway Commission or its Game and Fish Commission. Despite his claims to have reformed the Arkansas school system, Governor Clinton did nothing to change the grafting and other corrupt practices.

The first governor that the Tysons had a hand in creating was Orval Faubus. He was a politically ambitious country newspaper editor whom Don Tyson's father supported in the early 1950s. A famous segregationist who opposed the integration of Little Rock high schools and provoked President Dwight D. Eisenhower in the autumn of 1957 to send in one thousand paratroopers from the 101st Airborne, Faubus was a master of the Arkansas machine. He was also the first Arkansas governor to break with the state's tradition of serving no more than two consecutive two-year terms. Faubus served six. Coincidentally, the next governor to win six terms was another Tyson protégé, Bill Clinton. To have compared the two at the outset of the Clinton presidency would doubtless have illicited sneers from Clinton's sophisticated friends at Oxford and Yale, but would they continue to sneer as the months wore on and the reports of so many irregularities from the past accumulated along with the indictments, the plea bargains, and the jail terms? Both men had played the machine deftly, but Clinton outperformed even Faubus. Assisted by the innovative commissions and agencies that his brand of progressive government prescribes, Clinton soon had as much power as any urban machine boss. What is more, he had the sweet reputation of being progressive in the tradition of, say, Woodrow Wilson. No Mayor Daley or Boss Tweed could have imagined such a dispensation.

Upon returning to Arkansas after Yale Law School, young Clinton got off to a fast start thanks to his education and his established political connections. His claims to have led a Huck Finn youth, shoeless and shirtless in Hope, Arkansas's shantytown, are obvious hooey. Only his first few years were spent in Hope, and it is debatable how poor he was even then. At age six it was off to Hot Springs, the famous Southern gaming resort. There he was raised among Arkansas's versions of the Borgias, always in comfortable homes, occasionally in fine private schools. There was adequate money. Late-model Buicks gleamed on the front drive, and young Clinton's connections quickly extended beyond the orbit of Uncle Raymond's Buick dealership. During his Rhodes scholarship interviews Clinton attracted the favor of two senior partners at the Rose Law Firm, Gaston Williamson and William Nash, both of whom had been Rhodes Scholars themselves. Their endorsement assisted him en route to Oxford, and when Clinton returned to Arkansas six years later they provided introductions to the oligarchy. When Clinton challenged the four-term congressman, John Paul Hammerschmidt, in Arkansas's lone Republican redoubt, the Third Congressional District, the Rose firm feted him. It held a reception for both Clintons, where they met the giants of Little Rock. Henceforth the fledgling politician had access to plenty of money and campaign support. In a matter of months he had matched Hammerschmidt's war chest. His campaign ended in defeat, but not for want of funds. He outspent Hammerschmidt by $20,000, corralling friends from the AFL-CIO, the United Mine Workers, and the Arkansas Education Association, as well as the oligarchs.

Clinton entered Arkansas politics just when an aged generation was passing on. Clinton was part of a rising crop of exceptional Razorback talent. The magnificent Faubus had retired in 1967. In a 1970 attempt at a comeback, Faubus was knocked off in the Democratic gubernatorial primary as though he were an unknown by one of the prodigies of the new generation, Dale Bumpers. Bumpers then walloped Governor Winthrop Rockefeller. In 1974 he retired the aging Senator J. William Fulbright, taking over the Senate seat that Fulbright had held for twenty-nine years. Three years later, declining health forced eighty-one-year-old Senator John L. McClellan to vacate the Senate seat he had held for thirty-four years. Kaneaster Hodges, Jr. was appointed to fill the vacancy. Barred from running for the seat, the appointee wandered into oblivion. Instead, another marvel of the 1970s appeared. David Pryor landed in old Senator McClellan's seat. It was now, in 1976, that thirty-two-year-old Attorney General Jim Guy Tucker set his eyes on Washington. Despite his youth, he won the Second Congressional District. Eventually he would be Clinton's replacement in the Governor's Mansion, and the first of Arkansas's big-time machine politicians to be indicted in a Whitewater scandal.

Among all these political talents Clinton stood out like a colossus. His initial loss to Hammerschmidt slowed him not at all. Within weeks he was planning a run for attorney general. He won that position in 1976. Two years later he was governor. Clinton's political libido had not been in repose since puberty. After Yale Law School, however, it became nymphomaniacal. Of all the political newcomers scrambling for high office in the 1970s, Clinton was the most tireless, relentless, and—that quality so essential to political success in our time—adaptable. Neither a hippie wife nor his own Beatles haircut could slow his early ascent. It helped to be politically well connected, but something within Clinton set him apart. He was so ambitious, so inexhaustible, so political, as to be a freak even by the standards of Arkansas. Commentators attempting to explain Clinton's lust for power frequently resort to some psychoanalytical interpretation of his childhood in the shaky household of an alcoholic father and a party-happy mother. That is plausible. Also the messianic conception of politics that Clinton picked up from his left-wing profs may have helped fire his passion. Whatever the correct mix of his motivations, Clinton's ceaseless political urges were unmatched.

Of course, during his first term in the Governor's Mansion he stumbled. Forgetting that Arkansas is not New Haven, Connecticut, he ran afoul of the oligarchy. He neglected his vow to Tyson. He and his wife brought in a team of young bureaucrats devoted to regulation and to red tape and disdainful of the profitable inefficiencies of the Arkansan symbiosis. The oligarchy threw its support to his opponent, forcing Clinton to undertake a fateful two-year sabbatical. During the course of his second term he mastered all the details of the Arkansas machine and added a few innovations of his own. Clinton accomplished this consolidation with the usual payoffs. Friends and financial supporters were rewarded with comfortable and lucrative government positions. Out in the countryside agents of the machine—usually crooked sheriffs, judges, or commissioners—chastised the politically wayward. A threatening mutter was usually sufficient; occasionally some rough stuff might be applied. For the most part, Clinton's machine was amiable, and in Little Rock after hours, it was even good fun, especially with such parvenus as Dan Lasater.

Clinton's innovations after his comeback included the use of bond issues as patronage, first through the highway authority, then through his brainchild, the Arkansas Development Finance Authority. Prior to Clinton, the machine might have used an occasional bond issue as boodle. No Arkansas governor, however, had envisaged the state's bonding authority as expansively as Clinton. As a reward for his imagination, his campaign contribution reports from 1984 on are flush with large donations from Wall Street bond underwriters, such as PaineWebber; Donaldson, Lufkin & Jenrette; First Boston; and Blyth Eastman PaineWebber Health Care Funding, Inc. Word had undoubtedly reached the financial districts of the Northeast that the progressive government of Arkansas would henceforth become a lucrative source of commissions for its ambitious bond issues. He also created scores of new boards and commissions, all promising progress and good government while affording the governor ever more opportunities to pay off his growing army of cronies. After twelve years as governor Clinton had mustered three thousand appointees to serve humanity and his political campaigns. No taint of Tammany Hall was perceived by the press, but then Tammany predated Harvard's John F. Kennedy School of Government and all of the Kennedy School's clever sophistications for a wheeler-dealer's political immortality.

Governor Clinton's long tenure had made him significantly more powerful than Faubus and strategically far better positioned for national office. Faubus's segregationist politics scotched any ambitions that he might have had for national office. Without the impediment of a segregationist past and with all the rhetoric of progressive liberalism gathering wind in his sails, Clinton could set his course for the White House assisted by three thousand hell-bent-for-Washington government-appointed supporters. In 1992 no other Democratic candidate had such a cadre of political foot soldiers. Nor did any have the financial wherewithal. As Clinton's record of tricky loans has revealed, Arkansas's banks stood solidly behind their tireless governor. In addition, he could raise millions from state employees and enlist them in primary campaigns outside the state. An April 1992 *New York Times* dispatch reports on Clinton's surprisingly productive fund-raising appearance before state employees in Little Rock. In a sudden effusion of gasconade he exhorted them to "Go when you can.... Call when you can. Stand up for what you know is true. Write when you see something that makes you mad. But always remember: Do not defend me. Instead, defend what we have stood for and fought for and believed in, because that is what America needs to embrace in 1992." [22] Of course, what they had stood for and fought for and believed in was boodle. The Yankee press did not catch on, but the machine's yokels did, and soon hundreds of these Arkansas political appointees were at work in primary states, dreaming of the thirty-hour week in Washington.

Another of the innovations Clinton introduced to the Arkansas machine was the politicization of everything from state bureaucrats, to state troopers, to the gubernatorial cook. Clinton's penchant for politicizing government employees began early and was a natural consequence of the atmosphere in which he was educated. The intellectual climate from Georgetown to Oxford to Yale Law School was statist; its prelectors perceived all life as political. For them, government was the ideal instrument for ridding all life of imperfections. Naturally Clinton would expect those employed in his administration to share the urgency of his mission. Even on government time his employees were expected to pass out campaign literature or distribute "walking around money," as various state troopers did. (At the same time, the troopers were called upon to expedite his goatish trysts.[23]) As early as 1977, Clinton is on record urging the politicization of government employees. He was acting as coordinator of federal patronage for the Carter administration in Arkansas, and he warned the president that "Entirely too many of these jobs have been made nonpolitical when they are not.... We've gone entirely too far in insulating some of these jobs that are policy-making instead of administrative."[24]

Here, in his brisk distinction between policy-making jobs and administrative jobs, one sees Clinton's lawyerly mind at work.

Equally visible is the Arkansan habit of thwarting the law. No Arkansas governor has made heavier political use of his bureaucrats than Clinton. Repeatedly he has been rebuked for this politicizing, but in one-party Arkansas the governor gets off lightly for what in Washington attracts congressional inquiry. Federal oversight is more severe than state oversight. As early as 1979 the House Appropriations Committee cited Clinton cronies for improper political activity while working as federal employees of the community service agency ACTION. They were handling mailings, distributing campaign literature, and designing flyers for Clinton's 1978 gubernatorial campaign. In that campaign Attorney General Clinton was caught producing ten thousand copies of an eight-page brochure at government expense. Titled "Attorney General's Report," it featured five magisterial pictures of Arkansas's First Lawyer, headlines that yelled his genius, cartoons that ingratiated, and a text that was sheer campaign oratory.[25] When journalists objected, the Clinton campaign cited an obscure law passed in 1911 that called for substantive reports from the attorney general. Only after the press derided Clinton's reports for their lack of substance and blatant electioneering did the campaign make restitution.[26]

During his 1986 gubernatorial race, political appointees from Governor Clinton's office were spotted distributing campaign materials on state property, in obvious violation of state law. About this time supervisors from the Arkansas Departments of Health, Pollution Control and Ecology, and Finance and Administration were distributing still more literature prepared by Clinton's campaign committee as well as invitations to a combined fund-raiser and birthday party for the candidate. Upon being apprised of the campaign violation by Clinton's opponent, Frank White, local prosecutor Chris Piazza admitted that the Arkansas Political Practices Act had probably been breached. He declined, however, to prosecute, informing White that he had received the assurances of Betsey Wright, Clinton's campaign manager, that such irregularities would not continue. The assurance was good for two months. Then, just before election day, the state mailed twelve thousand brochures featuring a smiling Governor Clinton boldly at work signing bills, appointing cronies to government commissions, and walking in shirtsleeves through freshly plowed farm fields.[27]

And so it has gone throughout Clinton's adult life; charged with improving the human condition and blessed with a numinous vision of government's capability to do so, he summons to humanity's cause policymakers, bureaucrats, state police cruisers, and— naturally enough—government-owned telephones. In 1988, when Democratic presidential candidate Michael Dukakis had Clinton in mind for a choice spot at the Democratic convention, Clinton and members of his staff were caught flagrante delicto in the Governor's Mansion, telephoning nationwide to sing the merits of candidate Dukakis—all at state expense. They also engaged in fund-raising for Dukakis on those telephones. When reporters sought evidence that Clinton had reimbursed the state for the calls, Clinton resorted to one of his lawyerly rationales. His exculpatory records were, he insisted, locked up among his "working papers" and beyond the reach of Arkansas's Freedom of Information Act for years to come.[28]

In the 1980s the Clinton machine sent its minions into Republican primaries to ensure that the party put its weakest candidates up against the boss. The machine was even more dangerous to potential Democratic challengers. When Attorney General Steve Clark was preparing a run against Clinton for the 1990 Democratic gubernatorial nomination, Clark's use of state credit cards was leaked to the press by the Clintons' pal Webster Hubbell, leading to Clark's conviction on charges of theft by deception.[29] Within months a promising political career was in ruins and Clark was departing Arkansas for friendlier climes. Throughout the 1980s the machine tightened its grip on the state. By the time Clinton announced his presidential candidacy he had appointed every member on every

state regulatory panel. The result was vast corruption. In the area of
bond trading alone, the incidence of securities fraud in Arkansas was
probably the highest in the nation. Little Rock's so-called "bond
daddies" were a national scandal. Arkansas also joined the savings
and loan follies with extreme abandon, and it accumulated one of the
highest rates of thrift failure in the country.[30]

Yet Clinton's machine was not famous for passing legislation or
for effectively administering the state. During his governorship
Clinton passed his education reform and some economic development programs; but compared with other governors, for instance
his successor Jim Guy Tucker, his legislative accomplishments were
meager. That was not because of partisan opposition in the legislature. Of the 135 state legislators, Clinton never had to deal with
more than ten Republicans at a time. His problem was not with a
powerful opposition, but with himself. Clinton always arrived at
legislative sessions disorganized. Rarely did he pursue passage of his
legislation to its completion, often changing his mind midway
through the legislative process when significant opposition developed. "He always wanted to be all things to all people," explains Rex
Nelson, the perceptive Arkansas political reporter. Then too, he
was often out of the state, establishing his national reputation at the
expense of effective government. The national press never looked
very carefully at Clinton's record as governor. If it had it would have
noted many ironies. For example, in December 1992, when the
president-elect was snaring headlines worldwide with the Economic
Summit he had convened in Little Rock to conjure up a more
robust American economy, Governor Tucker was just a few blocks
away, having called a special session to bail out the state's Medicaid
program. Owing to Clinton's negligence, it was bankrupt.[31]

CHAPTER SIX

IN THE SHADOW OF
LITTLE ROCK:
THE CLINTONS' WHITE HOUSE

I N THE FIRST year of the Clinton administration the damaging news stories were infrequent. There were, of course, steady reports of bizarre happenings such as the president's lengthy haircut at Los Angeles International Airport and Hillary's firings of cooks and ushers. After each pother the press would quiet down and return to optimistic accounts of the progressive legislation that the Clintons had on the drawing boards. Generally ignored were the occasional stories that would pop up about Whitewater, the Clintons' unusual campaign practices during the 1980s, and talkative women—the most damaging being the one charging sexual harassment.

At the end of 1993, however, the damaging news stories began to appear with alarming regularity. They were usually of two types, the reports of financial fraud and even foul play in Arkansas in the 1980s, and the reports of White House coverups of these improprieties in the 1990s. Preceding this extended unpleasantness for the Clintons was a very controversial story. It was a story that the press ultimately decided was low down, uninteresting, and dubious, even as reporters broadcast it around the world. This was the *American*

Spectator's Troopergate story. After that story was leaked December 19, 1993, on CNN, the trickle of disturbing news stories became a torrent. The next day the *Washington Times* reported that shortly after Vince Foster's suicide White House aides removed Whitewater documents from his office. The Clintons' press coverage grew deadly. The *American Spectator* and the *Washington Times* were joined by London's *Sunday Telegraph* and a reluctant and sporadic American media in publishing accounts of the Clintons' past campaign irregularities, their misappropriation of bank funds, shady real-estate dealings, obstruction of justice, drug use, and association with drug traffickers and thugs. No American president had ever elicited such a broad range of unsavory charges, but then no other president had come from a Third World state.

The news stories of sweetheart bank deals and other conflicts of interest had their incarnation in Arkansas's symbiosis of politics and commerce. Some of the loans were made for the Clintons' personal enrichment, such as loans from the Madison Bank and Trust and from the Security Bank of Paragould that found their way to the Whitewater Development Company. Others were made to fund Clinton's campaigns. Still others, supposedly made to expedite Clinton's legislative agenda, seem to have been made to create slush funds for the governor.

There were the news stories about illegal SBA loans suborned by the governor; Travelgate, the summary firings of heretofore unpolitical White House staff; the unauthorized use of military helicopters for private purposes; and the political pressure on the RTC. All these stories had their incarnation in the political practices of one-party Arkansas, where, as Vargas Llosa might note, "those in power oversee it [the state] as though it were their own private property, or, rather their spoils." The news stories of the Clintons' cavalier treatment of the tax code also originated in the practices of one-party Arkansas, though they also reflect the third defining characteristic of the state—lawlessness and violence.

After the Clintons entered the White House a series of news stories about violent deaths, drug trafficking, and other serious felonies
committed in the 1980s began to appear, though usually not in the
mainstream press and never with followup. When the *American Spectator* in the late summer of 1995 published reports that arms and
drugs had illegally passed through Arkansas's Mena airport with
Clinton's knowledge, the entire media, with the exception of the *Wall
Street Journal* and the *Arkansas Democrat-Gazette*, ignored the story.
This was the mainstream press at its most perverse. When it had ballyhooed the *Spectator*'s reports of Clinton's promiscuity, the press said
the reports were not news. Criminal conduct would constitute news.
So, here were reports of criminal conduct, and the mainstream press
went limp. Ignored were the *Spectator*'s reports of drug trafficking,
money laundering, and illegal arms shipments, all witnessed by a
member of the governor's security detail and corroborated by a half-
dozen other witnesses. The European press was more attentive. In
the summer of 1994 the *Economist* of London warned of "a peculiar
pattern of suicides and violence [that] surrounds people connected to
the Clintons or their associates."[1] From early 1994 onward Ambrose
Evans-Pritchard wrote a series of reports in the *Sunday Telegraph*
linking Don Tyson to drug trafficking, Clinton to drug use, and
questioning the unsolved murder of a Clinton security expert who
supposedly kept damaging files on him.[2]

It is too early to judge which of the damaging news stories that
have contributed to the Clintons' prodigious problems were accurate or most consequential. Of those that originated from
Arkansas's symbiosis of politics and commerce, the first serious
report came from Jeff Gerth. All the reports of slippery bank dealings in Arkansas began with his March 8, 1992, story in the *New
York Times*, wherein Gerth reported that the Clintons went into
partnership with James B. McDougal in 1978 to buy land along the
White River and establish the Whitewater Development Corporation, a "corporation [that] continues to this day, but does not appear

to be active." Gerth reported that "at times money from Mr. McDougal's savings and loan was used to subsidize it." And Gerth describes the savings and loan, Madison Guaranty, as a "failing savings and loan association," regulated by an agency of Clinton's government. He noted that the Clinton-McDougal arrangement ensured "that the Clintons were under little financial risk in what turned out to be an unsuccessful enterprise." Federal regulators judged the savings institution insolvent, according to Gerth, and subject to closure by the state. However, Governor Clinton "appointed a new state securities commissioner, who had been a lawyer in a firm that represented the savings and loan." Contrary to state law the new commissioner, Beverly Bassett Schaffer, did not close the insolvent institution, but in a splendid example of the workings of the one-party state, approved "two novel proposals" (neither implemented) to keep the institution open. The proposals came from Hillary Clinton. Gerth supplied evidence that the Clintons deducted from their taxes interest payments that had actually been made by their Whitewater company—a splendid example of Arkansan lawlessness. Moreover, many of the company's records had disappeared. James McDougal claimed Hillary had them shipped to the Governor's Mansion. Hillary denied the claim. Gerth's prescient reportage adumbrated many of the sordid revelations to follow, but the *Times* failed to follow up on Gerth's work, a dereliction that was to be repeated by the mainstream press for months.[3]

In his 1992 story Gerth reported that when the Clintons went into partnership with the McDougals, McDougal was serving Clinton as an aide for economic development. According to Gerth, Hillary received a $30,000 loan to pay for a modular home built by Whitewater Development on the Whitewater property. This loan came from the Bank of Kingston, which was operated by none other than McDougal and another Clinton crony, Steve Smith, who pled guilty in June of 1995 to misapplying loan funds with McDougal. The loan was unsecured. Incidentally, Hillary got the loan almost immediately after McDougal and Smith acquired the Bank of Kingston, which later became Madison Bank and Trust. Despite the incriminating substance of Gerth's piece—not the least of which was the many missing Whitewater records—more than a year passed before more evidence of cozy deals surfaced in the press. Then a spectacular series of stories reporting various hastily made loans from friendly bankers to the Clintons elevated the Arkansas symbiosis to national scrutiny. Frequently the loans were unsecured, and even more frequently the bankers were rewarded by Clinton with government plums.

On December 15, 1993, Gerth reappeared in the *Times* to report a $50,000 unsecured loan to Clinton from the Bank of Cherry Valley for refinancing his 1984 reelection campaign debt.[4] The owner of the bank was another Clinton aide, Maurice Smith. Some $30,000 of this loan was paid off in 1985 by McDougal, mostly with kited checks drawn from Madison. Some of the money came in cashier's checks, endorsed by people who later claimed never to have signed the checks. One of those disputed signatures supposedly belonged to McDougal's former boss, Senator Fulbright.[5] Following up on Gerth's story, the *Washington Times* reported in the summer of 1994 that investigators were "probing whether Madison funds were improperly diverted to Whitewater and to Mr. Clinton's 1984 re-election campaign."[6]

Also in late 1993 it was reported that the Clintons and the McDougals used borrowed funds to purchase their 230 acres of Whitewater property. They had absolutely none of their own money at risk. The initial down payment from the Clintons came from an unsecured loan of $20,000 from Union National Bank of Little Rock. The bank's board was heavily populated with Clinton's pals, led by one of the governor's major fund-raisers and cronies, Walter A. DeRoeck. The mortgage of $182,611.20 was from Citizens Bank and Trust of Flippin, Arkansas. According to Meredith L. Oakley, Marlin D. Jackson was one of the bankers involved in lending to Whitewater; he later was rewarded by the governor with an appointment as state bank commissioner [see Appendix B]. Jackson explained his side of the Arkansas symbiosis to the *Washington Post*. Said the veteran state bank commissioner, unsecured loans were "just a slight accommodation for people of prominence in state government. The notion is you somehow ingratiate yourself slightly by doing this."[7] Jackson was an experienced ingratiator. Another bank that he controlled, the Security Bank of Paragould, loaned the Clintons $20,800 to pay off Hillary Clinton's loan at the Bank of Kingston.[8] According to an early 1994 report in the *Los Angeles Times*, when the Paragould loan came due McDougal paid part of it off for the Clintons by drawing a check on a Whitewater account from his Madison Guaranty Savings and Loan for $7,322.64. In keeping with his practice of kiting checks, McDougal did not have sufficient funds at the time to cover the check, and in keeping with their lubricious financial dealings, both the Clintons and the Whitewater Development Corporation took a tax deduction on the check for interest paid on the Paragould loan.[9]

The damaging financial reports continued. On July 13, 1994, the Associated Press reported that as much as $400,000 in unsecured loans were made to Governor Clinton during the 1980s to promote his political agenda, though at the time his annual salary was only $35,000. The loans came from Maurice Smith's Bank of Cherry Valley. For assistance in retiring them, Clinton then turned to Arkansas's business elite, a tactic that Scott Trotter, executive director of the Arkansas chapter of Common Cause, called "an end run" around campaign finance laws.[10] Tyson Foods contributed $15,000; Arkla, $15,000; Union Bank, $11,500; banker Bill Bowen, $5,000; First Commercial Bank, $3,700; Worthen Bank, $2,000; Wal-Mart, $1,000; McDougal, $500; and Frank Hickingbotham, largest shareholder of TCBY, on whose board Hillary Clinton sat, $25,000.[11] (All appear to be in conflict with Arkansas Campaign Laws limiting personal contributions to $1,500. These were loans that raised suspicions that Arkansas's oligarchy had in the 1980s created a slush fund for its prodigal governor.)

Responding to these damaging news reports, Clinton's defenders resorted to the same tactic they had used to defend him against charges of sexual impropriety. They dismissed the charges as ancient history. Unfortunately, on August 30, 1994, the *Washington Post* brought the Clintons' shady bank dealings into the 1990s. During Governor Clinton's 1990 campaign he garnered nearly $200,000 in unsecured loans from the Bank of Perry County. Some of those loans were neither reported in campaign finance records nor repaid. One was the $50,000 loan that Clinton called on the Stephenses and their associates to guarantee just before the November election. The owner of the Bank of Perry County, Herb Branscum, a former Democratic party chairman and generous supporter, was thereafter rewarded with an appointment to the state highway commission (he later received another sort of reward, an indictment from Independent Counsel Kenneth Starr). Another Bank of Perry County board member, Robert Hill, was elevated to the state banking board. "It remains unclear," the *Post* reported, "how the regulated financial institutions—which have strict guidelines for granting credit to individual borrowers—could have made the unsecured personal loans at all, since Clinton at the time made only $35,000 a year as governor."[12] The Arkansas symbiosis working in a one-party political system was, of course, the explanation. (Early in 1995 the *Post* followed up on this story, reporting that after the 1990 election $35,000 of this money was set aside in a "special account for Clinton at the bank"—yet another slush fund.[13])

If the news accounts of sweetheart bank loans cast light on the practices of the Arkansas symbiosis, another sporadic eruption of stories illuminated the practices of the one-party state, namely, the sedulous abuse of power, misappropriation of state property, misuse of state employees, and—after all of the above—the requisite obstruction of justice. Toward the end of 1993 the *American*

Spectator's interviews with Arkansas state troopers began exposing how the chief executive of the one-party state treated state property and state employees, again as Vargas Llosa would say, "like private property, or... spoils." The corruptions ranged from petty to grave. As first lady of Arkansas, Hillary Clinton had sent state police on domestic errands, for instance, to bring sanitary napkins to her law office. She had staff serve as baby-sitters. And she was brutally rude to state employees, a practice that would attract more notice during the White House years.[14]

With astounding frequency the Boy Governor would oblige his security men to procure women, serve as lookouts during his rendezvous, and cough up cash during times of revelry or when the use of state funds might run athwart even the standards of Arkansas. Trooper L. D. Brown reported in a second Troopergate story in the spring of 1994 that when there were extra girls Clinton was known to invite his security people to party with them. The girls were referred to as "residuals." Brown also reported that state trooper credit cards were used for entertainment. Brown met his wife, Becky, when she served as the Clintons' nanny. Her paycheck from the state listed her as a courier. Though Becky Brown took care of Chelsea Clinton, and the Clintons' only expense was a three-day-a-week preschool, the Clintons claimed a child care tax credit, a clear case of tax fraud.[15] Trooper Larry Patterson, reported to the *American Spectator* regarding Clinton, "He was always having us research his opponents. If he had a source, he'd ask us to drop a dime on them and report back, even though he knew it was a violation of state law for us to take part in political campaigns."[16]

The Clintons brought the one-party state style to Washington, conferring on their political style a burliness rare for two Ivy Leaguers of the progressive school. They placed political cronies throughout the government. Some, for instance Harold Ickes and Patsy Thomasson, had felons in their closets and on their resumes. One of their most notorious cronies, Hubbell, of course was the man who finished off Clinton's rival, Steve Clark. When Hubbell got to Washington he finished off all ninety-three incumbent U.S. attorneys in one day in an unprecedented politicization of the Department of Justice. On March 23, 1993, Hubbell, who had not yet been confirmed by the Senate as associate attorney general, called Attorney General Janet Reno and had her demand the prosecutors' resignations, some of whom—not surprisingly—were actively investigating other Clinton cronies. In their places the administration planted still more cronies, Paula Casey being, perhaps, the most significant. Upon appointment as U.S. Attorney for the Eastern District of Arkansas, she swiftly rejected the first Resolution Trust Corporation criminal referrals on Madison Guaranty Savings and Loan, which mentioned the Clintons as potential witnesses and possible beneficiaries from criminal activities. Then she snubbed plea bargain offers by David Hale who might have brought the Clintons' corruption to light. A willing member of the Arkansas machine, Hale in the fall of 1993 faced indictment for Small Business Administration fraud and sought leniency in return for his knowledge of illegal loans by Arkansas's political elites, including Governor Clinton. After rejecting the RTC referrals and Hale's offer, Casey decorously recused herself from further meddling in these matters. Prior to the Clinton administration, it had been standard Department of Justice practice to replace U.S. attorneys when their terms expired or when a successor was found, but the products of one-party Arkansas were not accustomed to working with members of the opposite party. It made them uncomfortable, and at the end of the summer of 1995, hearings conducted by Congressman James Leach and another conducted by Senator Alfonse D'Amato began to reveal that their discomfort was understandable.

The first major White House scandal clearly born of the corruptions of one-party Arkansas was the Travelgate fiasco. On May 19, 1993, the Clintons' Arkansas crony, David Watkins, then White House assistant to the president for management and administration, suddenly fired seven employees of the White House Travel Office, giving them one hour to vacate the premises. As information about what was soon dubbed Travelgate seeped out, first in the news, then in congressional inquiries, it became clear that the scandal was attributable not only to the arrogance of one-party Arkansas but also to the venality of the Arkansas symbiosis. The firings at the Travel Office were also motivated by a quality at the time—early 1993—unrecognized by most observers, to wit, the administration's political amateurism. Embarrassed by such blunders as the Waco assault and the president's $200 haircut, the White House sought a public relations coup to mollify growing public criticism. According to a memo written at the time by Watkins and released during a congressional hearing in early 1996, the Clintons' newly arrived political maestro, TV producer Harry Thomason, advised that the firings at the Travel Office would supply the requisite theater to put the American people in mind of the Kennedys during the Cuban Missile Crisis. Mrs. Clinton seems to have agreed.[17]

Thomason's political advice was not disinterested. Thomason and his colleagues intended to enrich themselves by taking over at first the White House's and later more of the government's travel business. Call it privatization, Arkansas style. In reporting this scheme and the Clintons' abuse of the FBI to smear the seven vanquished employees long before congressional inquiries and an occasional mainstream reporter got the drift, David Brock catalogued the Arkansas political practices that had been imported to the White House. "The plot lines are familiar," Brock noted, "abuse of government power to benefit campaign contributors; violations of conflict-of-interest laws; a review conducted to deflect, not resolve, legitimate questions; improper contacts with independent law-enforcement agencies; efforts to deceive the press; a compromised Justice Department; and, at the center of the muck, with her 'strong moral compass,' Hillary Rodham Clinton."[18]

Watkins continued to be a figure in the Clinton White House

until he flummoxed spectacularly a year later, causing another news story to break and again reveal abuses learned from one-party Arkansas. In May of 1994 he was photographed by the *Frederick News-Post* as he transported himself to a golf outing aboard the presidential helicopter. The ensuing White House maneuvers followed closely to the plot line Brock had perceived a year earlier. The White House military office was prevailed upon to release a series of misleading statements interspersed with downright lies. Supposedly Watkins had taken the helicopter on a "training mission" in preparation for transporting the president to the golf course. The "training mission" was necessary so that the helicopter pilots could "familiarize themselves with all aspects of the course, especially those aspects related to actual time of play and associated impact of security plans."[19] All Washington was beginning to laugh, and then the news got out that not one but two helicopters had been involved. This went beyond the pale, and Watkins resigned. Thirteen White House aides promised to absorb the $13,000 cost of the flights. It remains unclear whether they ever did.[20]

Attempting to justify the firings at the White House Travel Office, the administration released a typically misleading report charging the Travel Office with "gross mismanagement." Eventually Watkins was interviewed by the General Accounting Office (GAO). In this interview Watkins admitted that he had rarely met with the head of the Travel Office, Billy Dale. According to the GAO report, "Watkins did not set any specific performance expectations with Mr. Dale. Mr. Watkins expected Mr. Dale to continue to run the Travel Office in the early months of the administration, but did not give him any specific goals." This is what Watkins himself told the GAO! Moreover, according to the GAO report, Watkins "does not know if any Financial Integrity Act reviews were done of the Travel Office in the past two years. He is not familiar with the Financial Integrity Act." And there is more: "Mr. Watkins does not know the definition of the term 'procurement official.'

However he does obligate funds for government purchases of goods and services. He is not aware of the Procurement Integrity Act or if he is subject to it."[21] This interview took place almost an entire year after Watkins had come to the White House.

There were many more examples of Arkansan abuses of power and misuse of government property at the White House. Some were risible. On May 18, 1993, the media cackled with reports that Air Force One had idled on a runway at Los Angeles International Airport for forty-five minutes, tying up two runways at a cost of some $76,000 to commercial flights. The president was getting a haircut. The work was being done by the celebrated Beverly Hills barber, Christophe, for $200. It turned out that this was a bargain. Several days later the *Times* of London reported that when *Family Circle* sought to do a piece on Mrs. Clinton the White House demanded that the magazine transport Christophe all the way from Los Angeles to prepare her hair for the cameras. This time his fee was $2,000. It was also reported that the *Los Angeles Times* and the *New York Times* had been similarly importuned upon.[22] Also in May came the embarrassing report that on a presidential visit to New Hampshire, a White House staff member of the oafish Watkins variety had asked a well-known local television anchorwoman to apply the president's makeup.

The Arkansans were extremely uncomfortable working with anyone not a crony of their one-party polity. Chris Emory, a veteran White House usher, was fired by the First Lady after Deputy White House Counsel Vince Foster, her former law partner at the Rose Law Firm, concluded that the traditionally nonpolitical ushers "plotted to have excessive costs incurred" during Mrs. Clinton's redecoration of the executive mansion. (The redecoration itself was widely ridiculed for its vulgarity, with critics split on whether the style had been lifted from that of the late nineteenth-century Pullman club car or that of the late nineteenth-century New Orleans bordello.) The immediate cause of Emory's dismissal was a report received by Mrs.

Clinton that her White House usher had been espied conducting a telephone conversation with his former boss, Barbara Bush. He was advising her on a computer problem.[23] Mrs. Clinton fired the White House chef, Pierre Chambrin, explaining with characteristic pretentiousness that she wanted only wholesome "American cuisine" served to her husband, while the president was at the time positively boastful about his McDonald's hamburger binges and the eager beavers on the White House staff were becoming famous for their dependency on nocturnal pizza deliveries.

Contempt for government procedures was another legacy of one-party Arkansas. In March 1994 the press reported that nearly one-third of the 1,044 White House employees were still without permanent White House passes. White House Associate Counsel William Kennedy, another of Mrs. Clinton's former partners from the Rose Law Firm, simply had not given the Secret Service completed FBI background reports on the employees. The *Washington Times* explained that "the FBI found cases of past drug use and drug convictions, years of unpaid taxes, unpaid debts and financial irregularities." As these reports would obviously have made it difficult for the Secret Service to give their subjects White House passes, Kennedy simply held on to the reports and dispensed with the customary process for securing passes.[24] In June the *Washington Times* struck again, reporting that four White House military aides, all officers, had been ordered to serve hors d'oeuvres during a state dinner, as if the Clintons were still back in Arkansas, where they regularly misused staff and even put prisoners of the state penitentiary to such delicate tasks. According to the Marine officer, the Air Force captain, the Navy lieutenant, and a lieutenant from the Naval Service Office, the White House staff ordered them not to mention the incident, though it was clearly improper, and in fact a breach of the Geneva Conventions barring officers from manual labor.[25]

Other news accounts of embarrassments committed in the White House but born of one-party Arkansas were decidedly more serious.

Governor Clinton's proclivity for putting the arm on individuals, politicizing government agencies, and making improper contacts with government officials continued once he was president. The result was a series of news reports detailing indiscretions that almost certainly would have meant indictments for lesser figures.

In November 1993 David Hale, after failing in his attempt to plea bargain, charged that in 1986 Governor Clinton pressured him on the steps of the capitol building to make an illegal loan to McDougal's wife. As Jim Adams and I revealed in the February *American Spectator*, this $300,000 loan was diverted to cleaning up a loan in which Mrs. Clinton herself had played a possibly criminal role and for some other harebrained projects. It was never repaid. In the months following State Trooper Brown asserted in a deposition that he was a witness to the event. Presently the *American Spectator* and somewhat later the *Wall Street Journal* reported on telephone logs that raised suspicions that Hubbell had, in the fall of 1993 when he was associate attorney general, conspired with U.S. Attorney Paula Casey to discredit Hale as a witness, a clear obstruction of justice.

A month later the president himself may have perpetrated an indictable abuse of power. As reported in the *Los Angeles Times* and the *American Spectator*, aroused by rumors that Arkansas state troopers were fraternizing with the press and revealing sordid tales about the Clintons, President Clinton telephoned Trooper Danny Ferguson and discussed possible jobs in exchange for information about what the troopers were saying. At a Renaissance Weekend late in December 1993, President Clinton again stepped onto ethically shaky ground when he sought counsel from Comptroller of the Currency Eugene Ludwig. Both had been friends since their days at Oxford and Yale. Clinton wanted to know how Ludwig might handle the various imbroglios included under the catchall term Whitewater. Ludwig demurred, warning Clinton of the seriousness of his imprudence.

As Clinton's presidency wore on, the stories multiplied. The habits of intimidating opponents, discrediting them, and putting thereunto independent government agencies to one's own purposes were as deeply ingrained in the Arkansas boy's nature as salivating at the sight of McDonald's twin arches. In late 1994, after ABC News taped an interview with Trooper Brown, Clinton went into another of his panics. He believed Brown was going public with his knowledge of drug and gun trafficking at Mena. Brown's actual subject during the interview was his knowledge of Clinton's contacts with Hale. At any rate, summoning his personal lawyer, David Kendall, Clinton asked him to abandon the afternoon's Washington Redskins game and fly to New York to dissuade ABC from broadcasting the interview. At Clinton's request, Kendall depicted Brown as a "pathological liar" who had failed state police psychiatric tests. Brown's superior, Colonel Tommy Goodwin, when asked by ABC, refuted both charges. Kendall also passed on Clinton's claim that Brown's mother had died years before under mysterious circumstances and that Brown had failed a CIA examination. Neither story was accurate, and the last one alerted ABC journalists that Clinton had obviously sent aides ferreting through Brown's CIA personnel file for dirt on him. Nevertheless, ABC, under White House pressure, killed the Brown interview. Perhaps Clinton's fortunes would have been better served if the interview had been broadcast. Clinton's treatment of Brown infuriated the ex-bodyguard, causing him to go public to me about Mena for the first time.

Another legacy of one-party Arkansas was the Clintons' habit of concealing evidence. It is now widely known that when Clinton ran for Congress back in 1974 his draft file mysteriously disappeared and would have been lost forever if a lone and indignant ROTC officer had not made copies of it or some of the most incriminating parts of it.[26] Gerth's March 8, 1992 *New York Times* piece reports that, while governor, Clinton tried to conceal many Whitewater documents in the Governor's Mansion, leaving the Whitewater file so incomplete as to render it for the most part inscrutable. The reports of concealing evidence continued through the Clinton presidency. The *Washington Times* in early 1994 reported that even after President Clinton ordered Whitewater records released to Justice Department investigators, the White House was caught dragging its feet and suspected of concealing documents until statutes of limitations might make indictments impossible.[27] McDougal's wife reported that Clinton ordered her to bring still more Whitewater documents to the mansion "sometime before" October 3, 1991. Contrary to his promise to Mrs. McDougal, Clinton never returned her documents.[28]

The night of Vince Foster's death, White House Counsel Bernard Nussbaum, Clinton's White House Administrative Aide Patsy Thomasson, and the First Lady's Chief of Staff Margaret Williams, entered Foster's office at around 10 P.M. and did not leave until nearly midnight. Nussbaum claimed he had been in the office only briefly and said nothing of his co-conspirators. For months the White House lied about the disposition of those files. Hillary lied publicly about the concealment in an April 1994 press conference, which she had called to put to rest questions about her Whitewater involvement and about those cattle futures trades that showed her to be either a capitalist of unsurpassed genius or one of God's favorites. When asked whether her chief of staff had removed documents from Foster's office, Mrs. Clinton answered, "I don't think that she did remove any documents."[29] Eventually not only was it learned that the Clinton aide removed documents, but also that they were removed at Hillary's orders and locked in a closet on the third floor of the White House.[30] Finally, there is the question of Hillary Clinton's billing records from the Rose Law Firm that appeared miraculously in the White House residence. They had been subpoenaed two years previously.

All of the above stories of scandal are marbled with the political vices of Arkansas, and the element most widely streaked through them is conflict of interest. Combining the habits of lawlessness of a one-party regime (with the statist megalomania of 1960s Coat and Tie Radicals), Clintonites, whether in Arkansas or in Washington, could no more separate their personal interests from government process than they could pass up an opportunity to moralize and lecture the public. As 1993 gave way to 1994, then to 1995, the Clintons' record of conflicted interests in Arkansas was becoming a matter of public record in the press. First there were the reports that Hillary in the mid-1980s represented her business partner McDougal in his bank's desperate attempt to avoid closure by state regulatory agencies in the power of her husband. Then came the *Chicago Tribune*'s report that Hillary and associates from the Rose Law Firm represented the federal government in legal action against her friend Dan Lasater, one of her husband's major financial supporters. Naturally Lasater came out okay, and there were other conflicts of interests reported—for instance, Hubbell's employment by the Federal Deposit Insurance Corporation through the Rose Law Firm to pursue a lawsuit against Madison's accountant, Frost and Company. As with the Lasater case, this case was settled for a fraction of what could have been obtained. Only later was it discovered that the lawsuit arose partly over bad loans made by Madison to Hubbell's father-in-law, Seth Ward.[31]

As the scandals of Whitewater rolled across the White House compound like a mist off a sewage treatment pond, the Clintons could not restrain themselves from their old practices. Having placed their deputy treasury secretary, a Georgetown pal of Bill's by the name of Roger Altman, as acting supervisor of the RTC "to keep the lid on" the investigation of Madison, they pressured him not to recuse himself from the case. When he did they became "furious."[32] The proclivity for conflicts of interest was now afflicting even the Yanks in the administration. Beginning in the fall of 1993 White House Counsel Bernard Nussbaum held meetings with the General Counsel to the Treasury Department, Jean Hansen, in discussions about the RTC's dealings with Madison. The meetings spread to other Treasury officials and to such White House officials as Mark Gearan and Bruce Lindsey. George Stephanopoulos and Harold Ickes made improper calls to Altman opposing the hiring of a former Republican U.S. attorney as fee counsel to the RTC.

When subpoenas were served summoning these and other Clintonites to appear before Capitol Hill congressional committees, many of the participants in these discussions, according to Senator D'Amato, placed "the personal interest of the president above the people's interest" and lied "to Congress and to the American people in order to conceal this misconduct."[33] One, Treasury Department official Joshua Steiner, after being caught in a discrepancy between his testimony and notes he had made in his diary, seemed to be saying he had lied to his diary. Even the Arkansan ease with sweetheart loans was picked up by the Yanks in the White House. In May of 1994, George Stephanopoulos received a huge sweetheart loan from NationsBank despite his failure to meet at least four qualifying requirements. The loan was approved when NationsBank, owned by Clinton's friend Hugh McColl, had important legislation pending before the administration.[34]

The lawlessness of Arkansas had obviously come to afflict many in the Clinton administration, but what of the violence? That is a murky question entoiled in partisanship, usually the partisanship of the ideologically transfixed. The liberal diehards deride any suggestion of homicides, mysterious suicides, and mayhem; the right-wing enthusiasts draw a line from every unnatural death in Arkansas directly to the Oval Office. Historians will someday settle the question as to whether the Arkansas machine had a hand in the untimely deaths that overcame the Clintons' friends, associates, distant acquaintances, and enemies during their rise to power. We do know that in the summer of 1994 the sober *Economist* listed eight unpleasant incidents in warning of the "peculiar pattern of suicides and violence" surrounding "people connected to the Clintons": Vince Foster, Kathy Ferguson (ex-wife of a Clinton bodyguard, a suicide),

Bill Shelton (Arkansas policeman, boyfriend of Ferguson, a suicide), Jon Walker (RTC investigator concerned with irregularities at Madison Guaranty Savings and Loan, fell from the top of a building, dead),[35] Jerry Parks (chief of security for Clinton's 1992 campaign headquarters, shot dead in Arkansas), Gary Johnson (Arkansas lawyer badly beaten in 1992 after claiming to have videotapes of Clinton calling on Gennifer Flowers), Dennis Patrick (endured three attempts on his life after he discovered millions of dollars passing mysteriously through his account at the firm of Clinton supporter and friend Dan Lasater), and Stanley Huggins (early investigator into Madison Guaranty Savings and Loan, found dead in Delaware).[36]

CHAPTER SEVEN

A SNOPES BREATHES
THE *KULTURSMOG*

NOT FAR BACK in Bill Clinton's ancestry the industrious genealogist will find grizzled old boys, who derived a delicious pleasure and even some prestige from holding between their remaining teeth a simple stalk of straw. It was the fashion in rural Arkansas in times past to twist that straw pensively 'twixt index finger and thumb, to suck on it lazily for its woody good taste, and to spit it out contemptuously when action was afoot. In the hamlet where Clinton's forebears dwelt, that straw clenched between the teeth was recognized as the mark of a suave, virile male by all the local dames—and with some urgency by the young 'uns. Clinton's hayseed ancestors had other distinguishing features. There was a time when few wore shoes. Their bib overalls often did not reach below their calves. Most went unshaven for days. Their necks were usually dirty. Even by the tatterdemalion standards of bygone Arkansas, Clinton's forebears were a mangy lot. He and his immediate relatives have come a long way. Except for certain persistent moral infelicities, the life of the forty-second president of the United States would be radiant with uplift. He might have been the

Abraham Lincoln of the late twentieth century, or at least the Rutherford B. Hayes.

Clinton is fond of saying that he was raised in pinched circumstances "in a place called Hope." Yet here again a Clintonian disclosure, like an Ozark duck call, is sounded not to inform but to deceive. As we have noted, Clinton spent most of his youth not in Hope, but in cosmopolitan Hot Springs, and in some comfort with new Buicks on the drive, a country club at which to golf, and a fine parochial school to engage an energetic mind. Nonetheless, a generation or two back his antecedents—at least those who appear in the public record—actually hailed from even meaner parts than Hope, and without the violin music that the sentimental presidential hopeful was wont to turn up whenever Hope was mentioned. His ma came from a remote settlement called Ebenezer Community. It never amounted to more than a tiny assemblage of tin-roofed shacks just over the hill from Bodcaw, Arkansas (population 100). It was dull and it was grim in those parts. For action or upward mobility one had to head down the road to the "oil towns" of Smackover and El Dorado, but then how would one get home? Cars were scarce and unreliable, and downtown Smackover was no place to leave one's mule overnight.

As Clinton's mother, Virginia Cassidy Kelley, attests in *Leading with My Heart*, an autobiography that casts more light upon her son's youth than any other book or governmental inquiry thus far, Ebenezer Community was inhabited by just three families, the Grishams, the Russells, and the Cassidys. "The Russells and the Cassidys," she relates, "had come to Arkansas from Alabama in the 1800s, already intertwined by marriage. The Grishams—my mother's family—seem to have been here forever."[1]

Where Clinton's father came from is still in doubt, for it remains uncertain who Clinton's father might have been. The putative father, William Jefferson Blythe, was, indeed, the marrying kind. He married at least four times in nine years. Supposedly Virginia

Cassidy was his last wife, he having met her in the summer of 1943 just before shipping out to military service in Egypt, then Italy. For the next two years Blythe served with the army in Europe, and Virginia was kicking up her heels in Hope. Then comes another of those discrepancies that make the lives of the Clintons so frustrating to the conscientious fact checker. Virginia claims she was reunited with Blythe in November of 1945. Yet military records show that he did not get back from Europe until December 1 and that he was not discharged until December 7. Clinton was born only three months after Blythe's death. Virginia explains her baby's early arrival as doctor's orders. She claims a doctor insisted that labor be induced early because she had taken a fall. As with other tricky issues involving the Clintons, we are asked to take Virginia's word on this. An alternative explanation that has circulated through Hot Springs for years is that Virginia had never even met Blythe and had a baby out of wedlock by some still unknown father. A well-connected friend, familiar with the last few months of entries at the morgue, the gossip says, provided the makings of an important branch for her son's family tree. For our purposes it is enough to observe that the child inherited his mother's cleverness, her appetite for fun, her affable nature, her yearning for acceptance and approval. He also seems to have inherited her knack for landing on her feet after the most reckless misadventures. Where Clinton got his indecisiveness, hollowness, and promiscuity remains mysterious. Blythe does seem to have been remarkably cavalier about commitments, so maybe the Hot Springs rumor mill was in error.

By comparison with the frank details imparted to posterity by Clinton's mother, other biographical treatments of her son have ranged from bland to vacuous. Some facts are rendered. The usual Clintonian discrepancies are duly noted; but yesteryear's Arkansas remains vague, and to most Americans the Clintons remain a statistical improbability. Even Mrs. Kelley's frankness leaves the reader hazy as to Clinton's origins. Fortunately William Faulkner, the distinguished Southern novelist who knew the South so well, has given us vivid depictions of the original Clintons in their natural habitat. Chronicling the decline of the Old South and the first stirrings of the New, Faulkner populated his Yoknapatawpha county with freed slaves; the remnant of white aristocracy; a gnarled white yeomanry; and finally the members of a seedy, coarse, amoral, rootless clan named Snopes. Violent, greedy, promiscuous, uneducated, and usually cagey—occasionally idiotic, insane, and criminal—the Snopeses slipped out of the hollows in which they had engendered from time immemorial and wandered into the hamlet of Frenchman's Bend. Steadily they worked and cheated their way to prominence and tolerable prosperity. They climbed over the backs of the yeomen and the blacks, giving both an occasional kick. They hustled and connived their way into the homes and the commercial holdings of the dying generations of Southern Bourbons. Some moved on from Frenchman's Bend to the more populous and dynamic city of Jefferson (do I hear Hot Springs?). After that they spread out. One even went to live in Los Angeles, where he made his way in the entertainment industry. (Bill and his boyhood cronies made it all the way to Washington.)

The most famous of the Snopeses is Flem, a cold, calculating sociopath who becomes the head of the family. He is too cheerless and cruel to serve as a prototype for Boy Clinton. Flem's cousin, Isaac, an idiot who falls in love with a cow, is obviously equally unsuitable, as is the dead-beat schoolteacher and restaurateur, I. O. Snopes. Cousin Eck Snopes looks promising. Being the rare Snopes who is actually somewhat the nice guy, he is likable enough to serve as a prototype for our forty-second president, except that, back in Jefferson, while trying to find a lost boy, he lowers a lighted lantern into an oil tank and blows himself to kingdom come. Bill Clinton would have had the sense to ask Bruce Lindsey to do that.

There is another personable and clever Snopes whose life prefigures Clinton's, at least in terms of manner and disposition, I. O.'s outgoing and comparatively energetic son, Montgomery Ward Snopes. In fact, the likeness is uncanny. For those of us who have thought that our roguish press conference prodigy was one of a kind in his smiling and fibbing, his ingratiating and conniving, his laying on of the country boy charm pursuant to nothing very coherent, Montgomery Ward Snopes is instructive. We find him greasing palms on the courthouse steps, gypping hillbillies at the county auction, or helping the occasional old lady across the street—at least halfway. He reminds us of Clinton. Even Clinton's war record bears similarities to Montgomery's. Montgomery Ward beats the World War II draft by joining the YMCA and going to France to run a U.S. army canteen. He recruits a French girl to entertain the troops in a back room. Then he returns to Yoknapatawpha, where he sets up a "French postcard" business. Eventually Montgomery makes good in Hollywood, and if I were to point out its similarities to Washington I would not be regarded as having made an original point.

The Snopeses at their best are salesmen and hustlers. At their next to best they are gamblers, traffickers in illicit goods, thieves, brawlers, and ex-convicts. Clinton's mother's first husband, William Jefferson Blythe—assuming they truly were married and that the marriage license was not merely a formality, ex post facto—had been a dairyman, a mechanic, a traveling salesman, an Oldsmobile salesman. But he was also a wife abuser, a bigamist, and a philanderer. His restless connubiality explains the embarrassing number of blanks who stepped forward from the American lumpen proletariat to claim half-siblinghood with the new president. It also explains why, just months into Clinton's first year, one of London's most prestigious newspapers, the *Independent*, could blare out that Our President was *nullius filius*.

Blythe was free in 1935 to marry Virginia Gash, the seventeen-year-old daughter of a saloon keeper, though having a child by her in 1938, two years after their divorce, was not in good taste. He was free to marry again in August of 1938, though when this second wife divorced him nine months later, the judge made it very clear that, far from an exemplary husband, he had been "guilty of extreme cruelty, and gross neglect of duty." Certainly his marriage in 1940 was legal enough, though as it was to Minnie Gash, his first wife's younger sister, his taste can again be questioned. (There are reports that he married Gash II only to escape the clutches of another girl, whom he had impregnated.)[2] But Blythe was almost certainly not free to marry Clinton's mother, Virginia, in 1943; for it seems that after his 1940 marriage he married again in 1941 to Wanetta E. Alexander, and his divorce from her did not come through until 1944.[3] Hence Bill Clinton, whether the son of Blythe or of an anonymous donor, is almost certainly America's first bastard to be elected president.

Whatever Blythe's relationship with Clinton's mother amounted to, it is obvious that the couple did not spend a lot of time together. Then on May 17, 1946, Bill Blythe died in a car accident. Virginia's next marriage was even more Snopesian. She packed six-year-old Billy up and moved an hour up the road to Hot Springs. One can understand her eagerness to settle in, for, as she notes, Hot Springs "had been one of the premier playgrounds in America. It had also been a place where gangsters were cool, and rules were made to be bent, and money and power—however you got them—were the total measure of man."[4] There, "in a town in which the con job was considered an art form," Virginia set up practice as a nurse anesthetist and married one of the town's gifted artists, Roger Clinton, whose surname was conveyed to young Bill. Roger was known to his friends as Dude, and by his signature line, "God dang it, let's all get drunk and talk about the chances we had to marry!"[5] As with Virginia's first husband, Clinton tried his hand at farming and sales. His brother, Raymond, had set him up with a Buick dealership in Hope. When he blew that operation, he began selling cars in Hot Springs; then, as the booze got the best of him, he ran the parts department at brother Raymond's dealership. He followed other callings. He ran numbers, dealt in moonshine, and eventually delivered liquor back to Hope, where Virginia's dad sold it illegally at that country store that Bill Clinton was to immortalize in his 1992 acceptance speech to the Democratic National Convention. Through a friend's drug store in Hope, Dude Clinton also supplied the local citizenry with bookies and slot machines from Hot Springs.

The Hot Springs that Billy Clinton grew up in was a banquet of bordellos, illegal booze, gambling (some legal, some not), and all-night clubs. Virginia and Roger abandoned themselves to the whole tawdry scene. Virginia danced, drank, flirted, and gambled. Roger competed in the same events and added the more manly competitions of fist fights, speeding (often under the influence), and philandering. In her autobiography Virginia relates the time he "bashed a Puerto Rican boy in the head with a cue stick" and "the night I danced with a man at the Tower Club and Roger Clinton beat him to a pulp." Their lives were not all drunkenness and violence. There was also room for art. Occasionally, at the end of an evening's revelries, Virginia would clear her throat, stand on a table, and belt out a song of her own composition, "I'm the Hempstead County Idiot."[6]

Roger Clinton was the roaring, hell-raising, drunken Snopes whom little Billy observed from childhood through college, at first with a mixture of fear and affection, then, as he matured, with anger, and finally resignation. In 1962, shortly after the Clintons' divorce, the older Clinton went into rapid decline. He lost thirty-five pounds, slept under the stars in front of Virginia's living room window, and three months after their divorce went through regained his ex-wife's hand in marriage. But the Dude was Dude no more. No longer was he the terrifying presence he had been to Billy; he was now a solitary, graying, silent drunkard. For hours he would sit alone in a favored chair in a room off to the back of the house, a drink in his hand, the reflection of the television set dancing on his blank face, or jazz from his record collection filling his ears with memories of more vivacious times. The household's center of attention was now young Bill. After he went off to Georgetown, Roger came down with cancer. Too vain to have surgery that might have disfigured his face, he suffered radiation treatment and died pitiably. Young Bill witnessed the final days and seems to have been deeply moved by his stepfather's death.

Virginia remained the fun-loving, gregarious Snopes, a female version of Montgomery Ward. It was her genetic blueprint that determined the character of the future president. During her son's early youth, Virginia may have lived a stupid life, but she was not unintelligent. She had been a member of the National Honor Society while attending high school back in Hope, and she passed her quick, albeit facile, intelligence on to Billy. Virginia expected him to get ahead, and though she spent much of her free time at the local race track, at the gambling tables, or in the clubs, she goaded Billy to success, both in the classroom and in the small-town ritual of being a joiner. Like Hillary Rodham later, Virginia was the dominant influence in Clinton's life. She discouraged his participation in sports, despite his interest. She was adamant that he avoid football, though his size would have given him an advantage. She patrolled his social life. True to his Snopesian inheritance of hustle and of carnality, Billy pursued the fair sex even at an early age, but mother was always there to see to it that Billy's girls were worthy of him. They never were. Even a former Miss Arkansas with brains failed to get the nod from the widow of Dude Clinton.

By the time Clinton was in high school, Virginia had transformed the living room of the Clinton home at 213 Scully Street into a museum dedicated to her first-born son. Her younger son, Roger Cassidy Clinton, sired by Dude, never matched his older brother's talents, save for a streak of roguishness whose trophies would be clearly out of place in the Clinton living room. The room's main wall was covered with memorabilia of Bill's miracles: pictures of him as class president, at Boys Nation, at summer band camp. There were, of course, no trophies from track and field and, as for the brutish football team, a trophy from a coed bake sale would have been more imaginable. Instead the museum at Scully Street was dignified with relics from scores of student activities triumphs, testimonials to distinguished scholarship, dozens of medals and ribbons from spelling bees, student debates, and the marching band. Through the early years, Roger would howl, break bottles, and brandish his shootin' iron (he fired over Virginia's head once). Through the later years, when Roger sulked in the back room, Virginia sedulously augmented the Bill Clinton Museum on Scully Street.

Hot Springs worshipped its student achievers, and by high school, Clinton was one of Hot Springs's "golden boys." Students avid for good grades would sit by him. Student organization types recognized his friendship as a potential asset. Hot Springs's paradoxical mix of gangsters and whores, Southern Baptists and American Legionnaires gave the town's youth conflicting role models. The Hero of Scully Street was too clever to emulate the model of the gambler or the gangster. Raised among car salesmen, and with the Snopesian hustler imprinted in his genes, he just naturally inclined towards politics.

Boys Nation was for him, as were church picnics, student organization meetings, and the marching band. Then while at Boys Nation in 1963 came that transilient handshake with President John F. Kennedy. Clinton's ardor for politics heightened, and perhaps that handshake with Kennedy got him to thinking about a duality that has characterized his political life: there is a moral standard for the clods and there is a more amorphous standard for the well-connected politico. Growing up in Little Rock, watching the politically connected Uncle Raymond and Uncle Roy (who sat in the state legislature from 1951 to 1954), Clinton saw how those whom his mother called the "Big Wheels" could bend the rules for themselves. Now, having acquired JFK as his political model, he would not have failed to notice that even well-connected Yankee politicos lived by two sets of rules. Kennedy, the rich playboy, always invoked the high ideals of the Boy Scouts while living the easy morality of the low life. Clinton would too.

The eternal candidate was stung by the political bug as early as high school, and by then he was—well, he was what we saw on the campaign trail in 1992 and in the White House during his every waking hour. He was a glad-handing, back-slapping, smiling, schmoozing, yuk-yuking, politicking maniac. His life at Hot Springs High marked the beginning of what has become a life of daily, weekly, monthly whirl. Like Flem Snopes descending on Frenchmen's Bend, Bill sauntered into Hot Springs High, sized up the place, and *whoosh*—he was Beta Club president, junior class president, band major, Key Club president, a fully accredited senator to Boys Nation. By senior year his frenzied acquisitions of sonorous titles and perks had alarmed even his teachers, though teachers usually esteem such student go-getters. They stepped in before Bill could hog the student body presidency for his senior year and in an unusual decision barred him from running. His response was an adroit volte-face and an unprecedented campaign to become senior class secretary. The senior class secretary had always been a girl. Clinton lost.

The world of the student politician is a vast delusion inhabited by narcissistic young people who assume that a title proffered by a majority of their fellow students really makes them a president or a senator. The university student gripped by the student government delusion is immensely amusing; the high school student is absolutely hilarious. The high schooler is not only playing the role of make-believe Roosevelt; he is playing the role of make-believe adult. It does not speak well for the American educational system that it provides the props for these patheticoes to gain their bogus prestige. Educators should not encourage students in their delusions. The students suffering them are almost always ridiculous and untrustworthy busybodies; nonetheless, their contemporaries frequently tout them as young people full of promise. Sometimes the commonweal gets stuck with them, though at other times they simply enter into long and happy lives of psychoanalysis.

In reading journalist David Maraniss's early biography of Clinton, *First in His Class*, readers are expected to marvel at the frequency with which Clinton's teachers, friends, and even the boy candidate himself predicted his eventual residency at 1600 Pennsylvania Avenue. In truth, *all* student body politicians are forever being boomed as potential presidents, whether they are hustling down the corridors of Hot Springs High or Peoria Central. What is truly marvelous is that Maraniss's volume of some 300 pages (only on page 286 does he leave Yale for Arkansas) brings Clinton only from his incunabular wailing in the manger up to his final glories in law school. Could a biographer spend 300 pages on Abraham Lincoln's youth and education, or on George Washington's? Could a Lincoln biographer locate hundreds of teachers and fellow students to testify that, yes, they felt certain that here was a young lad headed for the Emancipation Proclamation and a bad night at Ford's Theatre? Was there a vast correspondence from young Abe to his girl friends, his band teacher, an unsuspecting ROTC officer? Were there newspaper clippings of Abe's triumphs in student activities, academic exercises, student statecraft? Were there records of awards won, of class offices captured? I think not. Unfortunately, our educational system now provides many opportunities for the student body politician to amass such spurious biographical material. The only other type of modern-day student likely to leave such a trail of biographical residue is the student athlete. The student athlete, however, is really an athlete; the student politician is merely a make-believe politician and a make-believe adult. Some never grow out of the world of make-believe. A recurrent complaint about Clinton in office has been that he acts like an arrested adolescent, always at play with the facts and with people, never accepting responsibility for his blunders, always whining and blaming others.

The make-believe adult from 213 Scully Street never grew up emotionally. This upwardly mobile Snopes used his peers and discarded them. He ingratiated himself to adults. With no higher purpose other than holding some humbug office, the Montgomery Ward Snopes of Hot Springs developed intricate, manipulative techniques. "Speaking the idiom, wherever he was, ranked among Clinton's greatest talents," Maraniss observes. Like any other Snopes coming into town with a load of belt buckles to sell, or wild ponies, or Bibles that glow in the dark, Clinton perceived the vanities and anxieties of his easy marks, and he adapted to them. "By his second year," Maraniss continues, "in Fulbright's shop [Senator J. William Fulbright's office where he interned while at Georgetown] he was a certified Hill rat who knew the lingo of the place, the tunnels and subway shortcuts, the lore, all the latest rumors and inside stories about LBJ and the frailties of senators who only a year earlier he had viewed as gods... Clinton's manner with congressmen was similar in many respects to the way he dealt with professors: by showing a keen interest in their stories and special concerns, he gained insight and scored brownie points at the same time."[7]

Clinton's ascent from presidency of the Hot Springs High School junior class, through high office at Georgetown, and on to the highest elective office in the Republic, gave him thousands of opportunities to perfect the talents of the poseur, particularly the most critical talent of the poseur, the talent for lying. After the historians have had sufficient time to assess Clinton's career, I believe they will rate him the greatest presidential liar in the history of the country. Franklin Roosevelt launched his share of whoppers, but most suspected him immediately and many forgave. Kennedy was fluent in his lies, but they were no more plentiful or unusual than those of any other seasoned politico. Nixon would lie, and his eyes would dart madly about the room while perspiration arose on his upper lip. He was a ready liar, but not an expert liar. Nor was Johnson, who telegraphed his in sanctimonious tones that could cause nausea among those within listening distance. Moreover, the lies laid down by most of these statesmen were common political fare. Clinton is a constant liar who has, on occasion, devised lies that are truly extraordinary. He tells huge lies when a little white lie would be sufficient and perhaps even pardonable. He applies a modest lie when no lie is needed. Some of his lies are admittedly artful and possessed of a bland lawyerly elegance, but others are juvenile. Nonetheless he intones them all so smoothly, so coolly, so reflexively as to suggest that, for him, there is no reality beyond himself. He lies like a man totally unencumbered by conceptions of right and wrong. He lies like a sociopath.

His 1992 campaign was an operetta of lies. To hear him tell it, his draft records were in perfect order. He had never tried to skip service. In fact, in a moment of great heroism and self-sacrifice, he exposed himself to the draft. That would have been in the fall of 1969, in September, or was it October? And he did it by letter, or his uncle Raymond did it, or someone else—as is so often the case, Clinton's actions are concealed behind a drizzle of discrepancies. And then there was the Gennifer Flowers imbroglio; he never had an affair with her. And the Gulf War—he supported it, properly understood. As we have seen, he claimed that he was on record as having been for it, until reporters discovered that he had not been for it. But they did not truly understand that in Arkansas a governor can be for a war and for the position taken by the state's U.S. Senate delegation who opposed it. This hopscotching is an epistemological advance that looks like a lie but is not. And Mr. Clinton is taking his leave to visit a sick aunt—so no more questions.

Clinton boasted that his campaign was one of moral reform. Just as he and Hillary claimed to have brought a kind of spiritual rebirth to Arkansas, now they were bringing moral rebirth to a Republic corrupted by the knave Bush and the untrustworthy Barbara. Clinton's lies were at times breathtaking in their boldness. Despite the constant scrutiny of the press, this gifted beneficiary of a comfortable, well-connected Arkansan boyhood continued blatantly misrepresenting his youth as one spent in barefoot poverty. The press never caught on. The lie had been so finely woven into his campaign patter that, after a certain point in the campaign, it did not have to be fully enunciated, merely hinted at for the reporters to become teary-eyed. From New Hampshire onward all Clinton had to do was lugubriously blubber, "Ahh come from a place called Hope..." and his entire audience beheld visions of Huck Finn, shoeless, a bamboo pole on his shoulder, and lugging home a catch of catfish for ma. Sometimes his more reckless lies were spur-of-the-moment assaults on the sympathies of the gullible, as when the candidate told a *New York* magazine reporter that "One of the most difficult things for me was being fourteen years old and putting an end to the violence [between his parents]... I just broke down the door of their room one night when they were having an encounter and told him [Dude] that I was bigger than him now, and there would never be any more of this while I was there."[8] Theretofore he had never mentioned this fracas. Not only is there no evidence that it ever took place; there is actually evidence that it did not take place. [9]

Earlier Snopeses lied before the era of television and back in the swales of Dogpatch. Clinton lies with all the instruments of major media focused upon him, and he lies with the ease and grace of a great athlete at the pinnacle of his powers, of, say, the pole vaulter breaking another record. As he heads for the bar, his run is flawless; having precisely planted the pole, he releases it at maximum torque. Airborne, he floats across the bar. No extremity large or small touches it. Triumphant, he flops to earth. The crowd is amazed. Clinton, too, amazes the crowds, particularly the crowds of reporters attending his incomparable press conferences. There he proclaims blatant falsehoods, foiling those who might guffaw with the suave application of a lawyerly adverb: *mostly, chiefly, generally, almost invariably, golly dog that's what ahh thought ahh said.* The reporters are entranced. Only a few suffer nausea.

Posterior to the 1992 campaign, as the president-elect was beginning the first of what would be a continual series of policy reversals,
he backed down from his campaign promise of a "middle-class tax
cut." The reversal was similar to President George Bush's abandon-
ment of his 1988 campaign promise, "read my lips, no new taxes,"
except for one detail. Bush broke his promise without resorting to
complicated alibis and childish whines. Clinton chaperoned his
reversal with an elaborate, albeit brazen, deceit. (And remember; he
campaigned indignantly against Bush's reversal.) Clinton claimed
that by early 1993 a tax increase was now unavoidable because of the
government's sudden discovery of a looming federal deficit—$346
billion. No one had expected such a monstrous deficit, the new president insisted. Actually, Clinton himself, the summer before, had
publicly assumed a $400 billion deficit while repeatedly promising
his "middle-class tax cut." And though he now claimed that his tax
increase would spare those with annual incomes below $30,000, it
would obviously extend to those making but $20,000 a year. Among
the consensus journalists only a handful of stuffed shirts such as
David Broder objected. Most acquiesced in Clinton's bogus explanations. Many were expatriots from 1968, just like the president, and
hence accustomed to the sudden Ascents from Reality.[10]

The lies that our Snopesian president applied so effectively in
Washington unfortunately fell quite flat when he tried them
abroad. Foreign leaders seemed to be immune to Clinton's boyish
charm and shameless flimflam. Few fell for his lawyerly evasions
and explications of what appeared to be bold-faced lies. Most
quickly came to the judgment that the American people had
elected a president who was a vacillating perjurer of uncommon
flagrancy. During the first two years of his presidency his policies
on Haiti and Bosnia were continually being revised, usually
because his opposites abroad took him *cum grano salis* and refused
to submit to his policies. Foreign leaders said no to Clinton with
unusual regularity. In the summer of 1994 Panama's president,

who owed his office and possibly his life to the United States, refused to accept Haitian refugees after the Clinton administration announced that he would. About that time France blocked a trade initiative at the Naples economic summit that the Clinton administration had championed. China ignored Clinton's warnings on human rights violations and received Most Favored Nation trade status from Clinton anyway. Singapore ignored the president's plea that an American teenager be spared rough Singaporean justice. North Korea ignored Clinton's admonitions against its nuclear weapons development. Haiti's military reneged on its promise to restore Jean-Bertrand Aristide to power.[11]

Following upon each of these rebuffs Clinton would duly revise his policy with Snopesian lubricity, always misrepresenting his revisions to his fellow Americans. The press slept. The pattern was established early in the administration. In May of 1993 Boy Clinton sent Secretary of State Warren Christopher to Europe to persuade the continent's governments to accept his newly concocted policy of lifting an arms embargo against the Bosnians, concomitant with threatening air strikes against the Serbs ("lift and strike"). Christopher's mission failed abysmally. His knocks on the door became a thing of fun at every foreign ministry that he visited. Despite such a widely witnessed humiliation, Clinton showed up at a press conference on the South Lawn of the White House May 7 and coolly apprised the assembled journalists that, regarding Christopher's mission and the Europeans, "there is a lot more agreement than you think."[12] As with so many of Clinton's lies, the statement was plausible but completely untrue. Presently the administration simply dropped its policy of "lift and strike."

If Clinton's readiness to lie got him only slowly into trouble at home, it got him instantly into trouble abroad. The summer of 1994 witnessed two instances of the Snopesian president lying about his dealings with foreign leaders and suffering instantaneous comeuppance. On June 2, 1994, Clinton held a forty-minute meeting with

Pope John Paul II in the Vatican, after which he told reporters that he and the Pope had made "some progress" in reconciling their differences on abortion. Almost immediately the Vatican spokesman, Joaquin Navarro, denied the assertion and rubbed in some salt: "If he says there was a narrowing of differences, it's clear it can only be in one sense," that being that the American president had come closer to the Pope's total opposition to abortion.[13] Early the next month Clinton was even more firmly repudiated. At the Naples economic summit, after France's aforementioned rebuff, Clinton met with Russia's President Boris Yeltsin. During a rowdy press conference the American prevaricator announced that Yeltsin had told him he would order a withdrawal of troops from Estonia on August 31. One minute later an angry Yeltsin loudly denied he had said anything of the kind, shouting an old Russian standby from Cold War days to the startled crowd, "nyet."[14]

A peculiarity about Clinton's lies that sets him apart from other presidential prevaricators is that his lies are often so obvious as to cast temporary doubt on his intelligence or his contact with reality. "President Clinton yesterday minimized the likelihood that an explanation will be found for the apparent suicide of White House deputy counsel Vincent Foster Jr..." the *Washington Post* reported immediately after Foster's corpse was found in Fort Marcy Park. "As many of the Arkansans who came to Washington to run the new government began returning home for the funeral of their friend, Clinton and his senior aides repeated that no clues now exist to explain Foster's death."[15] Clinton may become the first American, contrary to the Menckenian adage, to go broke underestimating the intelligence of his fellow Americans. The obvious and stupid lies that he calmly deposed on the public record after Foster's death actually heightened public suspicion. "What happened was a mystery about something inside of him," Clinton ventured.[16] The ring of untruth was becoming a roar. The next day Clinton tried again: "I don't think there is anything more to know... I don't think there is anything else."[17] Adults continued to investigate, and in days it became clear that Clinton along with many of Foster's colleagues had been very much aware of his troubled state of mind. In fact, out of concern for Foster's state of mind, the president had invited him to the White House to watch a film the night before his body turned up. A suicide note of sorts had apparently been withheld from investigators, so had other documents. Then it was reported in the press that, before his death, Foster had been working on the Clinton's financial arrangements, among which were three years of delinquent income tax returns for the Whitewater Development Company. What remained unknown to the general public was that Foster had been involved in a long-standing affair with Hillary Rodham Clinton, though acquaintances in Arkansas knew. The affair was finally revealed by members of Clinton's governor's security detail in late 1993 and 1994.[18] Though the press picked up other revelations in these stories, it utterly ignored this revelation. Even during congressional hearings into the White House's handling of Foster's papers, no mention was made of his relationship with Mrs. Clinton, though its existence might explain the White House's efforts to conceal those papers.

Clinton's lies in the wake of the Foster death were completely unnecessary. Had he stated the obvious, to wit, that Foster was distressed by the burdens of his work and the various criticisms of him in Washington, the public would have understood; but Clinton seems to have a lust for lying. Of a sudden and out of the blue it is aroused. For two-and-a-half years after Foster's death, Clinton lied at first about Foster's state of mind and what might have been found in his office. Then the president lied—at times cleverly, at times gratuitously and rashly—about his personal involvement in the Whitewater Development Company, the Madison Guaranty Savings and Loan, and his administration's attempts to ward off various official investigations into his past. Late in 1995, as major media were beginning to add their mild accusations to the scores of serious accusations already leveled by the conservative press, Clinton launched one of his most amazing lies. By this time Republican politicians, even an occasional Democrat—for instance, Senator Daniel Patrick Moynihan and Bob Kerrey—were complaining of Clinton's forked tongue. Yet Clinton's lies persisted. The day before the White House, under threat of subpoena from the Senate Whitewater committee, gave up incriminating notes of an administration coverup, Clinton whined to the *Los Angeles Times*, "There has not been a single, solitary soul accuse me or my wife of doing anything illegal not only in the White House, in the presidential campaign, or in the governor's office."[19]

That was a kind of personal best for this ready prevaricator, but such reckless lying had been part of his act for years. In early December of 1993 the *New York Times* indignantly reported the departure of two powerful White House aides, Roy M. Neel and Howard Paster, "to take charge of lobbying enterprises at salaries of $500,000 a year...."[20] The next day the *Times* caustically editorialized against the Clinton administration's "income enhancement plan for well-connected Democrats."[21] By March the controversy had been forgotten. Then, during a press conference in the East Room, while answering a question about the White House Travel Office and White House security clearances, Clinton suddenly erupted with a whopper about his policy toward former aides lobbying, opening up the embarrassment of Neel and Paster's $500,000 jobs all over again: "People leave the White House; they can't lobby the White House. If they're in certain positions, they can't lobby the White House for a long time. If they're in certain positions now they can never lobby on behalf of a foreign government," and he bragged that "we have enforced higher standards against the ethical conflicts than any previous administration."[22] Clinton went on to attribute his administration's many vacancies to its unsurpassed ethics standards.

At least these gratuitous lies were uttered in defense of Clinton's

embattled policies and cheesy ethics. He has also heaved up gratuitous lies to defend merely comic pratfalls best left forgotten. In
June of 1994 the Snopesian president telephoned a radio call-in
show from Air Force One and delivered a twenty-three minute
denunciation of the "violent personal attacks" he was suffering from
conservative critics such as Rush Limbaugh, Gordon Liddy, and
Michael Reagan. "I don't suppose there's any public figure that's
ever been subject to any more violent personal attacks," the
aggrieved politico complained, "than I have, at least in modern history."[23] Also during the show Clinton dredged up his embarrassing
haircut incident at Los Angeles International Airport that had taken
place over a year before. "I could give you a lot of examples," he said,
expanding his complaint to include the press generally. "A year ago
there was a widely reported story that I kept airplane traffic waiting
an hour in Los Angeles to get a haircut in an airport. That wasn't
true either."[24] But it was. Precisely how much inconvenience he
caused may be debatable, but as the assembled reporters must have
recognized, even under the best conditions airplane traffic is delayed
when Air Force One lands. Moreover, immediately after Clinton's
luxurious haircut, he had apologized on *CBS This Morning*. Even the
loyal Dee Dee Myers had admitted the airport delays.[25] Why renew
a controversy for which he had already apologized?

In the same interview the president brought up a more current
embarrassment best left forgotten and engauded it with a lie easily
refuted. Contrary to reports that White House staff had stolen
embossed bathrobes and towels while staying overnight on the carrier *George Washington*, Clinton charged that it was reporters who
had made off with the souvenirs. The *New York Times* promptly
defended the press. "Although reporters certainly cannot be ruled
out as suspects, some who were on the ship said later that they could
not have taken any embossed robes or towels since none had been
supplied them in their rooms aboard the carrier." And the *Times*
concluded with a thud: $562 had already been paid by a White

House aide for the missing items after the aide failed to come up with a memo "about the missing items" for reporters.[26] Again— why would the president renew a controversy that the White House had suffered with so ignominiously?

"Inside my head," writes Virginia Kelley, "I construct an airtight box. I keep inside it what I want to think about, and everything else stays beyond the walls. Inside is white, outside is black... Inside is love and friends and optimism. Outside is negativity, can't-doism, and any criticism of me and mine."[27] There you have the makings of the sociopath at 1600 Pennsylvania Avenue. Surely this credo at least partially explains the flagrancy, frequency, and recklessness of Clinton's lies. Through the years of his presidency these lies have revealed the intriguing duality expressed by his mother: within the Clinton coco, an egocentrism verging on the delusional; outside the perimeters of his mind, reality. At a March of 1995 press conference, after months of news reports about Clinton's dubious bank loans, financial legerdemain, election irregularities, and adumbrations of even graver misdeeds, the president repined that, "I am the first president in history ever to have a special counsel involving activities that have nothing to do with my work as president... and that *arose when there had not been a single, solitary serious assertion that I had done anything illegal*" (italics added). Actually "serious assertions" were proliferating like bacteria in a sewer pipe, and no fewer than two independent counsels were scrutinizing them.

Clinton's capacity to, as Maraniss puts it, "speak the idiom" of those whose influence he sought was fundamental to his quest for political power. Given his charm, many of his influential targets were sitting ducks. Yet he had to choose the right ducks; and, most importantly, he needed the right duck calls. No time could be wasted courting has-beens or invoking controversial values. As for the ducks, in Arkansas they were well known. They were the automobile dealers, and in the black community, the proprietors of the local African-American funeral parlors. They were the local precinct lords and county sheriffs, the men of the cloth, Elks, members of the Loyal Order of the Moose, the Knights of Pythias, and members of service clubs unheard of beyond the borders of the great state of Arkansas. Then up there on the Gibraltar of Arkansan society sat the elites of the oligarchy. As for the values that a politically ambitious Arkansan might adopt, there has never been a lot of diversity in the state; the elites' version of the Good Life has usually been philosophy enough.

Choosing the "idiom" became more problematic when Clinton departed for college. It is a big world out there. Clinton recognized that the narrow range of values deemed socially approved in Arkansas would not play up North and could be ruinous to a young pol with national ambitions. So at Georgetown the Montgomery Ward Snopes fresh from Hot Springs had to listen carefully. In bull sessions he would defend the South, while usually condemning racial segregation—though apparently not always. There was even a period when he defended the Vietnam War. Almost certainly he put in a good word for the Elks and Rotary and small-town Arkansas. Even over in Oxford there were bull sessions in which it is recorded that he played devil's advocate against the regnant anti-Americanism. But Clinton is a clever fellow with an absolute craving for approval.

Eventually he discovered that the winning "idiom" was the same for charming the campus elites and for campaigning for a Democratic presidential nomination. The idiom was to be found in that great vaporous chaos of progressive ideas, noble values, momentous events, and baseless fears that floats over America and is identifiable as the *Kultursmog*. It touches ground on college campuses, in government agencies, in broadcasting studios, think tanks, even in museums and many churches, polluting all thought and every utterance. It is the culture of the American sophisticate, so-called.

Once that stratum of American culture dealing with the arts, ideas, and sophisticated values was diverse, lively, and relatively untainted by politics. Then in the late 1920s and throughout the 1930s along came those noxious isms to pollute the mind and befoul the spirit with a school marm's certitude: Marxism, progressivism, fascism. In the 1960s there arrived still more noxious isms—consumerism, environmentalism, feminism. Steadily the culture of the American sophisticate became a leaden, lifeless smog tainted by politics, mainly left-wing politics. This *Kultursmog* has contaminated practically every American institution that ever had anything to do with speculative thought and the imagination. It is repugnant to lively minds but immensely helpful to a Snopes in need of an "idiom."

American *Kultursmog* contaminates all aspects of American culture—music, art, horticulture, TV soaps—but its gravest consequences have been on our once vigorous and lucid American language. *Kultursmog* corrodes meaning. It obscures. Politicians, happy within the *Kultursmog*, now employ words for their pretty connotations rather than their substantive meanings. Besmogged audiences rarely catch on. The *Kultursmog's* corruption of language allows many politicians on the Left to engage in Masked Politics. Posing behind the masks of such worthy persons as the nature lover, the advocate of peace and sweet reason, the humanitarian, they steadily advance a left-wing agenda. The *Kultursmog* allows those who engage in Masked Politics to evade critical questions about their lovely goals. Finally the *Kultursmog's* debasement of language has allowed the Coat and Tie Radicals to pose on both sides of every issue, to have things both ways.

The *Kultursmog* might tolerate only one party and only one point of view, but it provides those who take to it all the heroes and heroines, ideas and ideals, anxieties and affectations that they will ever need to gain approval among America's self-proclaimed intellectuals. It also provided the governor of Arkansas with the patrons and values he needed to hustle the Democrats beyond Arkansas. Clinton is not the first presidential hopeful from the South to hustle the *Kultursmog*. In the 1970s Governor Jimmy Carter made a similar commitment.

Though Carter was a hick, his mastery of the *Kultursmog* won him the approval of the Republic's sophisticates. That approval brings with it certain dispensations. Those approved by the sophisticates can play both sides of the fence without being called hypocrites or—worse—conservatives. Even before Clinton, Carter identified himself as a new kind of Democrat. Thus he, like Clinton, later could claim to being at once conservative and liberal, hawk and dove. Carter had the reputation of being the special friend of blacks, though back in Georgia he had cultivated the Ku Klux Klan rather late in the day. "Both tactics—hedging, avoiding labels—were to become features of his later campaigns," wrote Betty Glad in an insightful biography of Carter in 1980.[28] You can be sure Boy Clinton studied those campaigns.

When a candidate has been active in the *Kultursmog*, inhaling its political particulates, adding a few if possible, he is presumed to be a strong friend of feminism, black resentment, homosexual militancy, consumerism, environmentalism, and of all the other isms mastered by our malcontents and mountebanks. Thus when he campaigns in middle America and, perforce, sounds unusually reasonable none of the above-mentioned fanatics takes offense. They recognize that their candidate is merely deceiving the unpolluted. Liberals realize that deviousness is the duty of the missionary.

American liberalism is mutable. Once it was for a color-blind society; then it was for a color-based society. Once it was for sexual revolution; then it became downright puritanical and consumed with something it called sexual harassment. Liberalism originally favored nuclear power, beginning with the Truman administration, and eventually came to envisage it as historians of the Middle Ages envisage the Black Death of the fourteenth century. Liberalism favored vigorous opposition to communist subversion in the "developing countries" during the Kennedy administration; then it favored "negotiation" and even unilateral disarmament. It ceaselessly advances "progress" throughout American society, but frequently changes its definition of "progress." For some three decades its passions have intensified; but there is only one political value to which it has always remained steadfast, namely, disturbing the peace. Liberalism is history's only political movement that has revered a common misdemeanor.

Its modus operandi is always the same: politics, which is to say, the amassing of power over the citizenry. Liberalism is *very* political. Its tainted political winds seek entry into every corner of society, for it considers all society in desperate need of its uplift: labor relations; sexual relations; racial relations; the proper care of children, of fresh vegetables, of language, history, art. Liberalism is the source of the politics polluting American *kultur.* It is the main perpetrator of the *Kultursmog.* In the *Kultursmog* there is a politically correct view of all the aforementioned topics and much more: diet, wrapping the garbage, treating illness, conducting scientific research, asking one's date to attempt a fox trot. The liberal impulse extrudes a smog of politics everywhere. It is almost impossible in modern America to escape its contaminants. In France we enter the Louvre and no uniformed attendant lectures us about the prevailing politically correct truths on the painter David or the sculptor Giacometti. A fur piece worn by Mademoiselle causes no alarums. French history and art are not constantly being revised to appease a new pack of balmy enthusiasts.

During the early years of the Clinton administration two controversies took place that, though they had little to do with the administration, reveal the workings of the *Kultursmog.* As there are unquestionably readers who doubt my claim that politics pollutes our museums, it is felicitous that the first example involves a museum. The Smithsonian Institution, in the course of devising an exhibit titled "The Last Act: The Atomic Bomb and the End of World War II," managed in 1994 to raise the Japanese militarists of World War II to a status unimaginable in their heyday. It raised them to the status of victim, one of the *Kultursmog'*s most prestigious positions. In the bizarre Smithsonian exhibit Japan was to be portrayed as the victim of Yankee "imperialism." The Smithsonian's proposed script actually used that word. American "imperialism" had supposedly caused us to commit "atrocities" against Japan.

The Smithsonian exhibit was to feature the fuselage of the *Enola Gay*, the bomber that dropped the atomic bomb on Hiroshima, along with an abundance of grisly pictures whose captions could have been written by the Japansese Imperial Army's most accomplished propagandists. There was to be no mention of the thousands of casualties suffered by the United States when the Japanese breached international law and mounted their covert attack on Pearl Harbor. Nor were there to be pictures of the Japanese Rape of Nanking, in which the Japanese army murdered 300,000 Chinese civilians. The Bataan Death March was left out, as was Japan's hideous incarceration of over 100,000 American, Australian, British, Dutch, and New Zealand troops—many of whom were summarily slaughtered. Others were tortured or subjected to gruesome "medical" experiments, in the best tradition of Japan's European allies, the Nazis (another victim of American imperialism?). Instead the original exhibit endeavored to demonstrate how, and I quote from the original text, Washington pursued "a war of revenge against the Japanese [who were] fighting to preserve their culture against imperialism."

Gassed by the *Kultursmog*, the politically correct pinheads at the Smithsonian just plumb forgot that it was the United States that had been attacked, and it was the Japanese who had an emperor, whose troops had swarmed across mainland China, the Malay archipelago, the Philippines, Southeast Asia, and lesser climes to establish their Greater Asian Co-Prosperity Sphere. These details were beyond the *Kultursmog's* interest, as were President Harry S. Truman's reasons for dropping the bomb, namely that Japan planned an energetic defense against invasion, and that American strategists predicted the deaths of millions of Allied invaders and Japanese citizens if hostilities continued. Even after Hiroshima, Japanese militarists were preparing to fight on. It took months of bitter negotiating by veterans' groups and Congress before the Smithsonian Institution's new secretary, I. Michael Heyman, scuttled the exhibit. But in the midst of the weird proceedings, air force historian Dick Hallion raised the evocative question, "Dealing with a morally unambiguous subject [Japanese militarism] why did they have to produce two and maybe three scripts to get it right?"

A few weeks after the sorely pressed Heyman scotched the World War II exhibit, he had to call for revisions in an exhibit on American science. Rather than celebrating American technology, "Science in American Life," polluted with the *Kultursmog*, stressed the Great Depression, DDT's darker side, accidents in the space program, and, once again, the atomic bombing of Japan.

The *Kultursmog* that young Clinton learned to manipulate in the 1960s was not nearly as extensive as the *Kultursmog* that Clinton had to adapt to as president. The difference is that the liberal impulse to politicize has grown more intense. By the 1990s it was even politicizing the contents of such reference books as *Bartlett's Familiar Quotations*. This polluting of American life was revealed by Adam Meyerson, the editor of the Heritage Foundation's *Policy Review*. Reviewing the sixteenth edition of *Bartlett's*, Meyerson discovered an egregious imbalance against conservatives and in favor of liberals. He found eleven quotations from John Kenneth Galbraith and only three and two, respectively, from Nobel Prize-winning economists Milton Friedman and Friedrich Hayek. The small number of quotations from Margaret Thatcher (three), Pope John Paul II (three), and Nobel laureate Alexander Solzhenitsyn (eight) revealed little of what those distinguished figures stood for; the Solzhenitsyn section contained only one quotation critical of communism, and that quotation was equally critical of the West. The new *Bartlett's* did, however, include two entries from rock singer Bruce Springsteen, two from singer Joni Mitchell, and four from the Rolling Stones. From *Sesame Street*'s Cookie Monster comes the imperishable line, "Me Want Cookie!" There also appeared a long inscrutable passage from third-rate novelist Erica Jong expatiating on something called the "zipless fuck."[29]

The most absurd imbalance was shown in the reference book's treatment of presidents. It included twenty-eight entries for John F. Kennedy, thirty-five for Franklin Roosevelt, and only three for Ronald Reagan. Reagan was the first president to complete two terms since president Dwight Eisenhower. During the eight years of Reagan's presidency, Americans experienced the century's longest peacetime prosperity. The "Vietnam Syndrome" was lifted. The American spirit was "reborn." Moreover, the Cold War was peacefully concluded, communism vanquished worldwide, and the Soviet Union dismantled. Though during his presidency he was called "the Great Communicator," the editor of *Bartlett's* could award him only the same number of passages as Presidents Zachary Taylor (whose presidency lasted less than a year) and Gerald Ford. The passages deemed memorable by *Bartlett's* editor, Justin Kaplan, were significant only in that they perpetuated the liberals' vision of conservatives as being fatuous and materialistic. The reader relying on *Bartlett's* might never know about Reagan's eloquent justification of force, delivered in his historic speech at the cliffs of Normandy in 1984. The reader would remain uninformed of his impassioned plea in Berlin in 1987—"Mr. Gorbachev, open this gate! Mr. Gorbachev, tear down this wall!" Or of his 1981 prediction of communism's demise as a "bizarre chapter in human history whose last pages are even now being written." For those dwelling in the *Kultursmog*, Reagan's eloquence did not exist.

By including pop figures and quotations from them that have no intellectual or stylistic distinction whatsoever, Kaplan has unwittingly demonstrated another attribute of the *Kultursmog*: its intellectual decline into near barbarity. Those who contribute to the *Kultursmog* have arrogated to themselves the claim of being enlightened even as they discern failure in one of the century's most successful politicians and immorality in the gibbering of the Cookie

Monster. Ultimately, the liberalism that supplies the *Kultursmog* with its contaminants is a liberalism lost in decadence. It embodies everything it claims to oppose: intolerance, mean-spiritedness, obtuseness, and stupidity. When the *Philadelphia Inquirer* interviewed Kaplan about *Bartlett's* treatment of Reagan, he hissed, "I'm not going to disguise the fact that I despise Ronald Reagan." And then he assumed his role among the "enlightened," saying that Reagan "could not be described as a memorable phrase maker," but only as "an actor masquerading as a leader."[30]

Actually, the Snopes who became president in 1993 is Reagan's superior as an actor. Almost everything he does in public is an act. Reagan was constrained by principles that he believed in. He might resort to his original profession to dramatize them but he was limited to one role, the president as conservative. Clinton has no limits because he has no principles. Thus during his presidency he poses today as a New Democrat, tomorrow as an advocate of nationalized medicine, next week as champion of "family values." Throughout his public life, Clinton has manifested the amorphous personality of a superior actor. He is whatever an audience wants him to be... temporarily.

That earlier Snopes who came out of the South and into the White House, Jimmy Carter, was often a very funny man. His moralizing was artless and laughable. Clinton's public moralizing is smoothly acted. It is laughable only to those who take morals very seriously and remember the revelations about him that keep coming out. What is laughable is his general incompetence, all those pratfalls in an office he supposedly trained himself for from college onwards. They are also unexpected, for Clinton is that kind of career politician that is supposed to know government as well as a television evangelist knows pop psychology.

CHAPTER EIGHT

THE CHRONIC
CAMPAIGNERS

O NE OF THE unforeseen consequences of the many decades
of government expansion that have followed the New Deal
has been the emergence of a new kind of politician, the Chronic
Campaigner. The old kind of politico was not equal to the many
exacting tasks of modern government. A government that reaches
beyond the historic necessities of a cop on the corner, paved streets,
and decent sanitation, and that endeavors, among other things, to
manage day-care centers, formulate ethnic balances throughout
society, and conduct a regular census on rare plants, animals, insects
and bacteria, while ministering to the hurt feelings of feminists,
"minorities," and other malcontents of astounding specificity
requires an advanced kind of politician.

Such energetic government requires the kind of politician that
lives government twenty-four hours a day, every day of the week,
every week of the year. He must be versed in the arcane terms that
the policy wonk uses to dizzy the bureaucrat. He must have an ear
for the galvanizing slogan that in a given campaign year agitates the
electorate. Neither at the federal nor at the state level is this a job

for part-timers, that is, for normal citizens. Once shopkeepers or
members of the professions could break from their livelihoods to
run a state legislature, but increasingly even a city council is run by
full-time political operators. In a polity whose legislature sits most
of the year, with legislators claiming to know just about everything,
Cincinnatus is obsolete.

At the national level career politicians became the norm sometime after World War II; at the state and local levels somewhat later.
But now even the career politician is being rendered obsolete. His
replacement is the Chronic Campaigner.

Since the 1970s the Chronic Campaigner has been proliferating
throughout the polity, and a review of the political landscape makes
clear that the Chronic Campaigner drives out earlier, more non-
chalant species of politicos. To understand the Clinton administration's peculiar mix of high drama and exiguous achievement we
must understand the new model of politico.

Back in Arkansas veteran Congressman John Paul Hammerschmidt may have defeated Clinton in the latter's first adult run for
elective office, but he could not have continued to prevail against
the tireless young hustler. Hammerschmidt was a normal American, by trade a timberman. It was a piece of good luck for him that
the restless Clinton set his sights on higher offices. Fortunately
Hammerschmidt's district was small beer compared to Clinton's
large ambitions.

No sooner had the hills and valleys of Arkansas's Third Congressional District ceased to echo with his last hoarse alarum about
the menace and injustice of Hammerschmidt than the Boy Candidate[1] began his campaign for attorney general two years down the
road. The attorney generalship won, his every utterance and policy
pointed him toward the governorship. Once there, his mind turned
toward the presidency. From his 1974 defeat Clinton kept on running and networking, running and raising money, running and filling out file cards on potential supporters, voters, enemies. His first

term in the Governor's Mansion was ill-starred; but during that term he actually tried to govern. He tried to make policy and to marshal support rather than to do the one political thing he does best, campaign. He would rarely again make the mistake of actually governing. Now Clinton lives The Endless Campaign. Any other endeavor puts him at a dreadful disadvantage.

After a brief spell of soul searching in the uncomfortable role of private citizen, Clinton enlisted Betsey Wright to sit outside his office at the Wright, Lindsey and Jennings law firm where he claimed to be practicing law. He had a computer installed, and the ever-present Wright transferred onto it the political information that Clinton had been squirreling away ever since his loss to Hammerschmidt.[2] Through the next decade his campaigning never slowed, which might explain why, despite all the years in office, all the proudly announced initiatives, all the policies passed, little of substance was ever achieved by the Clintons in Arkansas.

Through all his public life what Arkansans saw was not what they got; but then, illusory accomplishment is typical of the Chronic Campaigner. Prior to Clinton's race against Hammerschmidt it seemed Clinton was a law professor at the University of Arkansas. Actually he was an absentee law professor. Rarely was he in his office. Frequently his classes were canceled. He might be seen sitting around the law school lounge, chatting and joshing. He was almost never seen using the law library, and only a bit more frequently was he seen in his office. He filed grades late—often months late. In 1974 he did not post grades for his spring criminal procedure class until the end of the summer.[3] Once he even lost a bundle of final exams. Only six months passed after Clinton graduated from Yale Law School before the young law professor launched his ambitious campaign for a seat in the House of Representatives.

During his three-year teaching career at the University of Arkansas he was on leave most of the time. He took his first leave of absence three months after he joined the faculty. He applied for

another in the spring of 1975. So immersed was he in politicking by
then that he did not even have time or the presence of mind to
return to the Dean's office to find out whether his leave had been
granted. The next year he applied for another leave so that he could
run for attorney general.

After his defeat in 1980 it may have seemed that he was practicing law for Wright, Lindsey and Jennings, but after a depression-
induced lull he was actually bouncing about the state, campaigning
for the governorship. Typically he was engaged in a purely selfish
pursuit when he was supposed to be doing something else. All the
Chronic Campaigner is ever *really* doing is campaigning and
advancing himself.

The Chronic Campaigner was first spotted in large numbers in
the 1970s. John F. Kennedy has been identified as the prototype for
this political model. Says Richard Reeves, one of Kennedy's most
interesting biographers, "Looking back, it seemed to me that the
most important thing about Kennedy was not a great political decision, though he made some, but his own political ambition. He did
not wait his turn. He directly challenged the institution he wanted
to control, the political system. After him, no one else wanted to
wait either, and few institutions were rigid enough or flexible
enough to survive impatient ambition-driven challenges. He
believed (and proved) that the only qualification for the most powerful job in the world was wanting it."[4] All of that is true, yet
Kennedy did have a rich, well-connected political family goading
him into politics. And there is no evidence that Kennedy was ceaselessly campaigning his way through high school and college or was
driven by the bizarre narcissism of the Chronic Campaigner. In
truth Kennedy was a charming, party-going, rich boy who reluc-
tantly answered his father's summons to politics after the family's
first choice for president, eldest son Joe, died in World War II.

The true paradigmatic Chronic Campaigner was Jimmy Carter.
He too was "ambition-driven." No institution could withstand the

gush of his energy and ambition. Like Clinton, he came from a rural state and possessed but little national standing. He was not summoned by party leaders, as was Warren Harding. He was not the choice of sectional interests, as was George Wallace. Neither political principles nor ideology made him the logical choice of his party, as was the case with Ronald Reagan. Jimmy Carter was called to presidential politics by his own narcissistic yearning and by, I would suggest, a primordial desire to please Miss Lillian, his mother.[5] As he said over and over again, standing alone in a thousand New Hampshire doorways, "I'm Jimmy Carter, from Georgia. I'm running for president." Later he added the punch line, "I will never lie to you." Intellectually and philosophically that was about all he had to offer. A colossal drive made up for his mean circumstances and merely personal political purposes.

The Chronic Campaigner is always afire with ambition, whether he is running for city council, the state house, or the White House. While other politicians might take the evening off, the Chronic Campaigner is amassing file cards for elections scheduled somewhere off in the future, raising money, evaluating prospective consultants, canvassing. Once the election is under way, he knocks on doors himself. No matter the delicacy of his intellect, the exquisiteness of breeding, the inclemency of the weather, he never recoils at repeating yet again his standard banal anecdote about his childhood or his mother's gallbladder operation or worse. Gamely he intones for the ten–thousandth time his twenty-five second introduction to a startled citizen caught unawares on a front porch, a street corner, while exiting a public lavatory. In times past a candidate's credentials for nomination would include party loyalty or perhaps seniority. Today that which recommends a candidate is rarely anything more substantial than his invincible energy, ambition, talent for self-dramatizing, and animal exuberance. He need not have the political assets of a Hubert Humphrey or a Lyndon Johnson, but he must have the seductive qualities of Giovanni Casanova plus the energy of a geyser.

Most frequently the Chronic Campaigner is a Democrat. For many Democrats—those who might otherwise teach school or lead an aerobics class—the money is better. Moreover, Democrats since Woodrow Wilson's time have been believers in government's benignancy. Yet since 1994 the excited figure of Newt Gingrich sweeping across the political landscape and followed by scores of like-minded young Republicans suggests that now Republicans, too, are catching the bug of the Chronic Campaigner.

As Reeves mentions, our institutions lack the capacity to restrain these go-getters. Prior to Kennedy and to Carter, political parties were structured to allow party leaders some control over who would be nominated for what office. Then, too, ambitious young politicians had to pass muster with the intermediary institutions of their local communities, for instance, the Rotary or the Chamber of Commerce. All these relics from America's small-town past can now be circumvented.

The political parties have been opened up by years of progressive reforms. Today the Chronic Campaigner is free to bypass political leaders. All he needs is public status, and that is easily secured through the media. There he presents himself as a prophet, perhaps in some do-good cause, but increasingly simply as a prophet of his own cause, celebrated by the media primarily for his apparent or asserted electability.

Ambitious politicians once sought office out of a sense of mission or while riding the crest of one of the reform movements that from time to time sweep America, say, the late-nineteenth century's Progressive movement. Others of a more mundane turn of mind have sought office for the steady paycheck, as cutting hair is done for the steady pay, or collecting garbage—eight hours a day and quitsky. Today's Chronic Campaigner, usually a child of the 1960s, takes politics neither as a mission nor merely a job. He takes politics as a lifestyle.

For Chronic Campaigners such as Carter, Jerry Brown, Michael

Dukakis, Richard Gephardt, Gary Hart, Clinton, and now Gingrich, the political quest is so all-embracing as to be their lifestyle. Past politicians enjoyed wielding power for high purpose or for low gain. They were more apt to take risks and face defeat. Though he usually devotes more energy to politics, the Chronic Campaigner takes fewer risks. Power wielded is power that can bring the catastrophe of early retirement, and any retirement is early retirement. The Chronic Campaigner's goal is to stay in office forever. In modern America he often does. Politics is his life.

Few Chronic Campaigners ever identify closely with a controversial position. They may pretend to be taking heroic and controversial positions, but they usually do so by declaiming on nothing more controversial than "compassion," "full employment," "better education," or—casting the eye Hillary's way—"children's rights."[6] During the 1992 campaign Clinton was given to heaving off soliloquies on improving the nation's "infrastructure" and ending welfare "as we know it." Not surprisingly, once he took office nothing came of those sonorous vows. Though ideology is always in the air with the Chronic Campaigners, few ever stick resolutely with any body of principles likely to cost the candidate a significant number of votes. William Jennings Bryan championed labor and easy money, whatever the cost. Senator Robert A. Taft championed Midwestern conservatism and paid the price. The Chronic Campaigner might utter a platitude about the working man and woman or world peace, but the rhetoric will be gauzy and, under careful analysis, evanescent.

Clinton has often been evasive about his politics. "Governor Bill Clinton told members of the National Urban League today that Republican efforts to characterize the Democratic presidential ticket as liberal are a 'load of bull we've been paralyzed with for too long,'" the *New York Times* reported in 1992.[7] The story was about Clinton's resistance to being identified as a liberal. He usually sandwiches his New Democrat baloney between thick slices of white bread, the fashionable blah about the obsolescence of liberalism and

conservatism, and the blah blah about the terms having no meaning. In 1993, after campaigning as the candidate of middle America,
he immediately disrupted settled Pentagon policy towards homosexuals. He rescinded a standing rule barring doctors at federally
funded hospitals from counseling women to abort. He proceeded
with the liberal agenda. Mrs. Clinton has been equally mendacious
regarding her ideology. Once in the White House, after months of
denying charges that she was a lefty, she made her bid to national-
ize health care though no call for it from the people was heard,
while confiding to journalists that she was "conservative in the true
sense of the word."[8] It is unimaginable that Mrs. Clinton would
ever present herself at a liberal gathering—say, a national meeting
of the National Organization for Women—as "conservative in the
true sense of the word."

It is characteristic of the Chronic Campaigner of the left to jug-
gle political identities such as liberal and conservative. The Clintons
have been engaging in this legerdemain for years, with a flagrancy
that owes its origins to the 1960s Coat and Tie Radicals' trait of
having it both ways. True, there is intellectual residue in the way
they manipulate ideological terms that reveals how deeply rooted
within the American left they truly are. In 1995, when the Republicans were triumphing on all fronts, the Clintons commenced to
call Gingrich and his allies members of "the extreme right," "the
radical right," "the Christian right," members of a "national right-
wing movement," "a national thing which has access to unlimited
money," and "a spooky thing, really."[9] This sort of name calling had
not been heard since Barry Goldwater led the Right, when it was a
new political phenomenon, and embraced people and positions
which, relative to the politics of the day, really were shrill and
extreme. But for the Clintons in 1995 to apply these epithets not to
the fringes of politics but to established, sensible, law-abiding,
political opponents who had been winning elections all over the
country since the 1980 election of Ronald Reagan was to betray

one's own extreme ideological roots and the Coat and Tie Radicals' weird inability to learn from experience. The hard-wired brain butted up against the lust to please.

Chronic Campaigner that Clinton is, however, he would not forsake the comforts of ambiguity for long. He disparaged what he called "the old labels of liberal and conservative." He took a righteous stand for "practical, pragmatic solutions."[10] Taking refuge in ambiguity while concealing one's own ideological predilections typifies the Chronic Campaigner's political slyness, bringing to mind other Chronic Campaigners' evasiveness, such as California Governor Jerry Brown's boast in his late 1970s bid for the presidency that he would move to the left and the right "simultaneously."[11]

Though the Chronic Campaigner dislikes wielding power, the trappings of power are as indispensable to the lifestyle as is the frenetic schedule and the ceaseless appearances at hospitals to exploit misery and natural disasters, on television shows such as *Saturday Night Live* or on MTV where in 1994 Clinton conscientiously responded to questions about his underpants from a moronic teenage girl. All are places rarely deemed political until the evolution of the Chronic Campaigner. If a daring Chronic Campaigner did desire to wield power, he would encounter difficulty. For years the Chronic Campaigner has been handing power over to bureaucrats, to judges, to anyone who will protect him from having to make a potentially unpopular decision, so that elected officials no longer have the power that they once did. Mayor Richard J. Daley's son and successor can claim only a fraction of his father's power. The courts have moved in to police the city's electoral system. Reform has grievously weakened the machine. Federal bureaucrats prowl the city for infamies against various regulatory codes. Consequently one rarely hears an unkind word muttered against Daley II, but then he is rarely burdened by the responsibility of making an unsettling decision. In contrast to the days of the Imperial Presidency, Clinton, too, has his hands tied. He can say soothing things to both sides about abortion. Then he files the exculpatory codas, "My hands are tied." "I wish I could act, but...." Hopefully for him, the ultimate decision on serious issues reposes with higher powers: the courts, the bureaucracy, legislatures.

Modern government overloaded the system by opening it up to so many interest groups—minorities, environmentalists, and other self-appointed enthusiasts. Too many special interests have too many claims on a leader for him to invoke power decisively, even if he should want to do so. He would like to help the whites but all agree he cannot give offense to the blacks. He would like to assist the menfolk, but must not offend the women. In the spring of 1995 Clinton noticed the Republican Congress's popularity rise as it took aim at affirmative action. Soon Clinton was on the hustings promising a federal review of all affirmative action programs. Those found to be "unfair" would be eliminated, stomped up and down on, publicly rebuked, buried with toxic waste. Addressing a Democratic convention in Sacramento, the president lamented what had become, said he, "psychologically, a difficult time for a lot of white males—the so-called angry white male." He empathized. He announced that his support would extend only to those affirmative action programs that are "fair." But, this being a Democratic convention, out in the audience the placards grew agitated, proclaiming, "Stand Up for Affirmative Action" and "No Retreat." Clinton wavered. The next day the White House announced a forthcoming appointment of a bipartisan panel on the matter. [12] The president passed on. The bipartisan panel deliberated. Eventually it announced a reform that reformed nothing.

Actually, with the shift of real power to the bureaucracy and the judiciary, "leaders" such as Clinton have been totally freed of responsibility for government policy. Now responsibility resides with such bureaucracies as, say, the Environmental Protection Agency (EPA) or the Department of Housing and Urban Development (HUD), or with the courts. A classic display of modern

America's rule by bureaucrats, to the relief of the chief executive, occurred in 1994 when HUD began prosecuting private citizens for peacefully protesting a Clinton administration policy. Three citizens in Berkeley, California had to hire lawyers to resist prosecution and possible jail sentences for distributing leaflets against the policy championed by Clinton's appointee, Assistant Secretary for Fair Housing and Equal Opportunity Roberta Achtenberg.[13] She pursued her case until public protests fomented by the *Wall Street Journal* editorial page forced her to back down. Through it all Clinton could appear in his favorite position, firmly and forthrightly on both sides. Not only does this shift of power away from elected leaders insulate the Chronic Campaigner from public wrath, but it has the additional advantage of allowing him to pose as the electorate's bold defender against bureaucracy, or even better, its upright mediator in the face of bureaucracy. In sum and in fine, the Chronic Campaigner—now freed from actually governing—can exuberantly indulge in his favorite pastime and keenest talent, campaigning. This is the essence of the Chronic Campaigner's lifestyle, traveling through his constituency, offering compassion, soliciting advice, making bold and meaningless promises, weeping at a disaster site, laughing it up on festive occasions. The Chronic Campaigner has taken up the role once maintained by the clergy—but that is a vast topic beyond the modest ambitions of this chapter.

During his presidency, Clinton has spent more time campaigning than any of his predecessors. His pollster, Stanley Greenberg, and his top three political consultants, Paul Begala, James Carville, and Mandy Grunwald, were fixtures at the White House in the early years of the administration and influenced policy despite potential conflicts of interest owing to their simultaneously serving other clients.[14] No past presidency had ever been so attentive to the boss's campaign strategists. Indeed, for Clinton, being chief executive has always been secondary to carrying on The Endless

Campaign. He has spent much of his time posterior to his inauguration crisscrossing America, empathizing and bloviating. Clinton and his fellow migrants from 1968 call this sort of exhibitionism "public service."

The term has a ring more solemn than that musty term from yesteryear, "public trust," or the more appropriate term, "public trough." Moreover, the spacious term "public service" suggests the expanded concept of politics as a personal lifestyle. In the lifestyle of "public service" most of the Chronic Campaigner's expenses are borne by the taxpayer, the rationale being that every aspect of this politico's life is taken up in self-sacrifice during service to a higher calling.

Throughout their adult lives, the Clintons have been egregious spongers at the public trough. Though Clinton is wont to brag that the governor of Arkansas's $35,000 salary was the "lowest in the nation," Clinton's lifestyle was one of the swankiest. Arkansas state auditor Julia Hughes Jones reports that the Clintons cost the second poorest state in the Union more than three-quarters of a million dollars annually. Her estimate is conservative. The state picked up the tab for their food, shelter, transportation, security, housekeeping, administration, utilities, entertainment, and even their nannies. In her embarrassingly detailed report for the *American Spectator* on the Clintons' personal finances as Arkansas's First Family, Lisa Schiffren writes that throughout the 1980s the Clintons failed to pay Social Security taxes on nannies and baby sitters. That might explain why in appointing Zoe Baird, Kimba Wood, and initially Stephen Breyer (whose transgression was failing to pay his cleaning lady's Social Security taxes), the Clintons treated potential Nannygate problems so thoughtlessly—and why they dropped all three appointees so abruptly, though Wood had broken no law. Despite the state's payment for the Clintons' nannies and their failure to pay Social Security taxes, the Clintons actually filed for child care credits. Schiffren goes on to report that though the Clintons' income placed them in the top 3 percent of American families, they never missed a tax deduction, even claiming $3 on Clinton's used under-shirts and $1 on each pair of his and Chelsea's underpants given to the Salvation Army and to Goodwill.[15]

The Chronic Campaigner pops up everywhere, bringing the grime of politics to the most innocent of human endeavors. Charities once handled by private institutions have been co-opted. Counseling services once managed by churches have become government programs extending fanciful rights to their clients, costing government hugely and bringing the entire program to confusion.

Because of the Chronic Campaigner, government budgets go up faster and higher than they might otherwise. So do government deficits. The Chronic Campaigner, true to his primary mission of getting elected, is quick with government largess and reluctant to deny it to constituents. And in keeping with his desire to please, the Chronic Campaigner usually sees to it that the bills do not come due until well into the future—if possible, after he has left office. Raising taxes to pay for his big-heartedness would be inconsistent with his primary mission.

Another consequence of the Chronic Campaigner's lifestyle is that government's mistakes are repeated endlessly. Being a masterful campaigner, the Chronic Campaigner almost never has to acknowledge the botch he has made of governing. He knows what the venerable V. O. Key discovered while studying the electorate decades ago, namely, that the citizenry maintains only a general sense of how government is going. If the country is peaceful, if the milk and honey flows unimpeded, if the political leaders are amusing and give no offense, the citizenry will not fire the lunkhead. Key found that during most congressional elections over half the eligible voters are unable to identify either congressional candidate. Thus, with neither a carrot nor a stick goading him to rectify government's blunders, the Chronic Campaigner's government blunders on into the future.

Certainly Clinton's blunders have been given many repeat

performances. His record in Arkansas closely prefigured his record in Washington. Upon being elected governor in 1978 he immediately moved too far to the left, and almost immediately began to break his promises and welsh on commitments. He has followed the same course as president. By law his gubernatorial term was for two years, and he lost in 1980. His presidential term was for four years, but who doubts that had it been a two-year term he would have lost in 1994? Certainly enough other Democrats lost that year. During all his years in the Governor's Mansion Clinton bickered with the press. As president he continued bickering, though by all accounts the national press was predisposed to admire the boyish progressive from Georgetown, Oxford, and Yale. Clinton's premier reform in Little Rock, his vaunted education reform, differed from his 1994 health care reform only in that some of it passed. He proceeded with it much as he was to proceed with health care: vast promises and veiled threats; many Arkansans made hopeful, others alarmed; and everyone overwhelmed by a myriad of confused proposals. Finally a watered-down education reform passed, improving Arkansas schooling but little. None of it really survived into the 1990s. The Clintons' health-care package followed a similar route until it was mercifully killed off in September of 1994. The Chronic Campaigner is a bad governor, but the citizenry's pleasant disposition protects him from retribution.

Even friends and allies of the Chronic Campaigner have noted the fundamental weirdness of a human being devoting so much time to a political life that is so bereft of power or purpose beyond occupying office and making tiresome public appearances. Seeing the eager, energetic glad-handing of his boss, slogging through the New Hampshire primary, unfazed by devastating exposes, George Stephanopoulos confided to a reporter that Clinton was not "normal."[16] Nor, of course, is Jerry Brown, nor Gary Hart. It is not merely that Clinton's life is spent in The Endless Campaign. It is also that he must reach into the *Kultursmog* and boast about virtues that a gentleman would be embarrassed to claim in public and that, incidentally, the Chronic Campaigner manifestly lacks, for instance, compassion, decency, selflessness, sincerity, and idealism. Alas, the Chronic Campaigner is almost always compassionless, indecent, selfish, insincere, and cynical.

While repairing to the *Kultursmog* for seemly virtues, the Chronic Campaigner also latches on to the *smog*'s stereotype of the progressive president. The *Kultursmog*'s stereotype of the conservative president is either Richard Nixon, the devious crook, or Ronald Reagan, the philistine dimwit. The *Kultursmog*'s stereotype of the progressive president is more dynamic. Arthur Schlesinger, Jr., established the stereotype in *The Age of Jackson*. With Jackson came audacity, the common touch, and courage. With Woodrow Wilson, intellect and culture were added. With Roosevelt, all of the above remained plus gaiety, eloquence, charm, and tirelessness. John F. Kennedy embodied each of these attributes so prodigiously that those who wrote about him were driven almost insane. He added youthfulness, athleticism, a full head of hair, and glistening, flawless teeth. Clinton, ever the energetic striver, has endeavored to personify the stereotype's entire basket of attributes. The bags under his eyes, the thinning hair, the tired slouch in his posture that suddenly afflicted him during his third year in office all testify to the alarming fact that Arthur Schlesinger's progressive presidential stereotype has become a health hazard. Were Clinton's constitution any less robust, he would be dead from exhaustion.

For athleticism he jogged, or rather lumbered. For youthfulness he hired the youngest staff in White House history, attracting auspicious notices at first and then sneers as the greenhorns flummoxed both journalists and Washington politicos, conferring on the administration a reputation for incompetence that is without precedent in presidential history. Clinton's charm was genuine, except that he was given to temper tantrums and petulance. Naturally it was claimed that he slept only four hours and roamed the White

House late at night seeking more work, a snack, and books to read. A friend confided to the *New York Times* that Clinton read five or six books a week. Perhaps like his hero JFK, Clinton is a speed reader. Supposedly, he left over 4,500 volumes in the Governor's Mansion. All of this is in accord with the stereotype of the progressive president. As the *Times* reminded readers, "in modern times, such [bookish] interests put Mr. Clinton in the company of, say, Woodrow Wilson, Franklin D. Roosevelt, Harry S. Truman and John F. Kennedy."[17] His energetic style, his dynamism, his pandemonium were widely remarked. Remember Michael Duffy in *Time*: "Clinton is a complex, highly intense man who does almost everything at full throttle. He watches several movies each week—the White House refuses to release an exact number—and reads five or six books at once. He relaxes not by watching a basketball game on TV, or reading, or picking up the telephone, or doing crossword puzzles, but doing all four simultaneously, while worrying an unlit cigar."[18] All this "bookish" hustle and bustle is in keeping with the progressive presidential stereotype, but there were problems.

Courage presented difficulties for Clinton, given his war record, and it was a bit of bad luck that so many of World War II's fiftieth anniversaries had to be observed during his presidency. As for the stereotype's claim to verbal wonders, that too has presented Clinton with problems. He has had a dreadful speechwriting staff and seems not to have noticed. Yet he has shown genuine eloquence when speaking extemporaneously on matters of virtue, usually in a church—which, given his private life, should give churchgoers pause. Clinton's essays into gaiety have seemed forced. The common touch has frequently been cheap, as in his reference to his old pickup truck. It occurred just after his former security guards caused a furor by relating his ithyphallic sex life and after he piously disputed them. Then, before an audience at a truck assembly plant, he bragged of the pickup truck he drove in the 1970s. "It was a real sort of Southern deal," he crowed, "I had Astroturf in the back. You don't want to know why, but I did."[19] In keeping with another legendary component of the stereotype of the progressive president, Clinton promised a historic First 100 Days. Unfortunately the days turned into years, and after the failures of his second year it took the Republican Gingrich to deliver an historic 100 Days.

Gingrich's sudden prominence on the political scene suggests that America has not seen the end of the Chronic Campaigner. But his prominence also suggests that the *Kultursmog* may soon be fumigated and reduced to manageable proportions. No country's political culture can remain stagnant forever. And no free country's political culture can forever exclude the philosophy and values of a major political party. When the Republicans gained control of both the House and the Senate, captured the majority of state houses, and added another ten state legislatures in the 1994 elections, it appeared that large numbers of Americans had decided that the *Kultursmog* was unhealthy, radical, and contradictory. Its values were unreasonable and unrealizable. It created more problems than it solved. The conservatives' greatest weakness through the Reagan and Bush years had been their failure to develop cultural instruments either to pierce the *Kultursmog* or to insulate themselves from its pollutants. When George Bush became president he was almost asphyxiated by the *smog's* opposition to deficits, demands for taxation, quotas, and a vast and expensive bill for the disabled. On all these poisons President Bush succumbed to the fumes. It cost him reelection. By 1995, however, the *Kultursmog* was being pierced by talk radio, a growing network of conservative newspapers, and a vast growth in the circulation of the conservative magazines of ideas. The day was approaching when ordinary Americans might have access to intellectual and artistic values other than those that dominate a moribund Democratic party.

As for the ne plus ultra of all Chronic Campaigners, Clinton has demonstrated an historic irony. The Chronic Campaigner came into existence to fulfill the needs of energetic, full-service, all-purpose government. Yet, as Clinton has shown, the Chronic Campaigner is feeble at governing. He is a showhorse, not a workhorse. Moreover, the stereotype of the progressive president has accumulated so many fine qualities that it is no longer a thing to revere, but an impossible burden to bear. The sheer freneticism of running, reading, laughing, crying, the laying on of the human touch, the intellectual hankering, the saintliness, the earthiness, the full head of hair—all of it is absolutely killing.

Halfway through Clinton's first year in office, even the press had grown dubious, and began to monitor the frequency with which Clinton broke into tears in public. According to the *San Francisco Chronicle*, on November 5, 1992, he "dropped to his knees, teary-eyed" to console a lady who told him she was too poor to pay for medicine. He bawled again on December 13 upon introducing a boyhood friend as his chief of staff. He did it again on December 23 in introducing his nominee for the UN ambassadorship, a seemingly normal woman of impressive accomplishments. He cried again on January 11 after hearing "The Battle Hymn of the Republic" and on January 17 and January 21. On January 29 the press reported that a woman widowed by the Vietnam War brought Clinton to tears when she said she voted for him. On February 12 the father of a murdered child set Clinton to weeping, as did the brother of a cancer victim nine days later. March and April were okay, but on May 30 journalists spotted tears on his cheeks when he spoke of having "secretly" jogged by the Vietnam Memorial. Six days later, upon abandoning the appointment of Lani Guinier, he again lapsed into profound sorrow. The *Philadelphia Inquirer* reported him "shaken, somber, near tears."[20] In July the president broke down once more when he encountered twenty-four-year-old Christina Hein standing in a line waiting for a drink of water. After she said to him, "Mr. President, we need help," he hugged her. Then the woman reports that the president, presumably upon releasing her, "looked at me and said 'I'm very sorry' three times.

His eyes were very watery."[21] These are only the dolorous outbursts recorded by a watchful press. God knows how often he cried in private.

Perhaps Clinton's greatest addition to the stereotype of the progressive president has been a unique maudlinism, though President Carter was headed in this direction towards the end of his unhappy presidency. For Clinton the maudlin stirrings began when he moved from defending the little fellow to whining like a little fellow. Objecting to polls that revealed public doubt about his character in 1992, Clinton whined to an Arkansas audience, "… there's a lot of background for that…. A generation of disappointment in politicians. Somebody like me who's dumb enough to be honest and say, 'Hey, I like this. This is the only system we've got,' is automatically suspect."[22] And his whining has continued, as have his implausible efforts at sharing in everyone else's personal experience. Sentimental guy that he was, Clinton soon was claiming a piece of everything from manliness to womanliness, from poverty to living in middle-class terror, from understanding the Southern white mentality to understanding negritude. Though from a prosperous, well-connected family, he is still capable of reiterating his campaign bilge that his 1970s appointment to Senator J. William Fulbright's staff came "When I was nobody from nowhere. My family had no money, no political influence, nothing."[23]

By 1994 Clinton's attempts to touch everyone personally were attracting as much amusement in the press as had his public bawling and whining. During a trip to Central Europe and the Baltics, Clinton's maudlin theatrics were so risible that the *New York Times*'s report amounted to an extended put-on, abounding with such lines as "… Mr. Clinton was making out that his hometown, Hope, was a pretty worldly spot. 'I grew up in a little town in Arkansas that had a substantial Lithuanian population,' the president told a gathering of foreign reporters not long before he left Washington. 'So I grew up knowing about the problems of the Baltic nations.'"[24] And

Maureen Dowd had a grand time when she caught Clinton in a particularly transparent moment of sham sentiment. She traveled with him to Omaha Beach to commemorate the Normandy landing: "Originally, the White House told photographers they were considering a 'Where Have All the Flowers Gone?' moment, where Clinton and children would throw flowers into the sea. But they settled on 'a moment of solitude.' The president knew he was supposed to look reflective for the three cameras and dozen photographers who joined him. But after looking soulfully out at the ocean for a moment, he seemed at a loss for what to do next, according to a photographer on the scene, who was scared that Clinton was about to mouth the words 'What do I do now?' But then, spying some stones at his feet left by his advance staff to show him where his camera mark was, the president crouched down and began to arrange the stones into a cross. He gathered more stones to finish the cross, and then bent his head as though in silent prayer. The White House aides were ecstatic. 'Wasn't it great?' they asked reporters."[25]

But now let us turn our attention to the life and triumph of Hillary Rodham, Boy Clinton's wife and every bit the female edition of the Chronic Campaigner.

CHAPTER NINE

HILLARY AND HER MARRIAGE
OF CONVENIENCE

THOSE WHO HAVE studied the mating habits of humans often note that opposites attract. There are, however, exceptions to the rule. One is the famous partnership of Bill Clinton and Hillary Rodham or Hillary Clinton or Hillary Rodham Clinton or whatever she might be calling herself in a given decade. (As the Republic's hair stylists can document, change is a constant in her life.) The Clintons share many similarities. From the first hurrah of their public lives (beginning in high school for both), Clinton and Rodham have been energetic and steadfast in quest of political visibility. I employ the word "visibility" advisedly; it would be inaccurate to fall in with the consensus and assert that the Clintons have been pursuing political "power," which in their experience has often left painful blisters. They almost always settle for the semblance of power.

Their prodigious catalogue of honors and elective offices reveals almost none of the accomplishments resulting from power adroitly wielded. Contrary to their legends, little legislation has been passed. No significant policy shifts are recorded. From the Governor's Mansion the Clintons fashioned their much ballyhooed education reform, but it harvested mere weeds, then dust. Once in the White House they devised their famous health care plan, but after all the prenatal dramatics it died at birth. Its only consequence was the slaughter of the Democratic Party in the fall elections of 1994.

The closest the Clintons usually come to the actual exercise of power is leaking incriminating evidence or initiating an occasional police inquiry when a political opponent has loomed large, such as Arkansas's former attorney general, Steve Clark. No sooner did he rise up as a contender for Clinton's job than his expense account records mysteriously appeared in the press. All of a sudden he was indicted and exiled not just from the 1990 governor's race but from the entire state of Arkansas. And then there was the state audit of Cliff Jackson's tax returns in the summer of 1992, just when this long-time enemy of presidential candidate Clinton was beginning to dish out the dirt on Arkansas's favorite son. For such an audit to take place in the absence of a federal audit is almost unheard of.

Beyond their political precocity the Clintons have other qualities in common. They were good students—if grade grabbers are good students. Their intellects are quick, though facile. Both lack originality, illumination, and refinement. Deep knowledge and comprehension were less important to them than class standing. As students and ever after both have been assiduous masseuses and masseurs of the present moment and of whatever mentor or authority figure might be of assistance. Their public papers will in time reveal bottomless archives of friendly, at times earnest, communiqués to classmates, to teachers, and to other agents of influence. On holiday they send postcards. Once back at base they resort to letters and, of course, telephone calls. "She was so ambitious. She already knew the value of networking, of starting a Rolodex, even back then," recollects one of Rodham's Wellesley classmates.[1]

In the domain of student government the Clintons were giants. They were also prodigies in most other student activities, though not in sports. Consequently, their lives have long been enveloped in puffery, one of several abnormalities attendant with student government. In fact, there, puffery is required, and puffery begets puffery, occasionally exalting the most piffling stub-of-the-toe into the stuff of history. For Clinton and Rodham the puffery has continued into the present; in sum and in fine they have been student politicians all their lives. For them political life has been an unbroken chain of honors, high offices, and attitudinizing, from class presidency to American presidency.

The attendant puffery is frequently contradictory, particularly for Rodham. She has been billed as being practical and idealistic, compassionate and steely, liberal and conservative, a public servant of the workaholic variety, and a devoted mother radiating tenderness. She is tough but vulnerable. As her husband affirmed just after his inauguration to a distinguished interviewer, the world often misperceives Mrs. Clinton as "this sort of superstrong, brilliant person who seems to be almost mechanical" but "[t]here's that whole other more vulnerable, more human side of her."[2] The bold-faced contradictions have accumulated as a consequence of years of puffery manufactured for all the various audiences that she plays to, but being on both sides of every issue was essential to the Coat and Tie Radical from the beginning.

As a student government campaigner Rodham was accomplished, though not in a league with Clinton. At Emerson Junior High outside Chicago, at nearby Maine East High School, and later Maine South, Rodham was omnipresent in student endeavors. She graduated from Maine South in 1965, having become a National Merit Scholar finalist and been named "most likely to succeed." She had also been junior class president, though when she ran for senior class president she suffered the same fate as her future husband. She lost, but for different reasons. Rodham's classmates opposed her candidacy. Clinton lost because his *teachers* opposed his candidacy, because they thought he had been making a pig of himself in student government. Perhaps historians will someday offer a detailed account of why the senior class of Maine South turned thumbs down on Rodham. Possibly she ran an inferior campaign or maybe her opponent was positively Kennedyesque. Yet it is equally possible that her classmates had endured enough of her busy-bodied bossiness. They called her Sister Frigidaire, highlighting a problem that looms through all the clouds of puffery. She is not easy company. In fact she is a very difficult human being. "I've never been called arrogant in my life before," she complained to Leslie Bennetts once she got to Washington. "I find that the most astonishing charge."[3] How Clintonesque to serve up a big lie when a svelte little one would do.

Yet pictures of her in grade school reveal a sweet, graceful girl with an open, placid smile. Growing up in the middle-class suburb of Park Ridge, Illinois, she excelled in all she did, leading apparently a pleasant suburban life complete with lemonade stands, her games of cops and robbers, two younger brothers (both rather mediocre), and her standard-issue Park Ridge parents. They were Goldwater Republicans, a fact always noted in every account of Rodham's life. Yet, all three children had no trouble during college becoming sharply ideological Democrats.

Mother Dorothy seems to have been quiet, possibly diffident. A hint of tragedy or some dark episode during a restless Depression-era adolescence skulks through most interviews with her. At any rate, the unmentionable cloud occasioned her departure from the Alhambra, California, of her youth to chill Chicago and her nubile phase. In Chicago she, Dorothy Howell, met her future husband. She calls him "Mr. Difficult"—gloom again. After the war Hugh Rodham started a one-man drapery-making business that was to be successful enough to provide the modest home in Park Ridge and a life-long supply of Cadillacs—the family Cadillac is another fact sure to be found in all Rodham biographies. Hugh Rodham was gruff, demanding, and miserly with affection and money. He favored his daughter, whose name was chosen by his wife, who thought that in late-1940s Park Ridge, "Hillary" bespoke the "exotic." Why the Rodhams opted for the "exotic" when their daughter was born no biographer has yet explained. When the brothers came along the Rodhams settled for another Hugh and a Tony.[4] First Lady Rodham told an audience of New Zealanders that she was named for the conqueror of Mt. Everest, Sir Edmund Hillary. Well, perhaps, but she was born in 1947 when Sir Edmund Hillary was an obscure beekeeper. His fame did not come until 1953 when he topped that colossal mountain.

An exacting taskmaster for his three children, Father Rodham does not sound very agreeable. In adulthood his daughter would tell stories about his strict regimen. When she was Arkansas's First Lady, one of Chelsea's nannies overheard her lecturing her negligent daughter, telling her that back in Park Ridge she *always* had to replace the toothpaste cap. On one occasion when she failed, her father threw it out the window and sent her into the icy Midwestern morn to retrieve it.[5] Apparently Hugh mellowed. Arkansans who met him in the 1980s when he moved to Arkansas for good to participate in his son-in-law's campaigns remember him with marked fondness, even if they have little fondness for his daughter. Before the move he came down with his sons to participate in the 1974 congressional campaign. He and the boys would drive the Cadillac with its Illinois plates through the boondocks of the old Confederacy, tacking up Clinton posters. Actually Mr. Rodham's mission was twofold. He was also to keep an eye on the candidate's night life while his daughter, up in Washington, served on the House Judiciary Impeachment Inquiry. She had become apprised of at least two cuties he was—well, the polite word is "dating."[6]

Owing in part to the times in which they lived, to the politics of their mentors, and to similarities in their personalities, both Clinton and Rodham became paradigmatic 1960s Coat and Tie Radicals, spending their college days in protest, alienation, existential spelunking, and applying to law school. They attended "bull sessions," resounding with harangues on war and other contemporary Immensities. Yet there also was time for keg parties. There were lectures, cultural events, football games, fraternity or sorority dances, and the occasional drug overdose. I have detected no evidence that Rodham experienced marijuana, either in brownies or small pipes, as was the fashion for some college gals in that period. Nor have I detected any other coping mechanisms enhancing her student days, such as LSD or certain mushroom concoctions favored by some of her Coat and Tie Radical associates.

In addition to her protests out of doors which were undertaken even as she gunned for good grades and for faculty approval, she was an ornament in the Wellesley student senate, protesting curfews, the ban against men in the dormitories, and old-fashioned course requirements. She was at the forefront of the Coat and Tie Radicals' campaign to gut the curriculum. She also worked for including more minorities on campus. As with her peers, she had an admirable concern for civil rights, though they also were suckers for the Marxist class analysis. Through all the activism and protests, however, Rodham was never diverted for long from that one luminous goal so right for her increasingly bossy and disputatious humor, the study of law. In this she was among the cadre of pioneering co-eds who in the late 1960s would delay matrimony and motherhood for advanced training in courtroom confrontation and a life of litigation.

Rodham's testiness, first spotted in the waning days of her high school career, grew rapidly once she got to college; but then many of the left-wing co-eds from the 1960s became testy. They were to grow testier still. For decades their flinty anger has intensified, making them the clientele of an expanding complement of specialists whose professional services are essential for keeping them healthy and combat ready. I have in mind gastroenterologists, marriage counselors, cosmetic surgeons, psychotherapists, experts in lower back pain, psychics of various faiths, herbal medics, and aerobics instructors.

These sour, excitable dispositions were first observable freshman year when lecturers in Pol. Sci. spoke in comparative terms of Sweden's many government-funded amenities and America's vast deficiencies. They became more observable when lecturers in Eng. Lit. spoke comparatively of D.H. Lawrence's volupt visions and American Puritanism. Things got worse when these unhappy girls discovered that college boys were often referred to as "college men," while they were being referred to as "co-eds." In fact, by the late 1960s, the term "co-ed" made them mad as hell. So did the campus beauty pageant and the fact that there were no women on the varsity wrestling team. Next they grew mad as hell that males were not given free access to their dormitories. Their angers were productive. The term co-ed was banished, as were the beauty pageants and the prohibition against males in their dormitories. Soon the former co-eds were allowed free range in the theretofore all-male weight room and occasionally even in the men's toilets. Unfortunately, none of these reforms mollified Rodham's classmates, and male access to their dormitories in time made them even angrier.

Upon being welcomed into the young women's bedrooms, some of the young men, those unfettered by Christian chastity, attempted what young men attempt when placed in the vicinity of a nubile cutie's bed and lingerie chest. This turn of events really infuriated progressive women, and soon college towns became venues for "date rape," "sexual harassment," fear, and rage. University staffs expanded to include specialists in Rape Crisis Management. Codes of Sexual Conduct were adapted to guide young men from the first pro forma wink to the last carnal gasp. This historic evolution began in the 1970s, and by the 1980s on college campuses the rage of left-wing women was boundless. Anger and rage became as characteristic of the progressive young female as hope had been characteristic of Eleanor Roosevelt and her fellow valkyries of progress. Despite the ongoing march of personal liberation, ample job promotions, and handsome preferments, female progressives had moved from girlhood to womanhood getting steadily angrier. It is an Immensity that later generations of motherless and fatherless college students might want to ponder in their bull sessions.

Not that Rodham's female peers among the Coat and Tie Radicals did not have reason to be cranky. After becoming versed in the deficiencies of America, all were ready to take to the barricades with their male counterparts. Yet whenever there was a protest, or a campus revolt, what was their role? They were asked to lug provisions to the menfolk, declaiming from behind their barricades about peace, liberation, civil rights, or perhaps the immediate release of the kid arrested last week for taking his shirt off in Professor Buley's European History class. The guys did the exciting things. Shoving their books aside, they might even make a commando-style raid on the campus's Presidential Palace.

The Palace is surrounded by campus cops, negotiating a peaceful settlement through bullhorns as the guys burn the President's correspondence and use his wastepaper basket for a comfort station. Gamely the "activist" co-eds sneak past the cops with victuals—sandwiches, a case of beer, joints. Once in the Dean's office they engage in revolutionary acts of their own. A few heave their brassieres down at the cops with the bullhorns (a bullhorn filled with brassieres is almost useless). They shriek horrible imprecations. In the President's very office they copulate, though out of either revolutionary etiquette or vestigial modesty many will not remove their fatigue clothes completely or their heavy boots, which leave tread marks on the President's desk. Both sexes often wore army surplus dress in those days, despite misgivings about the military. Thanks to the theorizing of certain Central European academics, Eros had taken on a political dimension, transforming copulation into nonverbal political declaration. Incidentally, the introduction of sexual congress into campus politics also made female radicals very popular, even with Young Republicans.

Upon graduation, many of the Coat and Tie Radicals went to

graduate school, the young men in pursuit of draft deferments, the young women in pursuit of professional accreditation. (This was back before progressive women considered military careers a constitutional right.) For Rodham it was law school, with its promise of a life of structured ire and recrimination. Of all the professions, only the practice of law rewards its practitioners for getting angry at people in court, and, for that matter, even before arriving at court. Rodham's last act at Wellesley demonstrates the fully matured anger of this female Coat and Tie Radical.

Her graduating class of 1969 insisted on having one of its own speak to the commencement audience, and thus Rodham became Wellesley's first senior to address the departing throng. ("There was no debate so far as I could ascertain as to who their spokesman was to be," joshed Wellesley's president in introducing Rodham.[7]) Handed down through the puffery, the speech is remembered as "passionate and eloquent and wise [sic]."[8] Frankly, I find even the adjective "passionate" inappropriate, for the whole thing appears to have been staged. Supposedly, a previous speaker, Senator Edward Brooke, had provoked her to tear up her prepared text and sweep on into an ad lib fulmination on behalf of humanity. The speech she thereupon delivered was simply too contrived to be spontaneous. It had to be memorized. Leaning heavily on the abstractions of left-wing 1960s gurus and on some tortured platitudes of Transcendentalist origin, the concoction is expressed in that chaos of world-weary rhetoric and sudden urgency that is pure 1960s adolescent nonsense. Even the supposed provocation is improbable. Senator Brooke was a moderate Republican, the first black since Reconstruction to be elected to the Senate, and an outspoken opponent of President Richard Nixon. At any rate, according to first-hand accounts, Rodham's outburst left the senator smiling and seeping congratulations. Liberals of the era always treated their ideological progeny generously after an idealistic rant.

Being a United States senator, Brooke had spoken only in fashionable clichés about "relevance" and "empathy." Citing the percentage of Americans beneath the poverty line, he prescribed
empathy. That made Rodham mad, or so the legend goes. "Part of
the problem with empathy," she responded, "with professed goals,"
she continued, suggesting that she should have brought her dictio-
nary, "is that empathy doesn't do us anything... for too long our
leaders have used politics as the art of the possible. And the challenge now is to practice politics as the art of making what appears
to be impossible, possible. What does it mean to hear that 13.3% of
the people in this country are below the poverty line? That's a percentage. We're not interested in social reconstruction; it's human
reconstruction. How can we talk about percentages and trends?"[9]

Thirty-four years after this piece of effrontery, she recalled it as
First Lady. She had been asked to deliver a commencement address
at the University of Michigan, and there she demonstrated that
after all those years she was still at heart a school girl. After a message that was pure New Age flumdiddle, Rodham insisted that what
had provoked her 1969 oration was Brooke's inflammatory remarks
about the Vietnam War. I have been able to find no evidence that
she was provoked by anything Brooke said about the Vietnam War,
and it is unlikely that this mild liberal would have offended his liberal audience with any hawkish statement at that time. History
records only Rodham's dithyramb against "empathy." After her
Michigan speech, the students demonstrated the awe they held for
the First Lady by passing over their heads an inflated female doll.[10]

The radical gibberish she intoned in her spontaneous valedictory
address could not have come easily, even to a mind quickened by
indignation. It is tough going even to the reading eye. Said Rodham
to the two thousand Welleslians at her feet: "Words have a funny way
of trapping our minds on the way to our tongues but there are necessary means even in this multi-media age for attempting to come to
grasps [sic] with some of the inarticulate maybe even inarticulable

[sic] things that we're feeling. We are, all of us, exploring a world that none of us understands and attempting to create within that uncertainty. But there are some things we feel, feelings that our prevailing, acquisitive, and competitive corporate life, including tragically the universities, is not the way of life for us. We're searching for more immediate, ecstatic and penetrating mode [sic] of living."[11]

And that was not all: "Every protest, every dissent, whether it's an individual academic paper, Founder's parking lot demonstration, is unabashedly an attempt to forge an identity in this particular age. That attempt at forging for many of us over the past four years has meant coming to terms with our humanness. Within the context of a society that we perceive—now we can talk about reality, and I would like to talk about reality sometime, authentic reality, inauthentic reality, and what we have to accept of what we see—but our perception of it is that it hovers often between the possibility of disaster and the potentiality for imaginatively responding to men's needs... If the only tool we have ultimately to use is our lives, so we use it in the way we can by choosing a way to live that will demonstrate the way we feel and the way we know... The struggle for an integrated life existing in an atmosphere of communal trust and respect is one with desperately important political and social consequences. And the word 'consequences' of course catapults us into the future. One of the most tragic things that happened yesterday, a beautiful day, was that I was talking to a woman who said that she wouldn't want to be me for anything in the world. She wouldn't want to live today and look ahead to what it is she sees because she's afraid. Fear is always with us but we just don't have time for it. Not now."[12] Such passions and clarity of thought inspired professors of the 1960s to call Rodham's generation the brightest, most idealistic in American history!

Setting Rodham's college career side by side with Clinton's, she appears notably more ideological. Even Clinton's Oxford years are years of modest mischief by comparison to Rodham's protests, manifestos, and harangues, if we factor out his draft-dodging and antiwar organizing. Then, upon her entry into Yale Law School, Rodham's dispendious angers intensified.

With the utmost ardor she opposed the war and pioneered protests over the heartless scarcity of Tampax dispensers in the women's rooms. She smoldered on the board of editors of a radical quarterly, *Yale Review of Law and Social Action*. "Jamestown Seventy," an essay featured in the spring 1970 issue, will convey the adolescent quality of the journal over which she helped preside. Written by James F. Blumstein and James Phelan, it proposed "political migration to a single state for the purpose of gaining political control and establishing a living laboratory for experimentation."[13] "Now," Blumstein and Phelan explained, "a new frontier must be found to foster further experimentation, an environment relatively unpolluted by conventional patterns of social and political organization. Experimentation with drugs, sex, individual lifestyles or radical rhetoric and action within the larger society is an insufficient alternative. Total experimentation is necessary. New ideas and values must be taken out of heads and transformed into reality."[14] According to one of the editorial board's surviving members, Hillary offered a "detailed sympathetic critique" of the article, belittling it as "long on rhetoric, short on action." What "action" Rodham had in mind has never been revealed.[15]

Later, in a special double issue of the quarterly, Rodham appears as an associate editor. That issue features cartoon drawings of policemen portrayed as pigs [see Appendix C, item A]. In one, a group of grotesque pigs is depicted marching with guns, slop dripping from gigantic snouts. Thought balloons above their heads have them thinking "niggers, niggers, niggers, niggers.... " In another cartoon a decapitated and dismembered pig is squealing in agony. The caption reads, "Seize the Time!"[16] This episode in Rodham's career has never fetched much attention in the press. Having been a classmate with radicals in the 1960s, I can tell you that those who wrote this sort of primitive protest were radicals of a distinctly angry sort. They had moved to the outer limits of democratic discourse, to a fringe area where protest lunged easily into violence. One could be a bespectacled bookish disciple of Gandhi today and in a police lineup tomorrow for fire bombing, say, an ROTC facility. Rodham obviously was not guilty of heaving bombs—a very black mark on one's resume—but the evidence reveals that she associated from time to time with a very angry lot. The fashionable term for them was "alienated." Light-hearted Bill Clinton was never this "alienated."

Rodham's ideological fires did not bank even during summer holidays away from New Haven. In her first summer she took up a cause that was to attract her even during her years in Washington, Marian Wright Edelman's Children's Defense Fund. Rodham spent her next summer clerking for a far-left lawyer active in defending the Black Panthers. In 1972 she and Clinton took time off from law school. Under the moderating influence of her boy friend, she worked for the McGovern campaign in Texas. McGovern lost badly in Texas, but in the summer of 1974 Rodham got even. She went to work on the House Judiciary Impeachment Inquiry staff, where she became friends with Bernard Nussbaum. That fated soul was to be reincarnated in 1993 as the Clintons' first White House Counsel and one of the first members of the administration to suffer the Nixonesque undoing that has befallen so many members of the Clinton administration. History remains the greatest of literatures.

The enthusiasm of Rodham's first summer, the Children's Defense Fund, is an example of an expedient increasingly resorted to by contemporary liberals, the expedient of Masked Politics. The public has wearied of the Left's bold ventures into social engineering, and so the Left resorts to masks and disguises. As Masked Politics is played nowadays, the social engineering liberal dresses as some noble reformer, say, the environmentalist, or the consumers' rights advocate; campaigns for the noble cause with an aura of trustworthiness about him that is not available to mere liberal

Democrats; and surreptitiously advances still more government
control of private lives. In Edelman's case, behind the happy mask
of the children's rights advocate she and her acolytes steadily
advance policies that undermine parents' control of their families,
and shift power over children to the state. Edelman advertises herself as ensuring the rights of the young; actually she wants to
increase the rights of the state over the young.

Within a few years Rodham was devising rationales for these statist intrusions, though at the time of her theorizing she had neither
a family nor a husband. Her 1974 essay, "Children Under the Law"
(reprinted in a 1982 edition of the *Harvard Educational Review*), recommended three measures for promoting "children's rights": (1)
the abolition of the legal category of minority and thus the reversal
of a minor's presumption of legal incompetence; (2) extension to
children of all procedural rights that are guaranteed to adults; and
(3) an end to the legal presumption that there exists an identity of
interests between children and their parents, thus allowing children
to assert their own interests in the courts and opening the family to
further judicial intrusion.[17] Rodham goes on to equate the family
with slavery. "The basic rationale," she writes, "for depriving people of rights in a dependency relationship is that certain individuals
are incapable or undeserving of the right to take care of themselves
and consequently need social institutions specifically designed to
safeguard their position. Along with the family, past and present
examples of such arrangements include marriage, slavery and the
Indian reservation system."[18]

How do we account for the Marxist ring of these lines? Some of
this was to be expected of the Coat and Tie Radical, but how do we
account for the broader and angrier Marxist emphasis that made its
appearance during law school? The immediate cause was probably
the company she kept during her second summer of law school. That
summer she took a job that most biographies simply ignore. She went
to work for a communist lawyer. Most Coat and Tie Radicals drew

the line at associating with communists, stuffy fellows who could be quite unpleasant, and whose appearance on a resume was rarely helpful. Rodham's 1971 job was a bold move, a dangerously sincere concession to her predisposition toward the stuffy, unpleasant, no-nonsense reformer. The most influential mentor of her youth had been a Methodist spiritual advisor, which is to say, an advisor on transforming the planet earth into a no-dancing, no-drinking, totally middle class, ageless utopia.

The suspect is Donald Jones. He was Rodham's minister at Park Ridge's First United Methodist. He arrived when she was in ninth grade, and like so many Methodist clergy of the reformist variety, he too had an asperity to his thought. He induced his young charges to undertake serious readings: Paul Tillich, Reinhold Niebuhr, and Dietrich Bonhoeffer.[19] That is all to the good, but his general spiel had that Shake-Up-the-Yokels theme that is so characteristic and repellent in reformers of his type. Jones was a desperate adherent to liberalism's cardinal value, to wit, the moral imperative of disturbing the peace. Jones believed religion mere mood music unless it troubled people and slammed into their settled conventions. Hence, from blithesome Park Ridge, he took his charges on grim excursions to poor and squalid neighborhoods. On Sunday mornings he brought distress to the congregation at large by leading their children in discussions about teenage pregnancy and, who knows, perhaps condoms (in this he would have been ahead of his time, a not uncommon position for Jones). On other occasions he frightened adults and children alike with discourses on war and racism.

Rodham stayed in touch with him for years. Her letters often danced from trivialities to Deep Thoughts: "It is an interesting question you posed—can one be a mind conservative and a heart liberal?"[20] It was characteristic of Rodham and her colleagues to appear to let the mind speculate over broad reaches, to pretend to a dispassionate consideration of all political phenomena. During her historic 1969 commencement address she had said "There's a very strange [sic] conservative strain that goes through a lot of New Left, collegiate protests that I find very intriguing because it harkens back to a lot of the old virtues.... "[21] Yet when it came time for acts rather than words, the acts were always leftward. This has been the continual drift of liberalism for over three decades, a pretense to openness, a claim to tolerating all points of view, and then a leap further to the left, until by the 1990s, the liberal was howling for causes that no Roosevelt or Kennedy (pre-Teddy) would have dreamed of.

Certainly Rodham's movement from her undergraduate days to her law school days was ever leftward. Consider that second summer job. Casting the Masked Politics of her summer with Edelman aside, she accepted the recommendations of two radical law professors and went to Oakland, California, sans mask, to clerk in the law office of Robert Treuhaft, the communist husband of Jessica Mitford, known in her native United Kingdom as the "Red Mitford" perhaps to distinguish her from her sister Unity Mitford who became infatuated with Hitler. "That was the time we were representing the Black Panthers," said Treuhaft to the *San Francisco Chronicle's* Herb Caen, "and she worked on that case. Some people think she went to Sacramento with them—remember when they disrupted the Legislature?—but I'm not sure whether she did or not. Anyway, it was nice to have her around."[22] To get a sense of precisely how stringent Rodham's politics had become by this time, it might be helpful to note that Treuhaft had joined the Communist party *after* the Hitler-Stalin Pact. He and his wife were *Stalinists*. Even the most doctrinaire sort of 1960s radicals gave Stalinists a wide berth. For a radical of the milder strength, such as a Coat and Tie Radical, associating with Stalinists was almost unimaginable.

Once Rodham was in the White House, her critics began to call her a hypocrite for having publicly moralized about the "Greed of the 1980s." News stories were beginning to reveal that no sooner had she finished her work with the Impeachment Inquiry than she began wheeling and dealing exuberantly for the root of all evil. Her critics cited Rodham's string of bountiful commodity trades, real estate deals, sweetheart bank loans, and conflicts of interest that most professional women would be loath to incur—for instance, representing clients before boards controlled by her husband, the governor. The innocent wondered as to how she could repeatedly denounce the "Decade of Greed" after being so much a part of it. One minute she was assisting the idealists in banishing the crook Nixon, and in the next, she, the wife of the newly elected governor, was accepting $100,000 from a lieutenant of the Tyson poultry interests. (Although it is widely assumed that the money was a bribe on behalf of Tyson, there are other possibilities. The commodity traders themselves might have had errands that they wanted undertaken.) After all, according to the puffery, after leaving Park Ridge she had "grown up and out of the conservative materialistic mind-set which is typical of affluent suburbs.... She was not interested in making money or being affluent." That is one variation on the theme sounded so earnestly by her partisans, in this case a college boyfriend.[23]

Those who think it hypocritical for Rodham to protest materialism while indulging in it so wantonly and unethically have failed to comprehend not only the rich complexity of the 1960s Coat and Tie Radicals, whose grandiosity could justify the starkest of contradictions, but also how special Rodham was among her peers. Since college her testiness had grown to an anger just short of that feminist quality that was to become fashionable in the 1980s, Rage. Remember her associates from the early 1970s: law students who depicted police as pigs worthy of decapitation, Stalinist lawyers who defended Black Panthers, many of whom had committed violent crimes.

For decades there have been radical students intent on bringing socialism to America; usually they aspired to do so peacefully from an impulse of benevolence. As with their perennial presidential candidate, Norman Thomas, they respected America's history and saw socialism as a natural development from the Constitution's most admirable ideals. Yet also numbered among America's socialists have been the morbid types who long ago marked the Republic down as racist and fascist, its riches nothing more than plunder. As to how deeply in sympathy with the latter type Rodham has been, it is difficult to judge. She has played Masked Politics from the early 1970s. Her mask slipped, however, at the *Yale Review of Law and Social Action* with its decapitated pigs, and it slipped again with the communist Treuhaft. If she shared these peoples' basic insight into America as a thoroughly corrupt polity, it was not in the least hypocritical for her to take $100,000 from the chicken baron (or from others?). It was merely against the law. Seen through the eyes of her Marxist friends, American ethics are bogus. American wealth is ill-gotten. Why not pocket as much of it as possible, legally or illegally? To a Treuhaft the American legal system is a fraud. A 1960s idealist can always put a bribe of $100,000 into a good cause.

Through the 1970s and into the 1980s, Rodham combined wheeling and dealing with Masked Politics. In 1979 with her husband in the Governor's Mansion she became chairman of the Board of the Legal Services Corporation, a favorite liberal mask, which engaged in so many radical and illegal machinations that the Comptroller General of the United States censured it for contravening its own by-law. By the late 1980s, Rodham was on the board of the New World Foundation, which among other things was funneling money to the Palestine Liberation Organization and giving financial grants to a group supporting El Salvador's communist guerrillas. The foundation also supported the far left Christic Institute, the National Lawyers Guild (founded in the 1930s as an adjunct to the American Communist party), and such other left-wing groups as the Center for Constitutional Studies (co-founded by radical lawyer William Kunstler) and the Institute for Policy Studies (the self-styled "center for radical scholarship").

A rare opportunity to glimpse the mentality of Rodham and her peers in the 1980s was afforded by the Columbia University graduates of 1968 when they gathered twenty years later to swank

and commiserate. Twenty years before they all had been protes-
tors of one sort or another, rattling the cerebral calm of Morn-
ingside Heights.

The event has been convened in Earl Hall to commemorate the
student strike and subsequent takeover of university buildings. Coat
and Tie Radicals are in attendance as are the more doctrinaire radicals, and those who have continued to evolve: militant feminists,
militant homosexuals, perhaps one or two who have discovered
their ancestry as Native Americans or victims of CIA research. Naturally there are former members of the Students for a Democratic
Society, for instance, Mark Naison. He had been a stalwart in
Columbia's student strike, possibly even a commando in the raid on
President Grayson Kirk's Palace. Now he coaches his son's Little
League team and teaches history at Fordham, where he says his
course on the 1960s is very popular, and, I should think, very inaccurate. Three hundred and fifty survivors of those Great Days are
here with him.[24]

They have taken up two floors of Earl Hall, "giving way at one
point" the *New York Times* reports, "to a tai chi class." At Columbia
it is final exam week, and after the reforms of the 1960s, tai chi is a
popular scholarly pursuit. The assembled dine on fast food, dance
to the Rolling Stones, and drink beer, "but mostly," claims the
Times, "they talked."[25] Coming out of some Freudian revelation
from decades back, talk had become a therapy in the 1960s, an
instrument for resolving conflict, an avenue to The Truth—though
be it understood that the young talkers already were in possession
of The Truth. After the requisite marathons of talk, everyone,
according to the 1960s theory of talk, would assent to The Truth.
On National Public Radio Bill Clinton once urged moving beyond
mere "philosophy" and on to an orgy of talk between Republicans
and Democrats.[26] The Clintons' friend, Lani Guinier, has made yet
an even more witless endorsement of therapeutic talk: "we've got to
learn to talk to each other even when we don't understand each

other."[27] And Rodham adheres to the same stratagem: "I don't mind a fair, honest give-and-take," she declared with a wink during the health-care debate. "If somebody in Congress disagrees with our approach to health care on ideological reasons, let's just try to have a good, healthy debate about it."[28] Of course, all this praise of talk assumes that, after the last syllable resonates, the Clintons win.

But to return to Earl Hall—Eric Foner, once a student striker and now a history professor at Columbia, tells the *Times*, "This is not *The Big Chill*.... These people are still committed." Well, yes and no. Ken Eardley is here. Upon graduation he spent years as a letter carrier by day in Berkeley, California, and as an active Trotskyite by night. In the biography that he has prepared for this reunion he writes that he is now living on a Vermont homestead, participating in a sister city program with Nicaragua (communist Nicaragua!) and "unmarried—the life of a professional revolutionary made that difficult.... Still hoping to see socialism in the U.S.A." Along with him is Allen Young, a gay rights activist, who is taking a break from his "small-town brand of activism" in Royalton, Massachusetts, where "My latest political activity is stopping the road builders from building roads and paving over more of this planet." Yet along with the "committed" we find a decidedly uneasy fellow, James Simon Kunen, author of *The Strawberry Statement* whom we encountered in Chapter 4. Once the Tom Paine of his generation, he now writes for Time-Life's *People* magazine. This he recognizes as a clear sellout to corporate America. He fears that feeling will be running high against him. In fact he tells a reporter that he was "paralyzed" while filling out his one-paragraph biography: "I was trying to figure out the politically correct thing to say." Kunen knows, and surely all his classmates know, that in *The Big Chill* one of the oxidizing student activists writes for *People*. The *Times* goes on to report that Columbia's returning "student rebels" include many poets, novelists, filmmakers, and—forget not—legal services lawyers.[29] Yes, but the *Times* reporter fails to note that these creative types are at best mediocrities. One of the peculiarities of the 1960s generation is that, for all its proclaimed genius, by the time it had arrived at middle-age it had produced fewer distinguished writers and artists than almost any preceding American generation. One has to go back to the Jamestown settlement to find such primeval intellectual coarseness.

Of all the participants at the Columbia reunion, the truest facsimile of Rodham is Nancy Biberman, a lady lawyer. Biberman works in government as a New York City housing lawyer. Since 1968 she, like so many of her female classmates, has grown mad as hell. "I'm finally coming to terms with the anger and frustration of being a girl—or was it a woman, or a co-ed, or a chick?—in 1968," she fumes (Remember what I said about "co-ed"?). Once a female member of the student strike, Biberman has risen in stature to become a panel member in this impassioned (and one-sided) discussion of the Columbia strike. (In keeping with a custom that began in the late 1960s, none of the many students who opposed the protests were included on these panels.) Yet Biberman is the only female panelist, and her impatience intensifies; the panel is dominated by the same ingrate who dominated the 1968 demonstrations, Mark Rudd. He meanders on through forty-five minutes of narcissistic pronunciamentoes, singing of his passage from being a "nice Jewish boy" to becoming a "Weather Underground" fugitive from justice. It is all too much for Biberman. "The only difference between today and twenty years ago is that I'm up here following Mark at all," she flares. Reading from *Up Against the Ivy Wall*, a 1968 account of the strike written by the editors—all male—of the student paper, she notes that the word woman can be found only once, that being a reference to a striking student's *mother*. Otherwise the account describes "girls" "making peanut butter sandwiches, vacuuming floors and emptying trash cans."[30] Well, you can be sure that Biberman, lawyer and activist, brought no vacuum cleaner or peanut butter this time.

One classmate who cannot be here is David Gilbert. He writes from prison, where he is serving a seventy-five years-to-life term for nothing more serious than robbery and the murder of a policeman and two Brinks guards. Rudd pays tribute to Gilbert and to another colleague, Ted Gold. Gold blew himself up while making a bomb in a Greenwich Village town house in 1970. "[G]reetings and warm hugs," the murderer writes from his cell. "The struggle has turned out to be much longer, more difficult and complex than we had imagined."[31]

"Warm hugs?" One of the achievements of the 1960s protesters, whether Coat and Tie Radical or straight radical, is that they have done much to erase the moral order of our civilization. Murder and robbery are understandable if a proper cause can be perceived. Cigarette smoking and whistling at a pretty girl are pathologies to be treated by counseling or a stretch in the cooler, but a bank robber and cop killer is a cuddly creature at a class reunion. Another achievement of the 1960s protesters is that after tearing down ceremonies, conventions, standards, and traditions, they established almost nothing in their place. Look back over the era. A campus ball or beauty pageant is yanked out here, a dozen course requirements yanked out there, unhappy young women are injected into venerable social clubs whose male character evaporates. Faculty-hiring standards go by the board. The resulting vista is a wasteland enlivened solely by feuds about gender, race, and mythological histories of primitive people.

Rodham's 1975 wedding with the Snopes of Hot Springs is a bleak reminder of the 1960s brats' destruction of convention and ceremony and of their capacity to drain meaning from normal life. Shorn of most formalities save the required state certificates and medical tests, it featured an exchange of rings and a reception that was more like a statewide political convention. It took place after years of feuding between the two partners. Notwithstanding all the puffery about their ineffable love ("in countless interviews," a

Washington Post writer affirms in 1993, "close friends describe the couple as being 'still incredibly in love,' 'partners in everything' and each other's biggest supporter"),[32] what they indubitably saw in each other were qualities advantageous to their life's work—namely, acquiring office.

The ensuing merger was and remains a marriage of convenience. Long before they tied the knot, Rodham was as aware of Clinton's satyriasis as he was of her dispendious wrath. Thus her father's role as private detective in Bill's 1974 congressional campaign, to keep track of the young law professor's intense affair with an undergraduate campaign volunteer, and numerous flings with other girls in towns around the district. That Hugh Rodham would undertake such a mission suggests the family's pliancy before their bossy daughter. That he would report to her on her fiancee's infidelities without blowing his top suggests that Clinton was not the first weak man in her life.

Campaign worker Paul Fray has reported overhearing Rodham "raising hell" with Clinton when she called him from Washington after acquiring a proper intelligence report on his undergraduate paramour. She threatened to take revenge by sleeping with someone in Washington. Clinton "about broke down and cried," begging her, as Fray recollects, not to "go and do something that would make life miserable" for them.[33]

As for the wedding itself, it took place on October 11, 1975, in a little house Clinton had purchased in Fayetteville. Rodham took little interest in the event beyond purchasing a wedding dress and assigning the ceremony's particulars to a friend, Ann Henry, who even designed the reception. The ceremony was a pared-down Methodist service in the presence of a few friends and family members. Then there was the reception at Henry's, where acquaintances showed up from all over the state. Two undercurrents inhered through the conversation: Clinton's plan to run for attorney general; and a sudden fly in the ointment, Clinton's Yankee wife was keeping her maiden name. That disturbed Arkansans, which might have been Rodham's goal. Being an understudy of Donald Jones, Rodham places at the center of her moral universe the moral imperative of disturbing the peace. It is the jolt that edifies. As for the honeymoon, it was another shredding of custom. There might not have been one except that months after the wedding her father espied a cut-rate vacation package to Acapulco. The Rodhams and their new son-in-law traveled together.

Rodham is supposedly a political virtuoso with a special instinct for political strategy. Actually her last seventeen years reveal her as merely an intelligent woman with a spacious background in the nuts and bolts of politics. Sometimes she has been a help to Clinton and sometimes a hindrance. She had a large say in the staffing of his first gubernatorial administration, whose inexperienced young zealots cost Clinton his reelection. A friendly biographer writes of Rodham's consuming desire for "power," and the same biographer quotes another Rodham admirer, Arkansas journalist John R. Starr, saying that "most of the people in his [Clinton's] first administration were Hillary's friends."[34] The administration was a disaster, conducing to the unthinkable: a Republican governor of Arkansas.

Certain unchanging rhythms appear in her public life from Arkansas to the White House. A graph of that life moves from controversy to quietude, from the conflicts of a career woman to the proprieties of a loyal wife and homemaker. Both at the Governor's Mansion and the White House, Rodham—amid much fanfare—assumed a large role in appointments, often with unfortunate consequences. Both in Little Rock and in Washington her clothes became an issue, as did her hair, her demeanor, her disposition. Then too on both stages she had her special policy reforms to initiate. She is usually quite sunny in public, whether in the Razorback state or in the District of Columbia, yet from behind the scenes comes word of controversy: servants are fired, security personnel misused, lamps smashed. Finally, however, even in public there are those instances of stony abruptness during which the cat exits the bag. It is time for her handlers to announce another "image transplant" for their difficult client. These are the rhythms of the public Rodham; who knows what her private rhythms might be?

Perhaps it is an unavoidable consequence of the abundant puffery that the Clintons manufacture; perhaps it is a consequence peculiar to the 1960s brats' self-absorption. Whatever the reason, both Clintons get into oddly personal rows. Their responses to controversy are never dispassionate and surely never amused. They are almost always either overheated or too clever by half. Neither is capable of distinguishing a controversy that is minor from one that is serious.

Rodham has been accompanied by a hornets' nest of controversies, many of which have been stupefyingly petty. Her reaction is always colossal indignation, occasionally relieved by a sneer. The journalist Connie Bruck has described Rodham's temper in comparative terms that are useful to us here, for the comparison is with her similarly endowed husband. "Temper is a trait she and Bill Clinton share, but, while his is said to erupt with the force of a sudden squall and then be spent—leaving him, more often than not, eager to make amends—hers has inspired ongoing fear in some of those who have worked with her over the years. Grown men describe her as being, at such times, scary."[35]

It does not matter if it is her educational reform that is being hammered on the critics' anvil, or her latest hair style; Rodham gets mad. During her first stay in the Governor's Mansion from 1979 to 1981, Arkansans had her in scores of snits. "People thought she was a hippie," her friend Linda Bloodworth-Thomason has said.[36] She arrived at the mansion overweight, wore her hair long and unkempt, and went without make-up or perfumes. Her spectacles were as thick as bullet-proof glass, and the lenses were encased in impressively ugly frames. The dresses that she wore were frumpy, though she often wore pants, usually baggy corduroys or jeans. It was one of the dogmas of the day among young people of Rodham's persuasion that haircuts, clothes, style in general, were matters of no significance. "No one ought to be judged by one's haircut or clothes," was the popular line, while those who proclaimed it practiced a sartorial conformism that would have shamed lifelong subscribers to *Vogue*.

After Clinton's 1980 defeat, his wife repudiated her peers' dogma. Obviously, style did matter. Rodham went conventional and very deliberately. She got a haircut, a perm, and a new pair of glasses. She lost weight and began to dress like a middle-class Arkansan. She took up her husband's name and began attending his Southern Baptist church, Little Rock's Immanuel. Yet it is characteristic of the Coat and Tie Radicals that, as they age and their behavior refutes their youthful dogmas, they put the dogmas in storage to be retained for special occasions, *Big Chill* weekends, commemorations of the student strike, or an interview with *People* magazine conducted by a fellow sojourner from 1968.

The fly-blown belief that haircuts, clothes, and demeanor do not matter was to come up again when Rodham became First Lady, and to embarrassing effect. "There are more pressing things for her to do than dress up like *Vogue*," declared Sarah Phillips, designer of Rodham's wardrobe on the night of the 1992 Democratic Convention. About that time Rodham's soulmate, Susan Thomases, snapped, "Clothes are not something I [we] think about." Within months of these reiterations of this threadbare dogma from their youth, Rodham stomped on it again, and this time with a breathcatching brazenness. She appeared in a series of slinky, glamorous Annie Leibovitz pictures, and where were they published? I direct your attention to page 227 of the December 1993 issue of *Vogue*. The spread provoked some fashion writers to remark on Rodham's new "pussycat" look and "bedroom eyes."[37]

Well, as I say, in Rodham's public life there are rhythms that recur—controversies over her dress and demeanor and over more serious matters, as we shall see. Regarding the controversies over fashion and demeanor, her defenders will argue that they are merely the crosses borne by modern women in public life, but other public women powder their noses, change their hemlines, and rearrange the foliage. President Ronald Reagan's ambassador to the United Nations, Jeane Kirkpatrick, was every inch a modern career woman; but the controversies that befell Rodham rarely ensnared Kirkpatrick. Of course, had Ambassador Kirkpatrick regularly unveiled a new look as ceremoniously as Rodham does, the world would snicker and protest. Or think of Prime Minister Margaret Thatcher. Her sartorial revisions rarely raised a gossip columnist's glance. Why do Rodham's makeovers create a pother? Perhaps it is the frequency (manic!), or perhaps the pretentiousness. "The first lady has managed to transform her mousy tresses three times in the past six months," records the *Times* of London, "leaving even Linda Evangelista appearing frumpy."[38] Her frequent changes of hairdo in Washington reminded longtime friends that back at Yale Law School a notable aspect of her appearance was frequent changes of frames for her thick glasses. The only public woman remotely comparable to Rodham for stylistic strife in recent years has been Mrs. Ronald Reagan.

The changes of role and style that made Rodham controversial in Little Rock began early in Washington. As soon as the 1992 election was behind the Clintons, Rodham reverted to her role as public figure. To the usual accompaniment of brass and timpani she became a powerful headhunter for the administration, becoming so much a part of the process that she actually sat in on interviews of prospective nominees. Also she retrieved her maiden name. Now she was to be addressed as Hillary Rodham Clinton.[39] "For months on the campaign trail, Clinton had been criticized as an overbearing, career-oriented lawyer," the *Los Angeles Times* observed after the election, "To silence her detractors, Clinton was eased into a less prominent, more traditional role. A month before the convention, she was given a smarter wardrobe and a shorter, sleeker hairdo."[40] Hurrah, the "detractors" have been thwarted, the public duped, and so it is back to the offensive name, the offensive style, and soon she was being pictured with Vice President-elect Al Gore in quest of the perfect lady attorney general.

True to the rhythms of her life, a wave of rows followed. There was the row over charging *Family Circle* magazine $2,000 for Christophe's services in preparing her hair for publication. Another row erupted over Rodham's use of a military plane to fly her to Philadelphia on a personal matter, and there was the characteristically mean and dissembling way she paid for the trip upon being caught. She promised to pay the $390 she would have had to pay for a seat on a commercial flight. As for the $4,000 an hour that the military plane actually cost, again the public could be duped; the press would remain indulgent, ignoring even the impudence of her deception.[41] As we have seen in earlier chapters, Rodham fired an usher, supposedly for talking to Mrs. George Bush, but really because the Clintons cannot conceive of any position not being political and reserved for one of their politically reliable cronies. Her mistrustfulness ignited other rows. The distinguished White House chef got the boot, allegedly for infusing massive doses of cholesterol in the health-crazed First Family's diet. He got off easier than the head of the White House travel office, Billy Dale. After he and other travel office employees were fired in a plot to turn the office into a source of traditional Arkansas patronage, Dale was prosecuted. Soon the nature of the scandal and Rodham's role behind the scenes was revealed (first by David Brock in the June 1994 *American Spectator*, later in congressional hearings, and later still in the general press), but Dale had been chosen as a scapegoat and he had to spend the better part of three years and hundreds of thousands of dollars to gain acquittal while the Clintons went along with the travesty. There was a transient row over Rodham's appalling redecoration of the White House, which took a macabre turn when Vince Foster's reputed suicide note claimed that White House ushers "plotted" to inflate the costs of that redecoration. They had ballooned 60 percent.

Yet the most illuminating report of Rodham's mistrustfulness and its rancorous consequences came out early in 1996. A memo by ex–White House aide David Watkins revealed what had long been rumored—Rodham and Clinton's early mistrust of their White House Secret Service detail provoked them to order that the entire detail be fired to be replaced by agents who "were loyal."[42]

Rodham even created a row over the White House Christmas card. "First, the White House dropped Hallmark after its 50 years of making the cards," reported the *Washington Post*. "Then Hillary Clinton's staff commissioned local artist Susan Davis... to come up with a watercolor last August. Davis chose to paint the Truman Balcony, and was then asked to put Socks in, take Socks out, paint the front of the house instead, lighten the sky and darken the sky. Two color sketches, four watercolors and countless work-hours later, Davis was told the Clintons were now considering a plain photo of the White House instead."[43] All this was of a piece with the controversies that she provoked back in Arkansas, where, as First Lady, she was famous for misusing staff, on one occasion having convicts who worked in her kitchen serve cookies at a social function. In Washington she got into a flap for using military personnel as waiters.

If by the 1990s a change had overtaken the rhythms of Rodham's public life it was only that her controversies increased in frequency, taking on the floppy hats and baggy pants of sheer buffoonery. Early in the administration the Clintons decided for reasons still obscure that state dinners were, like cholesterol, to be avoided. A year and a half elapsed before they finally held one, and it took the Japanese emperor Akihito's presence to occasion the change of heart. Then, when their policy on state dinners changed (as so many of their policies did), without precedent or explanation single-sex couples began showing up on the guest list. These were not necessarily homosexual couples but suddenly men were bringing men to state dinners. For instance, at a dinner for German Chancellor Helmut Kohl, Carl Lindner, president of American Financial Corporation, brought a James Evans; at a dinner for South Korean President Kim Young Sam, Raymond Lesniak, chairman of the New Jersey state Democratic committee, brought a Wayne Weiner; and, at the same dinner, Samuel R. Berger, deputy assistant of the National Security Council, brought Daniel B. Poneman, a lesser fish at the NSC. It seemed that it would be only a matter of time before the invited could bring their favorite dog or cat.

Then there was that sudden, albeit brief, period when the press resounded with priceless accounts of Rodham's breathless espousal of "the Politics of Meaning" which, not surprisingly, culminated in another Rodham tantrum. Her vision of the Politics of Meaning was imparted to her during a meeting with Michael Lerner, the humbug editor of a New Age Jewish journal, *Tikkun*. The meeting should have been anticipated. He was pure 1960s fauna, an ex-radical, an intellectualoid, stuffed with semireligious/semiphilosophical jargon like a suckling pig with a Rubik's Cube stuck in its mouth. He had excogitated "the Politics of Meaning" in a series of *Tikkun* editorials, wherein he fitted the empty term out with nonsensical intellectual accessories sure to entrap pretentious middle-aged Yuppie women such as Rodham. Under Lerner's spell the First Lady would sweep into interviews bubbling over with such didactic swill as this: "As Michael Lerner and I discussed, we have to first create a language that would better communicate what we are trying to say, and the policies would flow from that language."[44] There was rude chortling even in the press. Rodham got mad. The authoress of "Michael Lerner and I," accused the wretch Lerner of *using* her. Soon it was back to hairdos and indignant reactions to the radio show of Rush Limbaugh. Rodham assessed Limbaugh "extreme," though he never had associates who conceived the police as pigs. Nor did he work for Stalinists or Nazis or even humbugs such as Lerner.

Yet perhaps Rodham's weirdest controversies were those little ones that began in 1994, when Rodham reported that about the time she contemplated marriage to her husband she tried to sign up with the Marines but was rejected.[45] This account sparked derision against the leathernecks from both Rodham and the audience of Clintonites she was addressing. Then she described herself to *Parade* magazine as "conservative in the true sense of that word—not in the kind of radical, ideological, destructive way that term is often used"—again, the alarming Limbaugh had gotten under her skin.[46] In Warsaw she announced that she would like to have more babies. A couple of months later, during an interview with Paula Zahn on CBS News, she again mentioned her longing for a more fertile motherhood, and she recommended to the heavily pregnant Zahn that she videotape messages to her children when she traveled. That is how this expert on children's rights was staying close to Chelsea. How intimate can a mother get? One can imagine the day when some future Rodham, scribbling in the offices of Marian Wright Edelman, decides that Mom on video is every child's right. But the tabloids were watching. After the Zahn interview, the clever *Weekly World News* reported that Rodham was expecting a baby in the spring of 1995. Humor!

As headhunter for the administration, Rodham's record was not as disastrous as it had been back in Little Rock during Governor Clinton's first term, but it was problematic. It was Rodham who set Clinton's staff in ardent pursuit of a woman attorney general.[47] Why a woman was so important to head the Justice Department has remained as much a mystery as the Clintons' unexplained disrelish for state dinners, but the consequence was that her first two nominees were lost in Nannygate controversies. The administration's tardiness in filling job openings was also probably at least in part a consequence of Rodham's insistence on gender quotas. And her quotas also presented the administration with an early morale problem, as seasoned men were passed over or allowed to tread water while Bush holdovers stayed in place for months, then years.[48] The administration's abrupt shift leftward away from the centrism of the campaign was another deleterious consequence of Rodham's role as headhunter.

Another of the rhythms one discovers in Rodham's public life in Little Rock and in Washington is corruption, sometimes quite serious. As we have seen, there was the Miracle of the Cattle Futures, deals she later said she made on her own with only occasional advice from James Blair and judicious readings of the *Wall Street Journal*. Actually, investigative reporter David Brock has determined that, owing to her schedule on the board of the Legal Services Corporation, it was "logistically impossible" for her to make those trades, one of which earned her $25,000! In his piece Brock points to the aggressive and dubious deductions that Rodham was taking at this point on the family's discarded clothes, furniture she allegedly used in her LSC work, and other phantom expenses.[49] The *Sunday Times* of London reported in 1994 that in the late 1980s "Hillary Clinton... and two senior members of the Clinton administration have been implicated in a multi-million dollar deal to profiteer from the sale of old people's homes. As a senior partner in the Arkansas law firm which oversaw the transaction, she received thousands of dollars from a shareout of legal fees."[50] Earlier in the decade Rodham engaged in repeated conflicts of interest, for instance, by representing the government in cases involving such friends as Clinton's crony, Dan Lasater, the convicted drug distributor, and against Frost & Co., the accounting firm that had handled her taxes.[51]

In 1978 Rodham and her husband entered into their Whitewater partnership with the McDougals. Now James Ring Adams and other investigative reporters are coming to believe Rodham and her husband as a consequence of this partnership engaged in false financial statements, false bank loan applications and falsification on their federal tax returns. In 1980 she began her shadowy bank dealings by putting her name on a questionable loan for $30,000. For the next decade this loan was refinanced by friendly banks just a few paces ahead of federal bank examiners. Several of the bankers Rodham dealt with, of course, were receiving favors from Rodham's husband, the governor, and one was the state bank commissioner. In 1985 as First Lady of Arkansas she began taking a $2,000 monthly retainer from McDougal's Madison Guaranty Savings and Loan, though the trust was under the scrutiny of federal examiners skeptical of its solvency. According to McDougal, her husband leaned on him for the arrangement.[52] In 1995 House Banking Committee hearings introduced reports from the Inspectors General of two federal regulatory agencies lambasting Rodham's Rose Law Firm for its failure to disclose conflicts of interest in its relations with seven of the seventeen failed savings and loans on which it did legal work for the federal government. One of Rodham's clients, of course, had been Madison. Two others were Illinois thrifts that charged they were defrauded by the Clintons' friend, Lasater. The record was so egregious that House Banking Chairman Jim Leach said the review of the Rose Law Firm is likely to be "a case study of legal impropriety at law schools for decades to come."[53]

Yet the revelations were not over. In late 1995 during the Senate's Whitewater hearings it was revealed that, as a Rose Law Firm lawyer, Rodham had handled the Castle Grande development project, which bank examiners discovered involved in part a series of fictitious transactions devised to inflate profits. Subsequently, an FDIC lawyer and friend of Rodham's crony Webster Hubbell, April Breslaw, hired Rose to handle the legal angles of Madison's receivership.

"She's made a lot of sacrifices for me to be in public life, but neither one of us has ever cared about getting rich," Clinton has said, contributing to the cirrocumulus clouds of puffery crowning the Clintons' legend.[54] Lines such as that appeared increasingly risible as revelations of their 1980s wheeling-dealing seeped out in the 1990s. As former associates and business partners began plea bargaining or were indicted, the legend took on a lurid spectacle.

Much is explained by the theory of experienced investigators that she personally guaranteed a $135,000 loan from a small Arkansas back to McDougal's Flowerwood Farms project [see Appendix C, item C-1]. The money went elsewhere, as usual, including a pittance to Bill Clinton's campaign kitty. (But a pittance is all one needs to buy off the politicians.)

The dates are suggestive. This loan, from Stephens Security Bank of Stephens, Arkansas, went through April 3, 1985. (The Stephens in the bank name refers to the small town where it was based, 100 miles south of Little Rock and the Flowerwood site, but the Stephens family network typically had a hand in its business.) Shortly before the loan to Flowerwood, the bank's owners, the Smith family, had bought it from the parent corporation of Worthen Bank and Trust. (The bank's lawyer had been C. Joseph Giroir, Jr., the chairman of the Rose Law Firm who had hired Hillary.) Two days afterward, on April 5, Jim McDougal held his notorious fund-raiser for Bill Clinton. The soiree in the lobby of Madison Guaranty's Little Rock headquarters raised about $30,000 to help pay off a personal loan Bill had floated in his 1984 campaign [see Appendix C, item C-2]. Three cashier's checks from Madison bore the names of people who later denied making the donations. Jean Lewis's criminal referrals charged that at least $12,000 from this bash came from the Flowerwood Farms loan. The Clintons' drew another favor from McDougal too. Within three weeks of the Flowerwood loan, by Hillary's own account, McDougal began paying the Rose Law Firm that $2,000-a-month retainer for her services.

If someone should have found Hillary's name on this loan and put it together with these benefits received, she (and her husband) could well have been facing federal charges of conspiracy to commit bank fraud. So the Clintons scrambled hard to keep this loan from the ken of the federal bank examiners, and in the course of their efforts could well have crossed the line into the dreaded territory of obstruction of justice, the fatal ground the late Richard

Nixon, for whom Bill has revealed such surprising empathy, dared to tread. A phone message in December from Stephens Security President Richard T. Smith first gave the warning that the heat was on. Jim McDougal's secretary jotted it down: "Bank examiners are after him to reduce their out-of-region real estate loans. Can you transfer Flowerwood note elsewhere?" [see Appendix C, item C-3]. This pressure coincided with McDougal's cultivation of Pulaski County Judge David Hale, whose access to Small Business Administration loan guarantees became highly interesting. Hale kept a lending company on the side, an SBA-backed Small Business Investment Corporation called Capital-Management Services, Inc. McDougal and his lawyer Jim Guy Tucker (the future governor of Arkansas) made discreet inquiries about the extent to which Hale could help out their "political family."

In February 1986, Judge Hale later testified in court, Bill Clinton himself joined the campaign for Hale's lending. With the Flowerwood note still in play, Clinton asked Hale to arrange a $150,000 loan via Susan McDougal. "Clinton explained that his name could not show up anywhere," Hale told the *American Spectator*. "McDougal made the statement that that was all taken care of." As Hale was soon able to boost the lending limits for his company (thanks in part to maneuvers for which Tucker and McDougal were later indicted), he raised the loan to $300,000 [see Appendix C, item B]. He wrote the check to Susan McDougal's "Master Marketing" (an unexplained variation of the real name of her PR firm, Madison Marketing) on April 3, 1986, the maturity date of the Flowerwood Farms loan [see Appendix C, item C-4].

This money was supposed to pay for water and sewer lines at Flowerwood Farms. Instead one large chunk, $125,000, went to retire the Stephens Security note. Another large portion paid for land the McDougals bought from International Paper in the name of Whitewater Development; they hoped that this tract, southeast of Little Rock, would make the killing that would salvage their fortunes. Much of the remainder went unaccounted for until the tail end of McDougal's 1996 trial.

So in spite of Clinton's denials and the strenuous efforts of defense attorneys to discredit Hale, the motives abound for Bill Clinton to have done just what Hale said he did, arrange an illegal loan to cover his tracks. And apparently Susan McDougal didn't perform that task to Bill's satisfaction. Hale reports his last encounter with Clinton several months later. Clinton rushed up to him in a state of perturbation by the posh University Plaza Mall. "Have you heard what that f——ing whore Susan has done?" he blurted out and rushed off, leaving Hale perplexed.[55]

The above-the-law arrogance that had become a way of life for Rodham in Arkansas continued when she came to Washington. Early in the administration, while her husband was publicly threatening the pharmaceutical industry, her broker was selling Rodham's health care stocks short from an account that had yet to be put in a blind trust— a clear violation of government ethics requirements. Rodham was also open to obstruction of justice charges for a series of telephone calls that she tried to conceal. The calls, involving the First Lady, her chief of staff, Maggie Williams; her friend and advisor, Susan Thomases; and White House Counsel Bernard Nussbaum, took place two days after Vince Foster's death and just before Nussbaum reneged on his promise to allow Justice Department investigators to examine Foster's files. It is also apparent that her secret health care task force withheld documents for over two years and concealed from the public that, contrary to administration claims the task force's deliberations had cost taxpayers only $100,000, in fact, it had spent almost 140 times that amount. Under court order the administration reluctantly disgorged documents that revealed the true cost of $13.8 million. By 1996 it appeared that any time there was a crisis in the White House, an unforeseen suicide, an RTC inquiry, a trooper going public, an Arkansas crony copping a plea, either of the Clintons or their lieutenants might simply pick up the telephone and obstruct justice.

Then they would lie. By early 1996 memos were coming from the White House and congressional inquiries revealing Rodham as a blatant perjurer. She had lied about her role in Whitewater, in Travelgate, and on the appointment of a special counsel. She even lied about the authorship of her book, *It Takes a Village*, denying that the book was by Washington writer Barbara Feinman whom Simon & Schuster paid $120,000. Rodham even neglected to mention her ghostwriter in her acknowledgment page. In fact, on that page she acknowledged no one in particular, saying instead, "They [those helping with the book] are so numerous that I will not even attempt to acknowledge them individually.... "[56] Such is the smallness of the Coat and Tie Radical in middle age.

Both in Little Rock and in Washington Rodham took on a Vast Reform. She and her husband would inflate its importance with the usual fanfare, blaring huge expectations. Rodham's Little Rock Vast Reform detumesced gently after being passed by the legislature. In Washington, her Vast Reform went bust overnight. Typically, the Vast Reform is accompanied with the Clintons' special goody-two-shoes vow to work, work, work. An obvious trait that had remained with them from their days as teacher's pet, the Clintons have a proclivity for publicly bearing witness as to how hard they work on almost any policy. It is as though they expect a pat on the head from a grateful nation. "My biggest weakness is that I tend to work too hard so sometimes I don't work smart enough. And I see all these problems and it drives me crazy that we're not solving them, and if I'm not careful I'll try and do too much," is how Boy Clinton narcissistically analyzed himself on the campaign trail in 1992.[57] Rodham is an equally sly braggart: "I've worked very hard on education reform, worked very hard on children's and family issues—to deal with the problems that are affecting this country."[58]

Her education reform—her vast reform for Arkansas—closely prefigured her 1993 health care reform. She called many meetings. She proclaimed a vast fact-finding undertaking. She acted as though

she were deeply interested in the public's ideas. Fearful rows mysteriously accosted her from all sides. In the end it became apparent
that her public posturings were mostly a sham. Her education
reform had been fully devised before she began her public conjurings, and the plan she finally got through the state legislature even-
tuated in naught.

Rodham's Vast Reform as First Lady followed a similar course,
before it was slain by an alarmed Congress. Initially undertaken
amid gorgeous promises about Rodham's openness to the public,
Rodham—aided by fellow Coat and Tie Radical from yesteryear Ira
Magaziner—promptly walled off the project's proceedings from
public scrutiny. She paraded triumphantly before congressional
committees and public panels prolix with fact and figures all abetting the Clintons' delusion that policymaking is a variation of the
board game Trivial Pursuit. "Hillary Takes Capitol Hill by Storm,"
hurrahed a friendly press. "I think in the very near future," said
Ways and Means Committee Chairman Dan Rostenkowski, "the
president will be known as your husband. 'Who's that fellow? That's
Hillary's husband.'"[59] Then, after months of deceptions and wild
rhetoric, the plan, now grown gargantuan, failed in Congress.
Whereupon Rodham engaged in the aforementioned coverup, concealing documents and fleeing from subpoenas until in 1995 a court
order forced release of the documents showing the task force's
$13.8-million overrun. The White House faced U.S. District Judge
Royce C. Lamberth's threats of fines for the administration's "mis-
characterization of the [health care] task force makeup and the
administration's delay in releasing documents."[60]

"I am surprised at the way people seem to perceive me," Rodham
told a group of women reporters in 1995, "and sometimes I read
stories and hear things about me and I go 'ugh.' I wouldn't like her
either. It's so unlike what I think I am or what my friends think I
am."[61] It was 1995, and Rodham's project of the moment was yet
another revision of her "image." True to the rhythms of her life she

was now reverting to home and hearth and playing the adoring wife. The press, without any trace of skepticism, was reporting the transition as though it is perfectly natural that adults adopt different "images" according to the demands of the moment.

Far from a sign of artificiality or deceit, Rodham's careful representations of herself are a sign that she is a holy person. On this her friends were emphatic. Their superlatives were as fulsome as the Clintons' contradictions. "She has fundamentally given of herself, physically, emotionally, to this subject of health care, to an extent unlike anything I've ever seen.... She *drives* herself so hard.... She would hate my telling this... she is in a state of constant fatigue," her friend Senator Jay Rockefeller said. He went on to report seeing a group of veterans approach Rodham about the fate of their benefits under her plan. A veteran offered his condolences, as her father had recently died. According to friend Rockefeller, "And she said one of these amazing things. It was very soft, barely audible—there was nothing contrived about it. 'I would have been proud had my father died in a veterans' hospital.'"[62] Savor that line as you think back over her career. In fact, think of the mentality of the people she brought into the White House. Just weeks before there was an unprecedented altercation occasioned by Lieutenant General Barry McCaffrey's incautious greeting of a young lady on the Clinton White House staff. While passing through the southwest gate of the White House, the general greeted her with a "Good Morning." "I don't talk to the military," was her reply as she "stomped" by.[63] And think back on her public life: the war protests, the opposition to the military budget, the frosty treatment accorded the Pentagon during the first three years of the administration, and such little details as her misuse of military personnel in the White House, where she had them serving drinks to her yuppie dilettantes.

Yes, from all the puffery and all the dubious testimonials of her friends, it becomes obvious that the Clintons—and their friends— are set apart. They are holy people. That is how we explain their fundamental artificiality and crookedness. They are like the Holy Men of Eastern mysticism, exhorting abstinence in their followers while the Rolls Royces accumulated on the lawns of their villas and estates. It all goes back to the Clintons' roots. Those who had a stake in the Great Events of the late 1960s all saw themselves as set apart. After all they had gone through or imagined themselves to have gone through, they had emerged as a holy people. They had suffered for a virtue that only they truly comprehended. They fought the Vietnam War, the Imperial Presidency, racism. They did good. They could do no wrong. Those who doubted had their motives impugned. The Clintons' superior virtue perhaps explains why no other presidential family has ever attracted so many allegations across such a wide range of vices.

CHAPTER TEN

1993

B ILL CLINTON IS a man of gargantuan appetites. From his famous interviews with four state troopers from Governor Clinton's security detail, David Brock reports the troopers' astonishment at Clinton's energy and voracity. "When he would eat an apple," the faithless Roger Perry recalls, "he would eat the whole thing, core, stem, and seeds. He would pick up a baked potato with his hands and eat it in two bites. I've never seen anything like it."[1] From loftier quarters come news reports of Clinton's sudden lunges towards the golf course or into crowds for an orgy of embraces and palm slappings or into bookstores to grab an armful of books for an evening's read. In the first two years of his presidency Clinton would sneak out of the White House for unscheduled jogs. He would break from his schedule for desultory bull sessions. He would roam around the White House late at night cramming for the next day's policy meetings or, quite possibly, in pursuit of a nocturnal dessert.

As a consequence of his harum-scarum impulsiveness, Clinton has been unscheduleable; he is usually late, occasionally *hours* late; in making presidential appointments, *months* late; in fulfilling campaign

promises, *years* late. Except for when he is watching films in the
White House viewing room, it seems that Clinton is incapable of
pursuing to its conclusion any activity that involves remaining seated.
Essaying Clinton's modus operandi after a year in the White House,
Time magazine's Michael Duffy surely gilds the lily: "Clinton is a
complex, highly intense man who does almost everything at full
throttle." (*Intense man?* Bill of the baggy suits and "aw shucks"
demeanor?) But Duffy does at least apprehend the lily: "He watches
several movies each week—the White House refuses to release an
exact number—and reads five or six books at once. He relaxes not by
watching a basketball game on TV, or reading, or picking up the telephone, or doing crossword puzzles, but doing all four simultaneously,
while worrying an unlit cigar."[2]

Clinton's impulsive nature accounts, in part, for the chaos of his
first year in office, though liberalism's own disordered condition[3]
surely staggered his presidency as well. Then, too, he relied on assistant presidents who, when the lights went on, exhibited more quirks
than the assembled zanies at a national convention of nudists.

Given these causes and a few occurrences that can be catalogued
only as freaks of nature, Clinton's presidency got off to a rockier
start than any other presidency in this century. Six months into
what was supposed to be a fresh chapter of progressive governance,
the *New York Times* reported the White House whiz kids glum,
"faced with what even Mr. Clinton's supporters concede has been
the most traumatic debut for a president in modern times...."[4] The
Times duly adumbrated the chaos but then reverted to the customary mood of Great Expectations. Clinton's young aides had a plan
for Resurrection. These mood swings would afflict the consensus
journalists even into 1996, despite the fact that mere weeks after
his inauguration the political prodigy of 1992 was beginning to
look not like a Roosevelt or a Kennedy but like a Quixote in Yuppie dress.

Truth be known, the full catastrophe had been prefigured in the dizzy weeks that Clinton squandered between his election and his inauguration. It was then that he should have consolidated his electoral base. He had won back most of the Democrats who in the 1980s had abandoned their party for Ronald Reagan and George Bush. These so-called Reagan Democrats voted two to one for Clinton, accepting Clinton's assertion that he was "a different kind of Democrat," a "New Democrat," one driven by concern for "the forgotten middle class." Immediately following his victory Clinton had the time to adopt policies for the middle class and to keep them in the coalition with the more extreme elements among his supporters. Instead, Clinton partied. He celebrated with his Hollywood friends, and wasted time at self-congratulatory dinners, political soirées, sham policy meetings, and adulatory public appearances, all contributing to the impression that the campaign was still going strong, which it was. After his unique glorification rites on January 20, Clinton, the Chronic Campaigner, kept right on campaigning, a prime reason for his administration's erratic record.

Two days before his inauguration Clinton and his wife were glad-handing their way across Memorial Bridge. On that day thirty-two years before, President-elect John F. Kennedy was meeting with President Dwight Eisenhower for a briefing on nuclear codes and such flash points as Laos and East Berlin. Twelve years before, President Ronald Reagan was making final appointments, lunching with Henry Kissinger, and polishing his inaugural address. Once across the Memorial Bridge the Clintons struck up a transcontinental conversation via television satellite with Hispanic-Americans, Asian-Americans, and blacks. Perhaps they also sent signals to America's theretofore voiceless gypsies, its gay Eskimos, and Mississippi's dirt eaters (the practice is known as geophagy, and in Mississippi it is centuries old; if anyone could politicize it, the Clintons could). Living up to the stereotype of the progressive president, Clinton had to reach out to still more unacknowledged victims of society, and by

1993 the pickings were slim. At any rate, Clinton never did get back to the white ethnics who had just elected him president, not through the first three years of his presidency.

Clinton, heir to the mantle of Roosevelt and Kennedy, lifelong aspirant to the role of progressive president, and reader of many books, had little in common with his progressive predecessors. The presidential predecessor he has had most in common with is that convivial bumbler of Republican legend, Warren Gamaliel Harding. Harding and his bossy wife could almost pass as role models for the Clintons if their differing political philosophies could be factored out. Both the Clintons and the Hardings came from rural parts, albeit Harding had a more exalted pedigree. Both couples included a clever, assertive, and forbidding wife who had displayed above-average competence in business and politics. Both families were compact. The presidents were handsome, their spouses less so. Both presidents were personable and charming to the fair sex, whose nicely turned ankles fetched their wandering eyes. When not boldly at the helm of the ship of state, both presidents vigorously pursued the masculine pastimes of their day, golf and poker for Harding, golf and jogging for Clinton. Harding, of course, was less driven than the Boy Governor of Arkansas and obviously more dignified. He had a better tailor. He seemed to age more gracefully and less abruptly in office even if one evening his heart did go pop. Then, too, while alive Harding was freer of scandal. History remembers Harding as an amiable dolt whose scandals were revealed only upon his death. Clinton, the stereotypical progressive president, should have been as free of scandal and blunder as Woodrow Wilson, but his blunders began early and the shadows of scandal crossed him earlier still.

At first the new president's blunders were minor embarrassments, but in late January and early February 1993 they became daily events. To begin with there was the matter of Clinton's jogging. Though popular with many at first, it began to wear thin. Unlike President Bush's jogging which was decorously confined to military bases and golf courses, Clinton's was out the front door and into the traffic, tying up rush-hour commuters and causing security risks. Clinton had been jogging through Washington for weeks, occasionally accompanied by his fellow Baby Boomer, Vice President-elect Al Gore. They would pad down streets and through parks attired in diverting hats, sometimes wearing sweat shirts bearing slogans and logos pungent with social or political significance. Usually they wore t-shirts (it was a mild winter) and abbreviated shorts that looked like boys' underpants. Clinton and Gore were that variety of American male that finds middle age bearable only if he can preserve certain of those teen-aged enthusiasms that excited the admiration of his peers. Belching in public would not do, but being sporty would.

Clinton and Gore were very sporty, though they also claimed as their own many of the 1960s other youthful enthusiasms. Rock and Roll? They grooved to it. Hot Rods and pickup trucks? They dug them—and Clinton boasted of how he had transformed the bed of his pickup truck into an altar of love. But playing the role of dilettante jock was a special favorite for both. By the end of January many adult Americans became impatient. Two men who had recently been elevated to the highest elected offices in the land and become two of the most powerful men on earth were forever being photographed lumbering along public thoroughfares, tossing balls in the air, playing with household pets, and occasionally wearing the official t-shirt of *Rolling Stone* magazine. What would come next? Would they begin wearing baseball caps backward after the fashion of disturbed teenagers? Would the president let fly with paper airplanes at press conferences? Would he skateboard along Pennsylvania Avenue while Gore and his pretty wife were flying kites on the White House lawn?

It was January 28 when the *Washington Post* reported public rebellion against Clinton's matutinal trots. Pedestrians were no longer charmed by a glimpse of presidential leg. Motorists preferred getting to the office on time to waiting in downtown traffic as the Boy President chugged through the rush-hour. The *Post's* story marked the beginning of eleven straight days of embarrassing news stories. Months later, when the president was complaining that the media had denied him the traditional honeymoon from criticism, perhaps he was referring to this dismal string. But the traditional honeymoon is from criticism, not from reportage. Whether the mild criticism the media occasionally applied to him was exorbitant can be argued either way, but it cannot be denied that Clinton did jog through congested streets and motorists did complain.

From January 28 and for the next eleven days, the Clintons sired one peculiar story on a daily basis, occasionally two. The media duly reported each occurrence. If the Clintons did not want the coverage they should have stifled their impulse for yuppie show-off stuff. After the jogging story came the New Age séance. On January 30, President Clinton brought his cabinet and top aides to Camp David for a two-day "bonding experience." According to the *Washington Post*, the White House put the affair under the direct supervision of persons called "facilitators." Under their watchful eye, the president invited cabinet members and lesser eminentos to "build sharing relationships" by revealing something obscure about themselves or, better still, something humiliating. One observer reported that the president "talked about how he was a fat kid when he was five and six and how other kids taunted him." When this preposterosity was recorded, a Clinton aide admonished the reporter, "Don't try to make this sound weird."[5]

On February 1, Mrs. Clinton got into the act. With characteristic unctuousness she notified the *New York Times* that organic food would be encouraged in the White House and smoking prohibited, because neither she nor the president was a smoker. Two days later the White House had to clarify itself. Remembering photographs snapped during the presidential campaign, editors at the *New York Post* published pictures of candidate Clinton with a Churchillian stogy majestically protruding from his ample lips. The White House admitted that the pictures were authentic but insisted that they were misunderstood. The president "never lights it," deputy White House press secretary, Lorraine Voles, explained—laughter.[6] This chosen subtlety was too egregious for a press still mindful that Clinton "didn't inhale."

On February 4, the *Washington Times* published a Reuters report that a Vietnam-era peace protester, Mr. Clyde E. Petit, had shown up in Hanoi with a letter of introduction signed by President-elect Clinton. The letter presented Mr. Petit, now an Arkansas filmmaker, as an early opponent of the war; and it raised the possibility of improving relations between the two countries. Over Bill Clinton's signature the historic missive was addressed "[T]o whom it may concern." This time it fell to Dee Dee Myers to issue the White House clarification. Ever game, the appealingly girlish Dee Dee would soon become Boy Clinton's chief White House spokesperson, and through all the pratfalls that she was to encounter over the next two years of her service her cheerful explications of the inexplicable were to mark her as an exceedingly good sport.

Yes, she affirmed on February 5, the letter at issue had indeed been written on the governor's stationery, and yes that bold scrawl was the boss's own; but the letter was only a courtesy by him to a "constituent." The president hardly knew Petit. The Clinton administration would stand by earlier campaign promises not to change American policy toward Vietnam. The boss recognized the serious issues at stake. It did not make Dee Dee's job any easier when the *Washington Times* quoted a "former senior U.S. intelligence official" deploring "Mr. Clinton's loose language in the letter." The anonymous critic adjudged the whole episode as "very irresponsible."[7] All this took place on the same day that the *New York Times* published a front-page report that "Robert E. Rubin, a former co-chairman of Goldman, Sachs & Company who is President Clinton's top economics adviser, sent a letter in December to many of his clients urging them to continue doing business with the investment banking firm and to *stay in touch with him at the White House*" (italics mine).[8]

Next came the administration's second botch at naming a lady attorney general. The goal had become a matter of the utmost urgency to the Clintons, though why a lady attorney general was more important than a lady secretary of state or secretary of defense remains unknown. Clinton had ditched his first nominee, Zoe Baird, in January after the public learned that she had employed illegal aliens without paying their Social Security or workers' compensation taxes. Now on February 5 the White House revealed its intention to nominate Judge Kimba Wood. Mere hours later the White House ditched this nomination, too. Judge Wood had also employed an illegal alien somewhere back in the mists of time, though when she did it had been perfectly legal. Nonetheless the administration feared that the public was incapable of distinguishing between the two cases, and to the amazement of the nation Judge Wood was dumped and discredited. That blunder accounted for February 6's front-page embarrassment. February 7 yielded two embarrassing stories: feminist dudgeon over the White House's mistreatment of lady nominees was intensifying, and, as reported by the *Washington Post*, "The first targets of President Clinton's pledge to cut White House 'payroll, perks and privileges' are about two dozen lower-paid White House career workers with no job protection, some of them older women who have worked there for decades."[9] Here was an early instance of the Arkansans's distrust of anyone not totally loyal to them. February 8 again brought two more embarrassments: Commerce Secretary Ron Brown was under investigation for a series of petty irregularities, and the *Washington Times* reported that those twenty career workers fired the day before were being replaced by Clinton loyalists in need of work. The lineaments of the story were to reappear three months later in the far more damaging blunder to be known as Travelgate:

crass cronyism, a high-minded alibi, and the hint of darker machinations backstage.

By now a leitmotif was developing. A Clinton administration gaucherie is perpetrated. The press fixes upon it. The White House dissembles, usually attributing blame to others (political enemies, unenlightened bureaucrats, the gods). *Kultursmog*-bound alibiists in the press, such as Michael Kinsley, rush in to defend the Dogpatch regime. The press then subsides, spotting signs that the White House is improving. The administration's gaucheries were usually the consequence of some yuppie conceit, Clinton's waywardness, Arkansas cronyism, or political intrigue. After the press quieted down, weeks might pass with only the conservatives and a few radical leftists harkening. Otherwise most of the media simply purred over the presence of this new era of Kennedys and Roosevelts in the White House. It would take months, even years, before the rank-and-file journalists rid themselves of the widely held appraisal of Clinton that Mickey Kaus expressed as late as fourteen months into the administration: "Clinton is... the best president we've had in a long time."[10] And Kaus is an honorable man. Kaus, however, had been gassed by the same pollutant that enervated so many of his peers. It is one of the most prevalent pollutants in the *Kultursmog*, the stereotype of the progressive president. Unfortunately, Clinton kept falling from the Rooseveltian-Kennedyesque heights into, nigh, unto Nixonian depths. Then once again the sirens would sound from the *smog*-bound press. An example is Leslie H. Gelb's patronizing alarum sounded on the op-ed page of the *New York Times*, late in Clinton's first April, "From Washington and around the world, the grumbling has begun about President Clinton's leadership, his ability to wield power and his willingness to do what's necessary to prevail."[11] Seasoned students of the *Kultursmog* recognize that Gelb wrote this bilge in the belief that Clinton would read it, get the message, and clean up his act.

Through the first two years of the administration and well into

the third, members of the media could not resign themselves to the
horrible fact that the happy warrior who triumphed after George
Bush wilted was a klutz, and a corrupt one at that. And so for a
month or two the crude bungling would again be ignored. Hope
would revive. Camelot would be perceived at 1600 Pennsylvania
Avenue, whereupon another of history's banana peels would send the
cracker Kennedy sprawling headlong into the orchestra pit or his
cronies to court, thence to jail.

Michael Kinsley, returning from a sabbatical, boldly sounded the
leitmotif of hope-depression-hope in the summer of 1993: "During
my six months of leave from this column, Bill Clinton has gotten off
to what most agree is the grimmest start of any presidency in generations."[12] Presently, of course, Kinsley was back in the pro-
Clinton claque denouncing journalist David Brock for reporting
Clinton's voluptuous sex life, a sex life that the slightly hypochon-
driacal Kinsley considered inconceivable. Resigning himself to the
licentiousness, the incompetence, and the perfidies of a fellow
Rhodes Scholar yuppie was painful business for this yuppie prude.

It is, I believe, the fixedness of Clinton's deficiencies, combined
with the media's reluctance to face up to them, that explains the leitmotif of Bronx cheers following the fanfare that sounded throughout Clinton's presidency. In assessing Clinton's first year, political
observers frequently employed the term "roller coaster." They
resorted to it in their year-end summaries again in 1994 and in
1995. The term fit, not because the Boy President occasionally rose
to prodigious heights when seen on the upgrade, but because the
journalists of the *Kultursmog*, having assigned Clinton the role of
stereotypical progressive president, had to assume that he would
ultimately succeed and ascend to glory.

A sense of the ups and downs that lay ahead can be grasped by
reviewing the *Washington Post*'s coverage of Clinton in his first year.
Compare the conflicting judgments interred in the *Post* at the end of
President Clinton's first January with those at the end of his first

March. At the end of his first January Dan Balz and Ann Devroy reported, "Week Two of the Clinton presidency was if anything more chaotic than Week One. Hoping to convince the country that he was focused on the economy and health care, Clinton was thrust instead into a contentious debate over homosexuals in the military."[13] Clinton's botches were in fact more numerous if less grave than this one fling at homosexual politics. Nevertheless, the *Post* was accurately conveying Clinton's erratic entry into presidential politics. Yet a few weeks later, the *Post* was again full of hope, introducing its sanguine report under the triumphal headline "Beginner's Luck or President's Prowess? Dazzled Capitol Wonders if Clinton Can Keep Lighting Up the Board." "Professional Washingtonians," reporter David Von Drehle enthused, "impressed by Clinton's proficiency at the game—his command of the airwaves, his ability to connect with voters, his smooth touch on Capitol Hill—are giving him high marks, some enthusiastically, others grudgingly. 'I will say this: He is as formidable a political figure as I've seen in my lifetime,' Republican strategist Ed Rollins allowed recently."[14]

Yes, yes, but creeping into the end of Von Drehle's story there appeared, alas, the shadows. Though the president had an overall approval rating, his negative ratings were "unusually high." Then Von Drehle allowed as how "The whole wild *roller coaster* has been extraordinary"[15] (italics mine). A few days later columnist George Will had suffered enough. He derided the roller coaster cliché and the hackneyed "dazzle." Noting the dissatisfaction within Clinton's own Democratic coalition, Will anticipated Clinton's calamitous future.[16]

In truth, Clinton's approval rating had been slipping since the promiscuous jogging of his second week in office. Then voters began to notice that he was backpedaling on campaign promises. Rather than giving the middle class a tax cut, his government floated the possibility of various tax increases. After much artful legerdemain about the federal government's anticipated deficit, he revised his promise to cut the budget deficit in half. During the

campaign he had denounced President Bush's policy of returning
Haitian refugees. Once in office Clinton embraced Bush's policy,
leaving those Haitians who had believed his campaign promises in
ticklish condition. Some had aroused the interest of the authorities
as they withdrew money from the bank and hurriedly hammered
together ocean-going boats. Others actually put out to sea and were
lost. Survivors often returned and were arrested by the Haitian government. Up in Washington Clinton was backing away from his
earlier suggestion of government-paid child vaccination. He moved
back and forth on adopting either a political or a military solution
in Bosnia. Finally, despite his boasts to have his government "look
like America" or perhaps on account of that promise, he fell hopelessly behind in replacing Bush appointees with his own people.

Staffing his government was to be a problem for the youthful
president far into his second year. In the first year unfilled vacancies
and botched appointments were reliable cues for the media's leitmotif of hope-depression-hope. By Year II the staffing problems
were simply a fact of life. A year after Clinton's glitzy inauguration,
the *New York Times* confirmed:

> "...the state of the Clinton administration remains troubled
> by appointments gone awry.
> More than any other recent president, Bill Clinton has
> stumbled when it has come to choosing whom to place in top
> Government jobs....
> ...Mr. Clinton is also beginning his second year with other
> major jobs unfilled, leaving his White House still lagging
> behind the pace set by Presidents Ronald Reagan and Jimmy
> Carter in installing its appointees in Federal departments and
> getting them in motion."[17]

Thirty-six percent of the jobs at the Justice Department were
open. Thirty-three embassies were without ambassadors.[18] All these

vacancies existed notwithstanding the Clintons' obsession with placing loyalists throughout their government. By the end of the administration's second year the Clintons had infiltrated their political henchmen all over the bureaucracy, placing loyalists in agencies theretofore insulated from politics. Still, top spots remained empty. In fact, not even the White House was properly staffed. As late as March of 1994 one-third of the White House staff, more than three hundred people, still had not secured permanent White House passes.[19] The reason that the passes had not been secured suggests the Clinton administration's heritage within 1960s youth culture and the fraying standards that attended that cadre throughout the ensuing years. According to the *Washington Times*, "Of about 1,000 FBI background checks of White House personnel, more than 500 revealed derogatory information that would have prevented the people from obtaining security clearances at the FBI, Defense Department or CIA, said an administration source, who asked not to be named."[20]

Bungled appointments and broken promises were not the only blights ruinous to Clinton's early performance in the presidency. During the campaign and right up to his inauguration he had made boasts that were stratospheric. Even Presidents Kennedy and Roosevelt would have demurred from such rash claims. Having been cast in the mold of the stereotypical progressive president, it was natural that the Hot Springs prodigy would see his arrival in Washington as rattling the china and unsettling the dust. But he might have restrained his heroic vows just a bit. By the end of his first year, the disparity between his promises and his dismal performance created a deep sense of unease even among the faithful. By the end of his second year both the press and many Democrats, at least in private, had grown disgusted.

President Reagan had surprised by outperforming his critics. Clinton surprised by underperforming. Yet Reagan rarely gasconaded as Clinton did daily on the campaign trail, "I'll have the bills ready the day after I'm inaugurated. I'll send them to Congress and we'll have a 100-day period.... It will be the most productive in modern history."[21] This was characteristic. He was forever vowing to "send to Congress... a 100-day plan to revitalize the economy by reinvesting in America again, giving business new incentive to invest in our country—but no more tax breaks to move our jobs overseas—to control health-care costs and provide a basic package of health care to all Americans, to open the doors of college education to all Americans, and to give two-year apprenticeship programs to those who don't want to go to college... "[22]

It was surely imprudent for an incoming president with no national experience whatsoever to promise such a grandiose 100 Days. His boasts naturally elicited comparisons with the master and originator of the 100 Days, Franklin Roosevelt. In the 1930s, within his allotted hundred, President Roosevelt presented Congress sixteen major pieces of legislation, reforming agriculture, banking, industry, labor, and unemployment relief. Clinton could not hope to match him. For one thing, Clinton was not propelled by the exigencies facing Roosevelt: no Depression, no bank crisis, nothing comparable to 1933's catastrophic unemployment rate. Then too Clinton did not have a Congress beholden to him. What is more, by the time Clinton arrived at the White House America had undergone six decades of progressive government; there was only one gigantic welfare-state program as yet unperpetrated. That was government control of medicine, and no consensus clamored for it.

After serving as governor of Arkansas for twelve years, during which he became derisible for missing deadlines, Clinton should have recognized the hopelessness of suiting the deeds of his approaching 100 Days to his boasts. But like his cohorts from the late 1960s Clinton does not learn from experience. During his inauspicious first few months in office his alibiists in the media spread the legend throughout official Washington that Clinton "never makes the same mistake twice." Anyone familiar with his record in Arkansas recognized the statement as balderdash; Clinton always repeated his mistakes. At times it was his only consistent quality.

Vico, the eighteenth-century Florentine philosopher, speaks of the historian's talent for *fantasia*. It is the capacity to bring an historic figure to life on the page by going beyond the prosaic facts of his life and attempting an "imaginative insight" into the figure's feelings and thoughts at a given moment, as a novelist might do. The ambitious historian, Vico tells us, will endeavor to imagine what the statesman actually thought on a given morning as he greeted his wife, his lawyer, the hangman. Peering into Clinton's brain as he made these impossible boasts early in his administration, my guess is he was thinking that which he so often thinks—*"Ah'm so smart, and thare so stupid."* Or he was thinking the same thing he often thought as he retreated behind the press's questions about his loves or his draft record—*"Ah'll throw 'em so much bull shit that they'll be rail confused."* The tactic often worked. In the case of his 100 Days, it did not. April, May, June, and July turned out to be dreadful months for Clinton. The press could not fail to report the steady jitterbug of missteps. Each month his approval rating hit historic new lows.

Beginning in February and extending into March, serious business was afoot. The president delivered a State of the Union message promising a national health-care program and a "reinvigorated" economy. In February the president by executive order killed off former Vice President Dan Quayle's Council on Competitiveness, lifted the prohibition on fetal tissue research, and ended the abortion "gag" rule that prohibited physicians in federally funded hospitals from counseling abortion as a legal alternative. Having named his wife to head his Task Force on National Health Care Reform, he gave her 100 days to produce a program that would extend health care to all. On into March he signed two bills that his party had been advocating during all the bleak years of the Republican ascendancy: a family leave bill, albeit watered down; and a bill allowing citizens to register to vote when they got their

driver's license. Then after all the hoopla about his "Economic
Summit" in Little Rock and after his campaign oratory about
"growing the economy," he announced his budget balancing plan.
It would raise both taxes and spending. Through the smoke and
mirrors he pointed to a "balanced budget." Talk of his "dazzle"
spread throughout the *Kultursmog*.

Yet there was grousing also. Clinton's young staff repeatedly gave
offense. Its members were insensitive to the press and to Congress.
The new president failed to make courtesy calls to potential congressional allies such as Senators Daniel Patrick Moynihan and Sam
Nunn. Moynihan seemed especially put out. A year later he would
be the first Democrat to urge an independent counsel for Whitewater. Equally ominous, though the budget resolution passed the
House of Representatives on March 29, twenty-two Democrats
defected. The resolution, consistent with no economic theory
known to man, was attracting critics both left and right. Echoing
Clinton's campaign vow to cut the deficit, it nonetheless raised
spending in scores of categories and boasted a $16.3 billion stimu-
lant; echoing Clinton's campaign vow to pursue economic growth,
it nonetheless raised taxes. Coat and Tie Radicals Bill Clinton,
Hillary Rodham, and Robert Reich were having it both ways again.

February and March had witnessed other disturbing stories. The
Clintons bungled their second nomination of a female attorney
general and failed to assuage feminists. Moreover, party pros were
sensing the Clintons' fragile loyalties. Then, after the president
spoke out against the pricing policies of the pharmaceutical industry, the news began to circulate that the Clintons were selling pharmaceutical stocks short while their value plummeted under the
pressure of the president's attacks. The Clintons had yet to put
them in a blind trust. Such an ethical faux pas, Americans were to
learn, was not new to the Clintons.

April began a string of bad months for the Clintons not unlike
the string of bad days that they suffered in late January and early

February. Both periods interlarded the odd with the silly, the deceitful with the inept; but this second period's calamities were on a grimmer scale, and when they ended in late July the media's sense of hope seemed to have taken a gigantic dose of saltpeter. As always many in the press still yearned for a 1990s Camelot, but reality kept taking them down to the McDonald's where the stocky jogger, amiably stuffing himself with cheeseburgers, insisted that he was there for a salubrious helping of tofu and vegetables before jogging back to a National Security Council meeting.

In April homosexuals and their opponents began sniping anew at the president for his agile repositioning on their presence in the military. He saw his budget pass the Senate earlier than any president since Nixon in 1974, but the Republicans successfully filibustered his $16.3 billion stimulus package. Genuine disaster finally struck on April 19 when federal agents moved ferociously against cult leader David Koresh's fortified compound in Waco, Texas. Since late February they had besieged the compound following a poorly organized raid. The raid by nearly one hundred agents from the Bureau of Alcohol, Tobacco, and Firearms cost five lives, four of them agents. Through the subsequent negotiations, the Justice Department kept revising its complaint against the Davidians. When the government attacked the second time it used heavy military equipment and gas that caused the compound to go up in flames. Seventy-eight of Koresh's followers died horribly. At first, most Americans supported the move. Then, as investigations revealed the government's disorganization and shaky rationale for attack, the public began to perceive the Waco siege less hospitably. It was an alarming use of police power. Attorney General Janet Reno was ill-informed about conditions before and during the attack. Prior to the assault she had not even read the Justice Department briefing book. Waco was to be remembered as one of the Clinton administration's most serious catastrophes in a catastrophic year.

All of this came out later. What made Waco an immediate embarrassment was the president's poorly concealed fainthearted-ness. It was the most dramatic display thus far of his gelatinous character, a display more illuminating than his dissemblings about the draft, his broken campaign promises, or his sudden abandon-ment of nominees under fire. Clinton distanced himself from the decision to use force. He actually hid from public view. When he did appear in public, the *Washington Post* leaped on his evasions: "Clinton's comments yesterday differed in tone and substance from his earlier reaction. On Monday, when the federal authorities were moving on the compound but before the fire began, Clinton was asked if he had authorized such action. He said, 'I was aware of it. I think the attorney general made the decision.' He referred ques-tions to Reno and the FBI. Pressed, he said, 'I knew it was going to be done but the decisions were entirely theirs.'" Then the *Post* added, "But yesterday, Clinton said Reno phoned him on Sunday and the two had a 15-minute conversation. During the call, Clinton sought to assure himself through a series of questions that, while there was a chance that the action would have a bad outcome, things could get worse if authorities continued to wait Koresh out. 'Hav-ing asked those questions and gotten those answers, I said that if she thought it was the right thing to do that she should proceed and that I would support it, and I stand by that today,' Clinton said."[23]

This *mousse de confusion* following the Waco assault contained many of the elements that were to flummox the administration in the months ahead: a president irresolute and devious, a policy amorphous and poorly executed, a sudden eruption of the arrantly bizarre. The rest of cruel April's embarrassing stories were not as dramatic as Waco, but they did display Clinton's spinelessness and the bizarre trail that so frequently attached to him. (In this it could be said that he was merely being presidential. Like so many presi-dents after Eisenhower and Kennedy, the bizarre was his shadow. Of a sudden the post-Kennedy president would pull up his shirt to display a surgical scar to the world (Johnson!), arrive unbidden at the Lincoln Memorial late at night to inflict himself upon a group of hostile students (Nixon!), repeatedly fall down in public, often smacking his head on hard surfaces (Ford!), come under attack from an amphibious rabbit while fishing in a rowboat (Carter!), vomit on a nearby prime minister while at a state dinner in Japan (Bush!). Reagan again was exempt from such weird presidential mishaps, though, like Kennedy, he suffered an assassin's attack.)

Ever since the Clintons appeared on *60 Minutes* to assure the world of their marriage's incomparable normalcy, tales of their marital friction had circulated through Washington. In the second week of April a two-inch claw mark appeared on the president's right cheek, adjacent an inflamed right ear. The ever-game Dee Dee Myers attributed the damage to a shaving nick, an alibi plausible perhaps if the president shaved with a chisel. Then the president, with absurd joviality, tried this one out: he was "rolling around, acting like a child again." And George Stephanopoulos complicated the confusion saying, "He, he was playing with Chelsea, and I guess he just got scratched.... I didn't get all the details, minute by minute.... It was, was just, just some confusion.... It looked like a shaving—I mean, I just wasn't sure."[24] From the White House staff the rumor leaked out that "Bill and Hillary have recently had some rip-roaring rows, during which Mrs. Clinton... threw things at her husband."[25] One of the missiles mentioned was a lamp. Later in December when the Arkansas troopers came forth with testimony to the Clintons' rocky marriage, the reports of husband abuse in the White House circulated again. The Clintons responded with laughter. Ha, ha, us two happy lovebirds? Stalwarts from college days insisted theirs was a love to melt the heart, but acquaintances and employees from Little Rock had witnessed physical rows for years, Hillary being the more physical.[26]

Late in April reporters found in their press kits an official White House media advisory introducing the Polish president, Lech

Walesa, thus: "His Excellency Lech Walesa, president of the Czech Republic."[27]

After the White House Correspondents Association's annual dinner the White House spent several days apologizing for a presidential address that was a wooden, self-pitying blunder. In the midst of it Clinton delivered humorless and inappropriate jokes about Senate Minority Leader Robert Dole and radio talk show host Rush Limbaugh. It was now that word began to circulate that the White House staff was composed of greenhorns.

In recent years Washington figures and members of the press corps have come to depend on hackneyed terms. Such bundles of tired straw are the verbal coin of those "in the know." Even if a commentator is drunk by 10 A.M. and asleep by noon he knows that to utter sonorously the phrase of the moment while upright is to earn one's place on a weekend public affairs show. Just as "dazzle" or some variant thereof was being episodically resorted to in discussing Clinton's ditherings during his first three months; by the fourth month, and after Waco, the tiresome term was "focus." The president lacked it; and Official Washington settled on an explanation for this sudden lack of focus, Clinton's callow companions gamboling up and down the halls of the White House complex. Quite unexpectedly, Clinton's youthful staff, which for three months had been perceived as a charming asset for all its brash iconoclasm, became, by late April, a grave impediment, a hemlock to "focus." As Senator Dole put it after Clinton's impertinence at the Washington Correspondents dinner, Clinton had "sophomoric kids working for him, engaging in minor-league politics."[28]

Clinton's solution was to bring what *Time* described as a "grown-up" onto the staff. Roy Neel was a longtime adviser to Vice President Gore. He would serve under Thomas McLarty as deputy chief of staff. And the White House was bringing in another "grown-up" whose "temporary" acquisition of an office in the Old Executive Office Building *Time* greeted enthusiastically. He was Harry

Thomason, the Hollywood producer of prime time slop. Thomason was, said *Time* after talking to a presidential aide, "the perfect person to bring in." Here is the evidence adduced by that White House aide and passed on by this venerable weekly: Thomason's three hit television shows, his $40 million fortune, and his personal devotion to Clinton.[29] *Time*'s innocent restatement of this green-horn judgment in a piece devoted to criticizing the greenhorns on Clinton's staff bespeaks the fantasies that the press continued to entertain for the Clintons. Would *Time* have been as respectful if Clinton had fortified his staff with a "grown-up" who was proprietor of the Grand Ole Opry or chief brain surgeon from Beth Israel Hospital or coach of the year's Super Bowl Champion? I think so, but neither Thomason nor any such eminences necessarily have any of the talents for managing any aspect of government. In a matter of days Thomason, in league with Hillary Clinton, was cleaning out the White House Travel Office and staffing it with Arkansas cronies the better to increase his $40 million fortune and her control of 1600 Pennsylvania Avenue. History would record this impending scandal as Travelgate.

By the end of April *USA Today* reported: "President Clinton ends his first 100 days in office with 55 percent job approval, the lowest 100-day rating of any elected president since such polling began with Dwight Eisenhower."[30] That was the good news. Other polls put Clinton below 50 percent.[31] It was now that Leon Panetta, director of the Office of Management and Budget, admitted that the president's entire agenda was in trouble including foreign aid and health care. Worse, health care legislation would not be ready for its May 5 deadline.[32]

Another pattern was being established. A month begins. Fumbling, pratfalls, and circumlocutions ensue. The month ends as polls find the Boy President's ratings at an historic low. In May the serious business of government was almost wholly eclipsed by comedy. In foreign affairs the president was exposed as erratic, feckless, and inept, though it would not be until September and October that the full scope of his incompetence in foreign affairs became manifest. Early in May the president announced that he would send troops and offensive aircraft to Bosnia, then only aircraft, then only Warren Christopher. Aside from this foretaste of foreign policy incompetence, almost the only major news stories originating from the White House in May were caused by the place's adolescent blundering, roguish turpitude, and ventures into Arkansas cronyism. By the end of May *Time*'s cover featured a tiny photograph of a poorly tailored albeit obliviously jovial Boy Clinton standing beneath a headline whose lettering was charnel black and nearly as large as the *Time* logo itself. It read, "The Incredible Shrinking President." *Time* reported that some of Clinton's critics were again complaining that "...Clinton has spent too much time courting the left wing of the Democratic party when he should be building ties to the middle. After promising to cut taxes on the middle class and 'end welfare as we know it,' Clinton has proposed a host of tax increases and disguised hefty new spending programs as 'investments.' Rather than reduce entitlements, he nearly succeeded in creating a program to provide free immunization for children, regardless of income," and *Time* quoted Senator David Boren, a Democrat from Oklahoma, doubting whether Clinton really was a "New Democrat."[33] Here a theme from the Clintons' first term as governors of Arkansas has reemerged: probably under Hillary's guidance the Coat and Tie Radical dominates the Chronic Campaigner and puts the Clintons on the exposed left flank of American politics.

As in April, so in May, Official Washington's lament was Clinton's lack of focus. Supposedly the president was sending the White House spinning into chaos with his impulsiveness. Eloquence, a gift always associated with a stereotypical progressive president, had departed him. He dragged a ten-minute meeting meant to advise him on Supreme Court nominees into a self-indulgent two-hour bull session. Picking up on the president's garrulousness the

Washington Post's Lloyd Grove accused Clinton in a headline of a "Bad Case of the Blah-Blahs" and went on to record that:

> "It seems like only yesterday" that he was being heralded as a dazzling [that word again!] communicator.
>
> ...But it *was* only yesterday—actually it was Monday in Cleveland—that he uttered according to Reuters, the following: 'I've been criticized for doing more than one thing at once. I've always felt—can you do one thing at once? Can you do—wouldn't it be nice if all you had to do was go to work and not take care of your family? Would it be nice if you could pay your bills and not earn any money to pay them? I don't understand this whole—you can't do one thing at once. But anyway, that's what they say.'"[34]

Such indulgent self-pity was endemic among the Coat and Tie Radicals, and this self-indulgence is probably what kept thrusting both Clintons into May's embarrassing news stories. A few days after Grove recorded Clinton's garbled transmissions the populist president turned Air Force One into a Beverly Hills beauty parlor. On May 18 the mammoth plane idled on the runway at Los Angeles International Airport, closing down two of the airport's four runways, delaying thirty-seven flights, and costing commercial carriers $76,479, while a ludicrous Hollywood coiffeur by the name of Christophe trimmed Clinton's frizz for fifty-six minutes at a cost of $200. It was another Clinton first. Nothing like it had happened in the history of the presidency.[35]

The previous weekend it was reported that even no-nonsense Hillary had luxuriated her skull with an apolaustic haircut, this one costing $275. It was the work of "one of New York's hottest hairdressers," one Frederic Fekkai.[36] This was about the time that we began to hear about Mrs. Clinton's infatuation with the New Age swami Michael Lerner of *Tikkun*. On April 6 in Austin, Texas, she delivered a rambling, sermonic, public address reminiscent of her famous valediction to Wellesley; though now her lapses into non-sensicality were mellow New Age rather than indignant New Left. This speech was so egregious that even the *Kultursmog* belched derision. The *New York Times Magazine* assigned its house skeptic, Michael Kelly, to profile the First Lady's intellectual and spiritual pretensions. His subsequent piece in late May featured a picture of Mrs. Clinton on the magazine's cover, all in white and wearing a weird smile that looked like it had been created by cosmetic surgery and might be permanent. The title of the piece was printed across her waist, "Hillary Rodham Clinton and The Politics of Virtue." The greatest First Lady in the history of the Republic had become a joke even to the *New York Times*![37]

Also in May came that descent into cronyism that was to become a kind of low-level Watergate for the Clintons, causing them to lie to government agencies, conceal documents, and perhaps obstruct justice. On the very day that Boy Clinton turned Air Force One into his own private barber chair, the White House announced that it had uncovered "gross mismanagement" and "very shoddy accounting practices" in its Travel Office, theretofore a quiet, apolitical White House service whose political and boodling possibilities had escaped the eye of all previous administrations. The Arkansans saw its uses immediately. As soon as Harry Thomason arrived he, with Mrs. Clinton at work behind the scene, had the office's seven full-time employees fired. The FBI was importuned on to investigate the employees and blacken their reputations. Catherine Cornelius, supposedly Clinton's "distant cousin,"[38] planned to coordinate White House travel through a Little Rock firm that had handled travel for the Clintons and through another firm that Thomason had ownership in. A noisy controversy followed almost immediately as the fired head of the Travel Office, Billy Dale, had friendly relations with the Washington press corps, some of whose members suspected the White House immediately. Soon five of the disgraced employees were returned to the government payroll. Acquitted from fraud charges late in 1995, Dale too was exonerated. The testimony of former Clinton administration official David Watkins to the House Government Reform and Oversight Committee in January of 1996 reveals the desperate condition the Clintons perceived themselves to be in. Watkins said he was pressured by the First Lady to fire the Travel Office employees. Concerned by the criticism they were receiving from "Nannygate," Waco, and the $200 haircut aboard Air Force One, Mrs. Clinton and her entertainment genius, Harry Thomason, believed the Travel Office firings would win them the respect of a grateful electorate. So much for Mrs. Clinton's political instinct.[39]

An immediate consequence of Travelgate was a further White House reshuffle. George Stephanopoulos, the communications director most closely associated with misusing the FBI, was moved to the role of "senior adviser." David Gergen, a Washington insider and a Republican who had held high positions in the Reagan administration, was hired by Clinton to position the president, Gergen said, away from the left and closer to the center. Thomason came under a cloud. The new charge spreading through Washington was that Clinton had "gone Hollywood." Barbra Streisand's frequent visits, Thomason's White House office, and the Clintons' friendships with other Hollywood figures such as Richard Dreyfuss and Markie Post composed the corpus delicti.

Along with these embarrassments Secretary of State Warren Christopher had to telephone news organizations to disavow Under Secretary of State for Political Affairs Peter Tarnoff's public declaration that the United States was retreating from world leadership, though other State Department officers had been saying as much for months. In a widely-quoted wisecrack Ross Perot asserted that he "wouldn't consider giving [Clinton] a job anywhere above middle management."[40]

May was not over. On May 26 the president arrived in Concord,

New Hampshire, for an interview with Nanette Hansen, an anchor-woman at ABC affiliate WMUR-TV. One of his staff insisted that the anchorwoman prepare the president's makeup if she wanted the interview. The astonished anchorwoman repaired to her studio and returned with the required powders and ointments. She got her revenge, however, by reporting the contretemps on the evening news. Now it was national news and another of May's embarrass-ments. Once again the sorely pressed Dee Dee Myers was called to the rescue. "We certainly didn't mean to embarrass anybody," Myers emphasized, "or make anybody uncomfortable. As you know we've apologized...."[41] The month ended with Clinton attempting one of the acts of impudence that in the past had disarmed opponents. He boldly delivered his Memorial Day address at the very same memo-rial whose war he had evaded, the Vietnam Memorial. Boasting that he was the first president to so honor the Vietnam veterans, he arrived at the podium only to discover that the veterans were neither charmed nor honored. Repeatedly his speech was interrupted with shouts of "Draft dodger," "Liar," "Shut up, coward."[42]

By the end of May only 36 percent of those Americans respond-ing to a *Time*/CNN poll approved Clinton's performance in office. In the postwar period no president at that stage of his presidency ever scored so low. Even President Ford, burdened by his pardon of Nixon, scored 6 percentage points higher.[43]

June was another combination of bathos, burlesque, and incompe-tence along with the usual *basso continuo* of deceits. The burlesque began on June 2 when the *New York Times* belabored Clinton for repairing to the golf course "at a time when his presidency seems under siege from everywhere, as crises are erupting in the White House and around the world." What seems to have provoked the *Times* story's censorious tone was Stephanopoulos's attempt to con-trol the story's "spin" with a typically Clintonian dissimulation. The president, claimed Stephanopoulos, was not at the golf course to play golf but to attend an awards ceremony for Marines during their golf tournament. ("He had too much work," Stephanopoulos opined, for golf.) Needled by the reporter, Stephanopoulos admitted his boss did play three obligatory holes with the Marines—"It was a good opportunity for them." Needled further, he admitted that the three holes consumed a substantial portion of his boss's schedule—"between an hour and a half hour." Some charitable *Times* editor did try to take the edge off the story. It was run under a picture of Clinton engaged in what modern liberals perceive as the serious work of the presidency. The picture showed the president attired in casual dress, a baseball cap on his head, industrial gloves on his hands, "demonstrating his credentials as a man of the people by participating in a trash cleanup in a gritty neighborhood in northeast Washington."[44] To nonliberals, the picture was another instance of the president looking silly.

Two days later Clinton's esteem among feminists and blacks blew up when he was forced to withdraw his support for fellow Coat and Tie Radical Lani Guinier. Nominated for assistant attorney general for civil rights weeks before, she had been besieged by conservatives for theorizing that only "authentic blacks" could represent blacks in government (Guinier, herself, was only half black). As conservative criticism became a blare, Clinton claimed that upon reading her academic work he came to the belated conclusion that, their friendship and her intelligence aside, she was not a fit appointment to be the Justice Department's chief monitor of civil rights. He dropped her. After his abrupt abandonment of Zoe Baird and Kimba Wood, the uproar was deafening. "A disgraceful performance by the president," said Roger Wilkins. "An enormous loss to the civil rights movement and women's rights community," declared an official from NOW's Legal Defense and Education Fund.[45]

June rivaled May for calamity, Clinton's only achievement being his appointment of Judge Ruth Bader Ginsburg to the Supreme Court and a negotiated deal with the Senate Finance Committee on a gas tax. Otherwise the administration's budget was just squeaking through. Relations with the press were entering an uncomfortable hostile period. Journalists reopened the question of Clinton's tardiness at filling vacancies, noting that the ambassadorships to Japan and Israel were empty, as were three assistant attorneys general. Clinton had yet to appoint a secretary of the army or the air force, and the heads of various bureaucracies were vacant. Then in Texas the incumbent Democrat lost his special Senate race to a Republican. Gergen stepped forward to repair things for the White House. The result was a debacle. He put the president in a prime-time appearance before the American people. With the kind of TV props that President Ronald Reagan used so well, Clinton was to explain his economy. Two of the three major networks refused to delay their prime-time shows. The president came on looking like hell, and NBC switched to other programming just as Clinton began crowing about his "remarkable progress." Disaster.

The month ended with a prominent Air Force general being widely quoted as calling the president a "gay-loving," "pot-smoking," "draft-dodging," and "womanizing" commander-in-chief.[46] The general would lose his job; but by now, even among Democrats, respect for the president was evaporating. Before June was history, Clinton got in one more foreign policy blunder. After weeks of vacillating on Bosnia, Clinton attempted a grand gesture. He wrote German Chancellor Helmut Kohl urging him to persuade the European leaders to support arming Bosnia's Muslims. Kohl did so immediately at a regional meeting of the European Community, braving the irritation of his fellow Europeans, especially the British and the French. Presently their irritation evolved into astonishment. The Clinton administration of a sudden disavowed Clinton's letter to Kohl. To the embarrassment of all, particularly Kohl, a senior White House official explained that "Clinton never expected anything to come of his letter. We didn't expect the Europeans to take any action," the official said.[47] As June expired, the polls reported Clinton's popularity again at historic lows. No president at the end of his first quarter in office had ever done so badly.

There was a superbly amusing news story that stretched through the entire month. Somewhere out in Paradise, California, a retired janitor emerged from obscurity to reveal that for decades he, Leon Ritzenthaler, had been Bill Clinton's half-brother, oblivious through all those years of the distinguished blood flowing through his veins. Leon, as folks around Paradise called him, stepped before the cameras and the microphones of an excited press corps to recite the cold facts. He even had a birth certificate recording that his pa was William Jefferson Blythe III, who was also Bill's pa—at least according to Bill's ma. And there was more evidence. The *New York Times* noted that both men have "blue eyes with bags under them and share a passion for junk food." Leon's daughter reminded reporters that they also have "hot tempers" and a tendency for being "chronically late."[48] That clinched it!

Now the president was vowing to confer with Leon, saying, "I placed a call today but there was nobody home." Confusion. The press was having no difficulty whatsoever contacting Leon. Soon Leon is on wing to New York City for a tour of the talk-show circuit. Still the president cannot reach him. Leon pops up everywhere. White House operators keep missing him. The press is perplexed. It begins to feature pictures of Leon, alfresco, diligently telephoning the White House whose communications system is supposedly in constant contact with the Leader of the Free World wheresoever he might be; but still no luck. The Leader's reputation for effectiveness suffers anew. When will these two long-lost siblings link up? Clinton's problems with the budget, Lani Guinier, and a smart-alecky general recede behind this historically unparalleled drama. Finally the White House issues only what the *New York Times* terms "a terse three-sentence statement reporting that a 15-minute conversation had taken place."[49] "President Clinton's popularity continues to languish," begins a June 30 *Washington Post* report. "Public disapproval of Clinton's performance has reached a new high in the poll," the paper reports, citing its *Washington*

Post/ABC News poll. "That is the highest level of disapproval recorded by any president in the post-World War II era at a similar point in their administrations."[50]

By late 1995 and early 1996 the press, realizing that the Clintons had been lying to them for three years, concealing evidence, engaging in repeated conflicts of interest and obstructions of justice, botching policies, and abandoning loyal allies, slipped into fits of open hostility toward the Clintons (always followed by guilt and increased severity toward Newt Gingrich and the Republicans). Yet all the elements provoking the press were present in the first few months of 1993. No presidency in this century began so badly. How did Boy Clinton, this latest edition of the stereotypical progressive president, take it? What was on his mind as the news reports came in: of the anger following Christophe's haircut, of the impatience with his shilly-shallying after Waco, of suspicion in the press corps following Travelgate, of the general with the sarcastic tongue? What were the private thoughts of the great man seated in the Oval Office where Harding once sat? And what was his mood when Leon Ritzenthaler's tale came out?

Relying on Vico's *fantasia*, I think we can safely say that while sitting in Air Force One, the famed Christophe snip-snipping at his ears, the great plane's engines sedately sipping their fuel, Boy Clinton mused: *"I am the handsomest president since JFK."* (Harding was also quite handsome.) In the bewildered aftermath of the Travelgate firings, as Stephanopoulos ducks and Hillary scowls and Harry Thomason sees another lucrative deal go aglimmer, there sits a perfectly composed Clinton breathing easy: *"I am the cleverest president since JFK."* To that general's rude obloquies Clinton probably thought, *"They said the same things about Jack."* And when Attorney General Janet Reno squared off with the press after Waco, manfully taking full responsibility, Clinton undoubtedly reflected, *"JFK had a better looking attorney general."*

Fantasia reveals the warmth and general humanity of even the

most powerful man on earth. What would our forty-second president have been thinking after reading Guinier's theories of a racially
configured society, superseding majority rule and democratic practices? On this we do not speculate ex nihilo. We have the testimony
of a chronicler who heard Clinton air his thoughts during a White
House soirée the night he cut himself free of Guinier. R.W. Apple
of the *New York Times* has written that when the president "joined
his dinner guests Thursday night, two hours late," there was a "star-
crossed look" on him. Guinier was neither victim of her own
inflammatory theories nor of his faintheartedness. Support for her
had to be withdrawn, Clinton told his guests, because of "a campaign of right-wing distortion and vilification," in the media.[51] As
always with the Coat and Tie Radicals (and Guinier had been a student with Clinton at Yale Law School), they were blameless. But
what was on Clinton's mind a bit later that June when out there in
Paradise, California, another of William Jefferson Blythe III's progeny met with the press? How about: *"Damn I dun been found out!"*

Well, only temporarily. This Snopes from Hot Springs had safely
accredited himself at Georgetown, Oxford, and Yale. He had net-
worked with Yuppie-Marxists of the dope-fetcher variety. He had
cast himself as the Kennedy of the 1990s. Experience had proven to
him that he could transform himself into anything he wanted to be.
Apple's report of Clinton's post-Guinier dinner is a fine example of
the contradictions Clinton could embrace with no protests from the
press corps. Its headline reads "President Blames Himself." Early in
the piece Apple writes "He blamed only himself," but for what? "He
blamed only himself for the hurt he had caused his friend and himself." Later in the piece we get to the real culprit, the "campaign of
right-wing distortion and vilification" in the news media led by the
op-ed page of the Wall Street Journal."[52] So actually he blamed
neither himself nor Guinier. The real malefactors were at the *Wall
Street Journal* and among his political opponents.

If Clinton's identification with Kennedy was in some instances implausible, at other times he made the cut. Richard Reeves in *President Kennedy* writes of how Kennedy was "determined not to be trapped by procedures."[53] Clinton would not be either. Like Kennedy in his three years, Clinton in his first three years insisted on having a large say in every decision, no matter how small. Both men served as hubs with all the spokes of government coming to them. Reviewing Clinton's turbulent first year in the Oval Office, *Time* magazine reported "he liked having 20 people report to him, feeding him volumes of information that he would sit and consider in solitude. He wanted to be his own chief of staff, his own legislative director and his own National Security Adviser. He wanted to be as involved in choosing the dozen presidential scholars coming for lunch as in wrestling with the wording of minor speeches."[54] Yet halfway through 1993 it was apparent that Clinton was no JFK. He entered the White House accompanied by what would surely be considered "the best and the brightest" liberals of his generation, but by now such liberals were incompetents. Moreover, as the congressional inquiries were revealing, these liberals were unusually corrupt. Unlike Kennedy and his peers, Clinton and his peers had ducked most of life's responsibilities. They were the sheerist humbugs.

Both generations lived by different texts. The Kennedys began their "public service" with World War II. Clinton and his generational cohorts began theirs with *The Strawberry Statement* wherein James Simon Kunen proclaimed: "I'll do anything to feel like I'm doing something."[55] Casting a glance across the broken furniture and spilled milk of Clinton's first six months in office, one suspects that Kunen's adolescent maxim became President Clinton's working philosophy. In July, however, sobriety asserted itself as the scene at the White House replayed another of Clinton and his peers' texts, *The Big Chill*, that 1983 film of 1960-youth's middle-aged crisis, apostasy, and continued hustle. On July 20, Deputy White House Counsel Vince Foster was found dead, an apparent suicide.

Consistent with the gravity of the event, the White House's

burlesques abated in late July, but its deceits and melodrama continued. The president performed professionally at the economic
summit of the leading industrial powers in Tokyo, his only gaffe
being that he kept addressing the wife of South Korean President
Kim Young Sam by the wrong name. He appointed a new FBI
director, Louis Freeh, after some arcane maneuvering with his predecessor William Sessions. The White House made public its internal report criticizing Cornelius and Thomason for abusing their
authority and that of the FBI.[56] But on July 20, the day the FBI
acquired permission to search the office of David Hale, a member
of the Arkansas "political family" suspected of Small Business
administration fraud, Foster died. He had left the White House
shortly after 1 P.M. At 6:02 P.M. an unidentified 911 caller reported
finding his body lying neatly next to a Civil War field piece in a
secluded park off the George Washington Parkway in northern Virginia. The death was reported as a suicide. The Clintons' conflicting statements began almost immediately, encouraging suspicion
for years.

Mrs. Clinton, who was in Little Rock visiting her mother,
expressed her sadness. The White House reported that she and
Foster were very close and that Foster had overseen matters of personal finance for her. In fact, as was suspected in Washington and
would soon be substantiated by disgruntled former Clinton bodyguards, the two had been lovers. As for Clinton, his chief of staff
Mack McLarty pulled him off *Larry King Live* to notify him shortly
after the death of his boyhood friend. Clinton proceeded to Foster's
Georgetown home in an unmarked Secret Service vehicle to condole Mrs. Foster, and then immediately began to lie. "What happened," Clinton said at the White House the next day, "was a
mystery about something inside of him.... In times of difficulty he
was normally the Rock of Gibraltar while other people were having
trouble."[57] The White House insisted Foster had not been
depressed and that no one knew of any problems facing him. Soon

the White House had to confirm a *Newsweek* story that the president had a twenty-minute telephone conversation with Foster the night before his death. He had asked Foster over to see a movie with Hubbell. And, yes, the president recognized that Foster was in difficulty.

Administration officials, many of whom were friends from Foster's youth, consoled themselves very publicly at local yuppie restaurants such as Nora's. Then they all flew down to Little Rock for the funeral. There the president eulogized the deceased as "one of the best and the brightest" with whom the Clintons would spend long evenings "listening to music and drinking spirits and being incredibly silly." To the *Washington Post* he elaborated that Foster's friends have "been up real late two nights in a row now, remembering and crying and laughing."[58]

Then it was learned that the Park Police had badly bungled the death's investigation. The White House had frustrated the Justice Department's examination of Foster's office. A note apparently written by Foster, though his fingerprints were not on it, was found torn in twenty-eight pieces (one of which was missing) and concealed by the administration for nearly two-and-a-half weeks. Questions regarding the death continued to multiply in the months ahead. In October of 1995 it was revealed that three handwriting experts, one an Oxford professor, denied Foster's so-called suicide note was in his handwriting. There were many irregularities with the investigation. The disposition and nature of documents Foster might have left in his office were in doubt.[59]

In the press, doubts began to turn to open disrespect. About the middle of July, two days before Foster's death, the *New York Times* playfully reported the visit to Hot Springs of a president "who has no home," whose "weekend getaway has about as much structure as a college road trip," who stopped in an old girlfriend's house for a scheduled one-hour visit and stayed two. Encoded in the *Times* report was the suggestion that Clinton was still playing around; he "decided to drop in at the apartment of another friend, David Edwards... fished in the trunk, unzipped his garment bag and grabbed a white shirt, still in its dry-cleaning bag. An hour, he promised again, as he walked into the high-rise. More than four hours later, Mr. Clinton re-emerged... wearing the clean shirt."[60]

After its girlish dissimulations following Foster's death, the White House settled down. Clinton's budget passed on August 6 with Vice President Gore casting a vote to break the Senate's fifty-fifty tie. As the months passed the administration went to work on the Brady gun bill, a comprehensive health care reform, and the North American Free Trade Agreement. In September Israel and the PLO signed a Middle East agreement on the south lawn of the White House. Though Norway, not the United States, secretly brokered the agreement, Clinton took prodigious credit. Throughout autumn Clinton's abysmal approval rating climbed, to 47 percent in October, 48 percent in November, and 54 percent in December.

Yet even as the clownishness and incompetence in the Oval Office subsided, Clinton engaged in one more instance of impulsiveness that would propel him into his most dangerous scrape since the campaign. At the end of the summer Clinton got wind of reports that state troopers who had worked on his security detail at the Governor's Mansion were talking to journalists about the gory details of life with the Clintons. The president promptly picked up the telephone and called trooper Danny Ferguson. In fact he called him twice, perhaps several times. Roger Perry, a trooper then cooperating with the *American Spectator*, told the *Spectator*'s David Brock that Ferguson told him that in one of the calls Clinton dangled the prospect of federal jobs for those troopers who would break off their conversations with the press. In another call, according to what Ferguson told Perry, Clinton offered Ferguson the position of U.S. marshall or regional director for the Federal Emergency Management Agency (FEMA) if Ferguson would tell him what the other troopers were saying.[61]

Clinton's impetuous telephone calls were to ensure that 1993 would end catastrophically for the Clintons. Since I, as editor-in-chief of the *American Spectator*, was one of the Clintons' leading catastrophizers at the time, the gentlemanly thing for me to do is to set the record straight here and now. That August Clinton's troopers were talking to two reporters from the *Los Angeles Times* and one from the *American Spectator*, Brock. Earlier, during the campaign, reporters and acquaintances of the Clintons invariably let fall morsels about their marriage that adumbrated a typical 1960s youth culture union gone to hell: anything-goes youthful moral relativism had given way to angry middle-aged careerists holding together an unhappy but career-advancing union. Following up on several leads, by the time of Vince Foster's death, I had enough information on him and Mrs. Clinton to report their affair in the *American Spectator*, but it was not until the next month, when Brock met with the Clintons' former bodyguards, that we developed sufficient sources to chronicle irrefutably the Clintons' *Big Chill* marriage.

In August Clinton's longtime foe, Arkansas lawyer Cliff Jackson, approached our Brock with a project. He had four of the Clintons' security men who wanted to talk. Their motives were not wholly public spirited. Two were miffed that the Clintons had passed them over when choosing cronies for their new government. The other two would most probably have remained silent had the Clintons provided them with jobs, but the immediate provocation for their disloyalty was nothing more dramatic than a typically reckless Clinton snub. After all the irregular demands he had made on them in his pursuit of parties and security for his illicit liaisons, he ignored their request for autographed pictures. That stung both officers, Roger Perry and Larry Patterson, and their retaliation did him enormous injury.

One of the salient features of the troopers' testimony is their utter disloyalty to the Clintons, a disloyalty the Clintons had worked diligently to earn. All four troopers had acquired a bland disrespect for the Clintons, for Mrs. Clinton because of her bitchiness and hypocrisy, for Clinton because of his lechery, childishness, and hypocrisy. Their grotesque behavior was unusual even for a political couple. Having witnessed the Clintons' grotesqueries, their body-guards, true to the contemporary American conviction that anyone who has witnessed unusual goings-on is somehow immediately invested with literary talent, thought there might be a book contract awaiting them. After Jackson's meeting with Brock all four troopers allowed themselves to be taped by him, apparently in preparation for their literary careers. It would take a while before they abandoned their unlikely ambition. From August through October Brock taped more than thirty hours of interviews, covering the Clintons from early 1979 to January 16, 1993, when they left for Washington. Meanwhile Jackson worked out the legal details. He was also work-ing with the *Los Angeles Times* reporters.

What his arrangement was with the *Times* I cannot say, but with the *American Spectator* Jackson tried to arrange a "whistleblowers" fund to protect the troopers in the event that they suffered punitive legal action or were fired. He also wanted to ensure that the *Times* could precede us in publication. All this made Brock's work difficult, for while attempting to verify the troopers' stories he had to con-tend with changing legal demands from Jackson and later from me. I had nothing against a public legal defense fund open to contribu-tions from individuals concerned that government employees not suffer for revealing the Clintons' misuse of state funds and abuse of authority, the serious misdeeds underlying the troopers' stories. Furthermore, I saw no reason why the *Times*'s story could not pre-cede ours. As a monthly, the *Spectator* could carry more detail than the *Times*, whose story might actually increase interest in ours. But after we had made good faith efforts to respect the troopers' rights I was emphatic that we publish the piece regardless of threats from anyone. Meanwhile the lawyerly Jackson kept dickering and Brock, harried but steadfast, proceeded to verify the contents of his tapes. Had Clinton been at a hotel on a given date? Did anyone else hear what trooper Ferguson heard? All such questions had to be answered thoroughly but also quickly.

I was getting impatient with the lawyers, and the troopers were growing restive. Threats had been made against them by Clinton supporters, for instance, by their former supervisor on the security detail Captain Raymond L. "Buddy" Young, now, by Clinton's grace, the head of a regional FEMA office in Texas. Ultimately only Perry and Patterson would let their stories be placed on the record, and as late as November they were hesitating. As for Brock and my colleagues at the magazine, they felt increasingly beset. We had been at pains since August to keep the story quiet. Most worrying, since Jackson's first contacts with Brock, our New York apartment and our Arlington, Virginia, offices had been broken into three times. We knew that Betsey Wright, already famed for her wizardry at suppressing "bimbo eruptions" during the campaign, had employed a shadowy investigator by the name of Jack Palladino. There were signs that our telephones occasionally were tapped. Subsequent investigations found no connection between the break-ins and the intrepid Betsey, but through November the well-insulated nerves of my staff were beginning to fray.

I repaired to the beach, the better to keep things in perspective and to slay bluefish in the surf of North Carolina's outer banks. According to my calculations we had the story ready to go. It revealed sexual irregularities by both Clintons—in the case of the male Clinton, irregularities of rather gargantuan proportions. It previewed the angry, devious, arbitrary Hillary Clinton that came out from behind the arras in late 1995 when her billing documents suddenly appeared in the White House residence after being under subpoena for two years. What is more, the troopers' testimony revealed abuse of authority, misuse of state property, and now blatant lies to the national press. It was a most important story. Yet the troopers were in rebellion. Jackson's desire for a "whistleblowers" fund was approaching the condition of a non-negotiable demand.

The fund itself, as explained by Jackson, was beginning to look like a payoff; and that we would not provide. It was now possible that we might not be able to get the troopers' release to publish our piece.

The time was ripe for the editor-in-chief to become unreasonable. We had the troopers' testimony, and I threatened to run our piece without their release. Down in Little Rock, Brock, adopting the role of Kissinger negotiating with the North Vietnamese, had to convince his sources that the boss up in Washington was a nutcase Nixon capable of a Christmas bombing. His condition there became tense. While I faced the surf and the bluefish, he faced restless Arkansans with guns and the full authority of the Arkansas State Police.

Our piece was in galleys and being polished for a December publication. It contained the most devastating sketch of a sitting American president ever written, and Hillary did not come off looking all that homey either. The information was about character, precisely the issue Clinton had hornswoggled the press into avoiding during the campaign and precisely the source of his administration's present failures—along with the deficiencies of late twentieth-century liberalism. I decided to publish the piece.

The legal maneuvering caused by the troopers' financial concerns combined with my premonitions that the *Los Angeles Times* would duck publishing its piece (the very good journalists working for the *Times* had already seen a piece of theirs on Clinton held up for a year by their editors) made me fear that our December deadline might be missed. I consulted one of the finest legal minds of the age, me, and concluded that Jackson's maneuverings had so disfigured our original agreement as to kill it. Returning from the beach I called my lawyer, apprised him of my considered opinion, and suggested that he see things as I did. He read the piece and agreed. Meanwhile Brock had hit upon a splendid alternative if any further problems arose. He would write not about the troopers' testimony but about how the venality of Arkansans was impeding journalists from reporting on the Clintons. In the course of this second story the contents of the troopers' testimony would naturally have to be reported.

While Jackson reviewed his options, Brock flew to Little Rock to review his galleys with the two irate troopers, both of whom are rather large and rough around the edges, elbows, knees, and knuckles. Before sitting down with Brock and his galleys, one placed a gun on the table while musing, "If we know anything, we know you can kill anyone today." It was a ticklish moment, defused I like to think by my telephone instructions to the writer: "Tell him," I advised, "that he watches too many movies." Personally I watch few, but I had seen all three episodes of *The Godfather* and espied the origin of the trooper's line.

In his next call Brock reported that Jackson's obduracy had evaporated. He had composed a letter freeing us to publish and emphasizing that "no monies have been paid by you or anyone else for this story." Still, I rather hoped that the *Times* would precede us in publication, lending legitimacy to our carefully substantiated story. We would be on the street on Monday December 20, but I could not be sure that our appearance alone would create the national debate over Clinton's character that I sought. Fortunately some sleuth at CNN laid hands on our piece in galleys. CNN interviewed Perry and Patterson. It broadcast its interview on December 19 and news reports of our piece on December 20 just as we hit the street. All hell broke loose, and December ended the Clintons' 1993 roller-coaster in glorious free fall.

On Tuesday December 21 the crisis spread from CNN to the newspapers, with the *Washington Post* reporting that "President Clinton and other administration officials engaged in an extensive effort in recent months to prevent publication of allegations that Clinton as governor of Arkansas used his security detail to facilitate extramarital affairs, the White House acknowledged yesterday."[62] The night before, presidential adviser Bruce Lindsey had issued a press release that only fueled the media's interest, demonstrating

once again that the one-party Arkansas style of coverup and dispar-
agement was not all that prudent so far from home. Admitting that
the president had called the troopers, he inadvertently tipped the
press that there must be something to the troopers' stories. Lindsey
did begin the Clintonites' grand strategy to throw the press into
confusion by denying that the president was bribing the troopers
for "silence or the shaping of any stories." He also denied that Clinton had used troopers to facilitate extramarital sexual liaisons.
According to Lindsey his boss merely telephoned the troopers to
discover what was being said about him. Then came another botch.
A day after the CNN news story, Buddy Young, once Clinton's chief
bodyguard, now ensconced in a comfortable FEMA office, granted
an interview to an ABC news crew. During it the dolt took a call on
his speaker telephone. As the ABC crew recorded the proceedings
in Young's office, Lindsey came on the line from the White House
telling Young that he might be needed to rebut the troopers'
charges on CNN. ABC broadcast this priceless moment of Clintonian *realpolitik* on its evening news. The Troopergate story was
taking off. The Clinton machine's efforts were seeing to that.

Also on Tuesday Mrs. Clinton denounced the *Spectator* piece as
"outrageous, terrible stories." She perceived conspiracy. "I find it
not an accident," she told the Associated Press, "that every time he
[her husband] is on the verge of fulfilling his commitment to the
American people... out comes yet a new round of these outrageous,
terrible stories that people plant for political and financial reasons."[63] The interview led the evening news. That day the *Los
Angeles Times* also came out with its piece corroborating our story.
It emphasized that four troopers had come forward (though only
two on the record), and part of the piece was written from telephone records of Clinton's calls to paramours. At least one of Clinton's trysts had taken place in the Governor's Mansion since his
election to the presidency, making a mockery of his promise on *60
Minutes* to err no more. Wednesday brought more distress for the

president. During three interviews that day, questions about Troop-ergate flew at him. An Associated Press interview broadcast on the evening news caught him glassy-eyed and stammering, "I have nothing else to say. We... we did, if, the, the, I, I, the stories are just as they have been said. They're outrageous, and they're not so."[64]

Events had, as they say, taken hold. The story whirled into that cyclonic phenomenon known as a media event, and soon it was worldwide. Italy's *La Stampa* was the first European news organization to get the story, its brilliant Washington correspondent Paolo Passerini having secured an advance copy of the piece and written it up immediately. Shortly thereafter the troopers' story was being broadcast and published throughout the industrial world.

From Dublin the actress Jeananne Crowley conveyed the comic effect the story was having in Europe. She had just heard the wags around the bar of the Shelbourne Hotel joking about the *Los Angeles Times*'s report that telephone logs revealed that Clinton had called one of his mistresses fifty-nine times from 1989 to 1991. The woman insisted that he was helping her with a "personal" problem. One of his calls was made at 1:23 A.M. and lasted ninety-four minutes. Apparently, the "personal" problem persisted, for after his election, Clinton had the aforementioned nocturnal meeting with the woman in the basement of the Governor's Mansion, a trooper standing lookout as Mrs. Clinton snoozed soundly upstairs (the consensus among the troopers is that Mrs. Clinton could have slept through the San Francisco earthquake). "There was no improper relationship," the lady told the *Times*. Those assembled at the Shelbourne bar roared over their whiskeys when one read White House Counsel Bernard Nussbaum's explanation: "This president calls lots of people."[65] Many supposedly worldly American journalists, on the other hand, insisted that these first-hand reports from bodyguards were unreliable. They found the reports of Clinton's strenuous amours far-fetched. No man is a hero to his valet as the seventeenth century wit Madame Cornuel put it, but apparently in the 1980s the Governor of Arkansas was an enigma to his bodyguard.

The Clintons' attempts to kill the story, by turns petulant then mawkish, at first seemed only to have attracted the media's fascination. Brock and I were both invited to defend ourselves on television and radio, though not on *Nightline* or the shows we might have been expected to be on. The *Spectator*'s tireless and valiant Polish cavalry, managing editor Wladyslaw Pleszczynski, weighed in on scores of radio shows. Newspapers and magazines called for interviews. Wherever I went in New York or Washington, piquant intelligence reports came my way. When Mrs. Clinton read our piece her violent screams alarmed the White House staff and sent the president scrambling down the elevator from the family quarters in a state of dreadful agitation. At a staff Christmas party the Clintons scarcely talked to each other and left after five minutes (Richard Reeves verified both stories over a year later in the *New York Observer*). For several days the White House canceled its daily press briefings to avoid Troopergate inquiries. After Mrs. Clinton barred Troopergate questions from Christmas interviews scheduled for the networks' breakfast shows, all three canceled her appearances. The news kept sweeping us along.

And yet ultimately the press shielded the Clintons, by shifting the focus of the story away from the question of whether the charges— some of which were criminal—were true, and toward the one issue the contemporary journalist really cares about: how the subjects of "the story" handle "the story." One interesting result of this media-centric standard is that today's most successful public figures are often sociopaths. Without consciences to prick, they can weather any amount of apparent public humiliation without flinching, and since how they handle the story is the real standard of success, the media version of guilt or innocence, unless they flinch they cannot be taken down by public disgrace. Indeed they cannot be disgraced. They can be sent to jail. Or they can lose an election. But no force of conscience or shame can drive them from power, actually or effectively.

Media coverage brings with it the sense that all life is illusory. Only the nice-looking semihuman face on the glowing screen is real. The media coverage of Troopergate carried with it not just the fantasy dimension of media but also a hearty serving of the irrational including the supremely irrational claim that Americans are not interested in sexual scandal. In the weeks during which we prepared the Troopergate story for publication we assayed the story's content. Never before had so much scandal been revealed about a First Family, but then never before had America had such a First Family, a 1960s First Family. The unhappiness of their marriage and the Clintons' arbitrary use of government was extraordinary; but the most newsworthy information in the story was the troopers' revelation that the First Lady had been having an affair with a recently deceased White House counsel whose suicide was that of the highest-ranking government official since James Forrestal, President Truman's erstwhile secretary of defense. Just before publication I sought others' views as to what aspects of the story would attract the most attention. I remember in particular showing it to Kenneth Lynn, the distinguished retired professor of history from Johns Hopkins University serving on our Editorial Board. From my living room he let out a shout. The active love affair between the First Lady and the White House lawyer, now dead, was, he thought, the stuff of headlines. Yet when the story broke, no mention of the affair was reported. Only Mrs. Clinton's stormy temper was mentioned, and even that soon slipped from view. Even a year-and-a-half later, when the Senate Whitewater Committee was probing Foster's death, no one mentioned the famous couple's affair. And yet, while insisting that the dull stuff of sex was beneath the American public's attention, our journalists boomed Troopergate worldwide.

The delayed response of the pundits was equally irrational. A few days passed in silence on the op-ed pages of the Republic, then the columnists depreciated the troopers' stories as "unbelievable" and "baloney" even while claiming that everyone was already well aware

of Clinton's sexual improprieties and the citizenry elected him president anyway. So the unbelievable was irrelevant because everyone
already knew it was true. Despite all the evidence to the contrary,
most pundits sneered at the troopers' stories as "uncorroborated."
Some adjudged them false because, as Joe Klein of *Newsweek* who
called them "baloney" asked, "where are the women?" If they existed
surely they would have come forward. Of course three had come forward—Gennifer Flowers, Sally Perdue, and Connie Hamzy—who
for their attestations were branded as "bimbos." Did Klein and his
colleagues really believe that adulteresses were eager for that sort of
publicity? As for corroboration, the stories of the initial three
women had been corroborated by the stories of Clinton's four bodyguards and vice versa. Brock and the *Times*'s reporters had verified
Clinton's proximity to the women and brought incriminating telephone logs. To the pundits the stories remained dubious.

A final serving of the irrational was provided a year later when the
Washington Post's David Maraniss came out with a Clinton biography
mentioning the Boy Governor's repeated extramarital affairs.
Maraniss's only source was Betsey Wright who, in an interview, told
him that she had dissuaded Clinton from running for president in
1988 because "she was convinced that some state troopers were
soliciting women for him [Clinton], and he for them." According to
Maraniss, six years before Wright orchestrated the administration's
campaign to discredit the Troopergate story, she sat down with Clinton and "started listing the names of women he had allegedly had
affairs with and the places where they were said to have occurred."[66]
In Maraniss's book he never mentions Brock's earlier, more widely
sourced story or Wright's blatantly dishonest assault on it. Nonetheless his book's allegations were honored as gospel. None of the pundits remonstrated with him for having but one source and that being
a source that quickly disavowed him, as Wright did. Only British
journalist Peter Hitchens noted that from the book's notes it
appeared that he had to know during Troopergate that Brock's story

was accurate. That he did not file a story substantiating Brock and exposing Wright was unethical. The *New Republic* remarked on the discrepancy between the saintly Clinton whom Maraniss presented en route to his 1992 Pulitzer Prize for campaign coverage and the fraud he sketches in his book. Of that prize the magazine mordantly observed, "We suggest it be awarded retroactively for fiction."[67]

Brock's story held historic consequences. The corruption of the First Family was revealed in vivid American lingo, and it prefigured many of the scandals that entoiled that First Family in late 1995 and 1996. Brock's troopers had seen the Lady MacBeth in Mrs. Clinton. In front of the Governor's Mansion in 1991 she exploded. "I thought something was terribly wrong, so I rushed out to her," trooper Perry asserts, "and she screamed, 'Where is the goddamn fucking flag?' It was early and we hadn't raised the flag yet. And she said, 'I want the goddamn fucking flag up every fucking morning at fucking sunrise.'" In 1996 the press began to report her coarse treatment of the president, but it had begun back in Arkansas in front of the troopers when she would call the governor to his face "a motherfucker, cocksucker, and everything else," according to trooper Patterson. "I went into the kitchen," after one such outburst, Patterson told Brock, "and the cook, Miss Emma, turned to me and said, 'The devil's in that woman.'" Clinton is perhaps portrayed as nicer but no more civilized. He was carrying on several affairs at a time, using government personnel to cover for him and to expedite meetings with the women and with various pick-ups. He bragged of his sexual gymnastics in crude language, for instance telling Perry that Gennifer Flowers "could suck a tennis ball through a garden hose." He engaged in sex in parked cars, frequently oral sex about which he was obsessed, once telling Patterson that "he had researched the subject in the Bible and oral sex isn't considered adultery." The troopers described violent assaults by Mrs. Clinton on her husband and whatever property she could lay hands on in the family quarters.[68]

Within a dozen or so days of Troopergate's eruption in the media the journalists went on to other matters, namely the Clinton administration's periodic signs of rebirth, and revelations of dubious financial and electioneering dealings. But in the *Washington Post* Sally Quinn, that creature of the *Kultursmog*, made a telling revelation a month after Brock's piece came out. She wrote "For people who have lived in Washington for any length of time, these stories are unprecedented.... the stream of allegations out of Little Rock has taken its toll.... an erosion of confidence in the important purpose of the presidency. When Clinton asks us to trust him on Bosnia or the defense budget or even welfare or health reform, some of us feel uneasy. Words like 'character' and 'trust' become codes for the president's private behavior."[69]

Another historic consequence of the piece came two weeks later. The stereotypical progressive president became the first president to be charged with sexual harassment. Paula Corbin charged that while she was working for the state of Arkansas at a program in Little Rock's Excelsior Hotel, trooper Danny Ferguson asked her to meet with the governor in his hotel room. "He took my hand," and loosed his tie, Jones reported in an affidavit. "You have nice curves," Clinton reportedly said. "I love the way your hair goes down your body." He then asked her for "a type of sex." What prompted her to come forward her lawyer said was a report of the episode in the January issue of the *American Spectator*'s Troopergate story.[70] Brock had mentioned her first name. It was an accident. The name had slipped into the story from Brock's notes, a hazard of electronic composition. In all the other stories that the troopers had related to him Brock had kept the identities of the women strictly secret. Some were married and had children. Corbin was neither at the time of Clinton's indiscretion, but still Brock had not meant to mention Corbin's first name. It was but an accident of history that even her first name was mentioned, but the historic accident pursued Clinton from that point on.

CHAPTER ELEVEN

BOY CLINTON AND THE LIBERAL CRACK-UP

HISTORY WILL SURELY note and long remember that the first presidency of the brightest and most idealistic generation in American history was a thumping bust. President Bill Clinton of Georgetown, Oxford, and Yale Law—like *Strawberry's* Simon Kunen, the Tom Paine of his 1960s generation of protest, head lice, and sexually transmitted diseases—is a premature has-been. Within weeks of his arrival in Washington, the capital's politicians and foreign diplomats had taken Boy Clinton's measure. Almost all esteemed him a posturing milksop accompanied by a know-it-all nag, who, like him, never seemed properly affixed to reality. From time to time optimism would rekindle in the Democrats and fear in the Republicans, but this early assessment was to be repeatedly validated by events. Clinton's major reforms, so solemnly promised on the campaign trail, Welfare Reform! Health Care Reform! A Middle-Class Tax Cut! A Balanced Budget! were all, by the fall of 1994, roadkill. History passed them by.

Under Boy Clinton's leadership, the Democrats in 1994 suffered their worst defeat since 1946. One had to look back to Woodrow

Wilson to find a Democratic president at midterm who had lost both Houses of Congress. Not even Richard Nixon in his fourth summer in office had so many scandals and lawsuits rising around him, so many political aides and former supporters in the dock or the hoosegow, and so many special prosecutors hovering over his perspiring cabinet colleagues. The Clinton administration had by 1996 three cabinet members looking over their shoulders and a First Lady nervously (and irritably) answering subpoenas. By then she had become the first presidential spouse to be summoned before a grand jury or to be flirting with indictments for obstruction of justice, perjury, and bank fraud.

Still America's yuppie press—though roused to the foul smell across from Lafayette Park and the plea bargainings down Arkansas way—was suffering its periodic digitalis of Hope. Journalists still believed that there just had to be a Kennedy somewhere under the skin of our great big lovable lug of a president. And, as was widely reported, the Republicans were falling into disarray. Well, no and yes.

The Republicans are often in disarray, but much less so under Newt Gingrich and Bob Dole than before. Oh yes, Newt was indeed a rascal too. There was the million-dollar book contract, the energetic PACs, and a slutty girlfriend off in the past who popped up in 1995 attesting that Newt had been pleased by her endeavors at oral sex. Nevertheless, Boy Clinton's was the least successful administration of the twentieth century, worse than Harding's, worse than Carter's.

Unlike Harding and Carter, however, Clinton has an excuse. His was an accidental presidency. Had the 1992 race been the customary two-party engagement he would have been spared his four-year trial in the big league. History would remember him as a promising governor in the American outback. Not so many of his friends would be facing jail terms.

Clinton won with 43 percent of the vote, three percentage points less than his Democratic predecessor, Governor Michael Dukakis, had amassed in losing to George Bush four years earlier. Clinton's ticket to victory was the gimcrack messiah H. Ross Perot. Had Perot not yielded to the sirens between his ears and campaigned for the White House, his bête noire, George Bush, would have been reelected.

Admittedly, national polls suggested that the second choice of Perot voters split fairly evenly between Bush and Clinton, but a state-by-state analysis proves that the Perot vote was the final blow to Bush's reelection. As the political scientist Peter J. Steinberger has written, though nationally Perot voters divided evenly in their second choice, "in particular [and critical] states this was not the case. In Montana [usually Republican in presidential elections], for instance, Mr. Clinton beat Mr. Bush 37 percent to 35 percent, while Mr. Perot got 26 percent. Without Mr. Perot, Mr. Bush would have won that state handily. Things were much the same in Colorado, Maine, Nevada, and New Hampshire, as well as in large industrial states like New Jersey and Ohio."[1] Clinton did not so much win in 1992 as the incumbent lost. Bush was unpopular and ran a listless race in which he struck not even a glancing blow at his opponent's gravest vulnerability, his character. Perhaps, as I have speculated, Bush had entered into a gentleman's agreement with Clinton to avoid personal attacks owing to their shared vulnerability on Mena. If so, Clinton got the better of the deal, bearing in mind that Clinton had not only to worry about illegal gun-running, but also drug smuggling and whatever he meant when he said to L. D. Brown, "That's Lasater's deal." At any rate, Clinton's exposure on Mena is now on the public record, making him more vulnerable still in 1996.

Clinton's reelection in 1996 would run contrary to the rules of evidence, normative human experience, and all known theories of history save those of Edward Gibbon, the diagnostician of civilizations in decline. To begin with, Clinton's record is against him as are various codes of conduct adopted by the Constitution, the United States Congress, and the Department of Justice. His economy is not that much better than the Bush economy that he disparaged, though the Bush economy was improving. Clinton's seems to be slowing. The Blue Chip Economic Indicator consensus of key forecasters in the winter of 1996 suggested that real per capita disposable income would increase at only 1.3 percent in the four quarters preceding the election. Since 1952 whenever disposable income growth has dropped below the long-run growth trend of 2.1 percent, an incumbent president has been shown the door.

Then too the simplest mathematical computations suggested by the distribution of votes in the Electoral College show Clinton's muzzle being duly removed from the public trough. Since 1968 Republicans have had a virtual hammer lock on the South, the Southwest, the Plains states, and the Rocky Mountain West. Add the electoral votes of such traditionally Republican states as Alaska, Indiana, Maine, and New Hampshire, and the Republican candidate, no matter how dull and ordinary, has 275. As he needs but 270 to be elected, Clinton is a goner regardless of results in California, Illinois, Missouri, Ohio, and Pennsylvania, all of which have very competitive Republican parties.

How did it come to this? How did this latest edition of the stereotype of the progressive president fall into such a low estate? What happened to the old competence, the legendary intellectual brilliance, the comparative freedom from scandal or at least from suspicion? One of the disaster's ingredients was the political corruption of Arkansas. Historians working apace with grand juries, independent counsels, and law enforcement agencies at the highest levels of American government are every day making that clear. Journalists too are catching on. Another of the disaster's ingredients is that agglutination of peculiar traits borne out of the 1960s by the Coat and Tie Radicals. These traits might have made them irresistible figures in student government circa 1968 and the apple of every progressive prof's eye. Their righteousness, self-importance, and masturbatory narcissism seems also to have made them welcome parasites in the worlds of government and of corporate America during the Wilderness years of the 1980s. But the peculiar traits that they picked up in the 1960s kept them insulated from the lessons of the recent past and facilitated their transformation into about the most corrupt political crowd since the days of Boss Tweed. Their arrogance deadened their consciences to charges of venality, conflicts of interest, abuses of power, and perjury, allowing all those vices to flourish. They began their public lives in the petty charlatanry of student government and ended in the 1990s as fit objects for grand jury inquiries, government subpoenas, congressional investigations, and massive rejection by the electorate.

Of course, there is another ingredient in the disaster that befell the Clintons' administration. It is the issue that they so cleverly kept out of bounds during the 1992 presidential campaign—character. In this department both Clintons are spectacularly bereft. Beyond being 1960s megalomaniacs, they are cheats, users, liars, and as greedy as their worst vision of a Republican. Both are without dignity. Four years of presidential flummoxing has revealed Boy Clinton as a vaporous cloud tossed about willy–nilly by the winds of an especially gusty day. The consequent chaos is what he and Hillary are pleased to call public service.

Clinton's essential vacuousness brought an additional ingredient to his failed presidency, an ingredient less personal than his flawed character, his Arkansas background, or those weird traits carried by Coat and Tie Radicals from 1968 to the *Big Chill* of the Clintons' Washington. It is the stultifying American *Kultursmog*. Back in his Georgetown days when this cunning Snopes took to the *smog* as his trans-Arkansas idiom, the fumes were very useful and certainly not personally dangerous. The *smog* did not force its adherents to cough up undeviating nonsense. It was cohesive without being repressive. Admittedly it was increasingly polluted by politics, but the pollutant was in those days mere liberalism, at the time still somewhat tolerant and relatively free of bugaboos. It had yet to be radicalized. The liberalism in the air in those days was about the same liberalism that had guided Adlai Stevenson in the 1950s along a well-traveled path not far from the center of American political life. It did the same for Hubert Humphrey in the 1960s and 1970s. Probably it helped young Clinton to win his class presidencies and impress his Rhodes scholarship screening committee. But liberalism was headed for a crack-up. Its constituent elements were becoming unmanageable. By the late 1970s it doomed the presidency of another Snopes who had left jerkwater for the White House, Governor Jimmy Carter. By the time Clinton was running for president liberalism's lack of cohesion, its radicalized constituencies, and its many con artists were even more unmanageable than in Carter's day. Boy Clinton may very well be the last American president to be undone by the Liberal Crack-Up.

From the days of Franklin Roosevelt, liberalism has comprised a coalition that in leaps and fits has steadily radicalized and as a consequence fragmented. Once, its composition of urban bosses and Southern agrarians, labor unions and reform movements could be held together by the practical guile that was FDR's genius. Truman too could keep the zealots from tearing the coalition apart. But throughout the 1960s and into George McGovern's 1972 Democratic National Convention the tensions worsened. After 1972 the liberal coalition's radicalized constituents, and the prehensile operators who are forever exploiting them, got the upper hand.

Whereas Roosevelt's union leaders and urban bosses, and his Southern pols and mild reformers sought practical objective goals, the 1970s constituents of the liberal coalition had become rapacious about their objectives, even as they widened their promises to include efforts that few political movements had ever made. They promised to minister to their constituents' feelings. They promised to assuage the feminists' feelings of rage, the blacks' feelings of powerlessness, the environmentalists' feelings of ecological despair. What was equally reckless, they divided their constituencies into

ever more specific varieties of malcontents: gays, animal rights advocates, sufferers of certain disgusting diseases, health nuts. To each
they would give power, a slice of the federal budget, and self-esteem.
Liberalism devolved from coalition politics to interest group politics
to group therapy. And as in group therapy, or "group" as it is known
to initiates, each voice grew steadily more angry, self-centered, and
demanding of a limited reserve of attention.

Even had Boy Clinton possessed the character of George Washington and been brought up in Hyde Park, adopting the *Kultursmog*
of the 1990s as his idiom would have doomed him. The former liberal coalition, now a testy collection of left political neurotics com-
peting for the title of most victimized, oppressed, or marginalized,
is thoroughly ungovernable. Clinton, the most self-obsessed,
weepy, and self-dramatizing president in history is the perfect representative of his core constituency, and they are a horrible burden
to him. Just as he and his short-tempered spouse seem incapable of
serving any cause beyond the next election or their own shadily
ensured financial security, the neurotic left factions seem incapable
of committing themselves to any higher common cause beyond the
tremors of their own emotional disturbances.

Once elected president, the centrifugal forces of his Liberal
Crack-Up were upon Clinton. His sudden and ineffectual attempt
to lift the ban on homosexuals in the military won him the further
contempt of the military but no applause from the Republic's militant gays. As with so many of his compulsive core constituents, they
merely wanted more. Then his attempts to balance the rights of the
spotted owl against those of loggers aroused hostilities among environmentalists and loggers alike—and no votes from the owls. Even
when he raised grazing fees in the West the environmentalists were
not appeased.

Then there were the shrieks that attended so many of his (or
should I say Mrs. Clinton's) nominations. As many were left-wingers
from the 1960s they brought with them biographical entries offensive

to the American mainstream—and to other patients in "group." As an
indecisive therapist will fall victim to his group patients' fury, Clinton's irresolute responses often offended everyone.

Consider the confirmation controversy over Tara J. O'Toole's
nomination as assistant secretary of energy. She was a feminist,
which was unexceptionable, but during her confirmation hearings
senators discovered that she had been a member of something
called Northeast Feminist Scholars, a Marxist reading circle originally called Marxist-Feminist Group I.[2] The end result caused the
new president embarrassment and won him few friends even among
lady Marxists. Even more controversial was the row over the nomination of Roberta Achtenberg as assistant secretary for Fair Housing and Equal Opportunity. A militant lesbian, Achtenberg, while
serving as a San Francisco supervisor, attempted to deny United
Way funds to the Boy Scouts because they barred homosexual
scoutmasters and referred to God in their oath. Then there were
the controversies surrounding the comic Dr. Joycelyn Elders, Clinton's surgeon general. Her history of outbursts against conservative
religious groups and on behalf of abortion and sex education kept
her in hot water with mainstream Americans from the time of her
nomination until she was relieved of her command for espousing
the sex educators' latest progressive cause, masturbation. Through
it all Clinton was battered on all sides. Feminists and blacks were as
unhappy with him upon Elders's departure as they were when he
failed to stand by Lani Guinier.

The Guinier controversy demonstrated how in the 1990s a liberal
president, in attempting to please newer groups in the liberal coalition, could find himself under assault from older groups. Guinier's
racial preferences appealed to militant blacks but elicited strong
opposition from Jews and older civil libertarians. When Clinton
backed off from his nomination of her as assistant attorney general
for civil rights he ended up with Jews, civil libertarians, women,
blacks, and the Republican opposition sniping at him. A similar con-

troversy befell him at the State Department. In making his ambas-
sadorial appointments he attempted to fulfill the old progressive goal
of allotting ambassadorships to career diplomats rather than to fat-
cat supporters. The results began to offend women and minorities
once they noticed that their gender and sex quotas were not being
achieved. When Clinton attempted to placate them with affirmative
action appointments, he raised the ire of Secretary of State Christopher and of old-line liberals in the diplomatic corps.

By August of his first year in office, observers were at pains to
explain the administration's rocky start. The president was criticized for being too quick to break his promises. His reluctance to
stand by controversial nominees was noted. Yet as the *Washington
Post* explained, there was another cause "…there is a larger, more
likely culprit: the progressive interest groups." They, along with the
press, "have forced candidates to make detailed promises they can't
possibly keep."[3] Writing in the *Wall Street Journal*, Paul Gigot cited
another problem hamstringing Clinton. The Democratic party had
moved still further left. In particular, the Black Caucus was more
rigidly left and less accountable to the Democratic majority.[4] Then
came the 1994 rout of the Democrats, particularly the moderate
Democrats, and the Crack-Up actually intensified. As columnist
David Broder noted, "The Democrats do not have a unifying goal
strong enough to brake the dizzying decline of their institutional
structure."[5] It is a condition with a long history, going back to the
McGovern revels of 1972 and before. Broder was right—but the
Crack-Up had worsened, and one of its main victims was President
Clinton, now moving toward the center and getting walloped by the
Left, next moving left and getting little gratitude.

Clinton's last two years in office were even less effective than his
first two. His Republican opposition was stronger than it had been in
four decades. His left refused to accommodate any attempt by him at
moderation. The Left ambushed his promise to moderate his stand
on affirmative action. Soon his crime bill was stymied by the Black

Caucus's demand that capital punishment take into account racial quotas, endangering even more moderate Democratic seats in Congress. When Clinton donned his New Democrat garb and made a gesture toward prayer in public schools, he was publicly shellacked by such core constituents as civil libertarians, feminists, blacks, and People for the American Way. Halfway through 1995, under pressure from unions and consumerists, Clinton even seemed to back off on his advocacy of free trade. Mickey Kantor, his trade representative, was threatening the Japanese in terms redolent of H. Ross Perot. It had become time to "stand up for America," Kantor bellowed. The horrified yelps from the left group threatened the last Clinton initiative that amounted to anything other than mere blather.

In the 1970s Theodore H. White, the distinguished chronicler of presidential campaigns, fretted that American politics had taken on too many promises. He was a liberal but one from the old school, one who believed promises mattered. In attempting to make good on its politicians' promises, the country, White feared, would tear itself apart. Boy Clinton is from the New School, the 1960s generation of brightness, idealism, and, as we have seen, guff. He and his impudent peers have demonstrated that, unlike White, they do not think promises matter, or words, or even deeds. Boy Clinton is a carefree nihilist. Thus my taste for justice has been agreeably satisfied by the fact that his presidency has been torn apart by those very same promises he has so casually made. Mr. President, you encouraged fanatics and crooks. You needed a broader coalition.

NOTES

PROLOGUE

1. Ronald Koziol, "Informant's Murder Puts Heat on Authorities," *Chicago Tribune*, April 13, 1986, 5.
2. All quoted statements from Brown are from interviews conducted by the author on various occasions from 1995 to early 1996.
3. All quoted statements from Becky Brown are from an interview with the author on May 19, 1995.
4. "Interview of Ernest Jacobsen," Executive Session, U.S. House of Representatives, Sub-Committee on Crime, Committee on the Judiciary, Washington, D.C., March 11, 1988. This information has also been independently corroborated in an interview with an employee at Stennis Airfield.
5. Dwayne Brown, interview with author, May 11, 1995.
6. Micah Morrison, "Who Is Dan Lasater," *Wall Street Journal*, August 7, 1995, A12.
7. Ibid.
8. Greg Hitt, "Inquiry: S&L Laundered Drug Cash," *Arkansas Democrat-Gazette*, July 28, 1995, 8A.
9. Ambrose Evans-Pritchard, "Bill Clinton and the Chicken Man," *Sunday Telegraph*, October 9, 1994, 31.
10. Interview with author, June 15, 1995.
11. "Inside Washington," *Time*, October 31, 1994, 19.
12. Interview with author, June 15, 1995.
13. Text of Clinton's speech on his administration's progress, CNN, October 7, 1994.
14. Jamie Dettmer, "Aide Swears Clinton Knew," *Insight*, February 12, 1996, 13.
15. In his book, Rodriguez also says he visited with Don Gregg on August 8, 1986. Gregg was Vice President George Bush's national security adviser. The book makes clear that Rodriguez met with Gregg frequently during this period and even with Bush.

16. Felix I. Rodriguez and John Weisman, *Shadow Warrior: The CIA Hero of a Hundred Unknown Battles* (New York: Simon & Schuster, 1989), 246.

17. Stephen Engelberg, "Nominee Denies an Iran-Contra Link," *New York Times*, June 16, 1989, A3.

18. Editorial, "Investigate Mena," *Wall Street Journal*, July 10, 1995, A14.

CHAPTER 1

1. Chuck Conconi, ed., "Capital Comment," *Washingtonian*, July 1993, 7.

2. Jessica Lee, "War Aftermath: To the Victors Go the Polls," *USA Today*, March 1, 1991, 2A.

3. R.W. Apple, Jr., "The Inauguration: A Grand Beginning," *New York Times*, January 18, 1993, A1.

4. Jacqueline Trescott, "Maya Angelou's Pressure-Cooker Poem: The All-Consuming Task of Composing Lines for a Nation," *Washington Post*, January 16, 1993, G1.

5. R. Emmett Tyrrell, Jr., *The Conservative Crack-Up* (New York: Simon & Schuster, 1992), 206.

6. Sidney Blumenthal and Thomas Byrne Edsall, eds., *The Reagan Legacy* (New York: Pantheon Books, 1988), 251-253.

7. Jeffrey H. Birnbaum and Rick Watrzman, "Representative from Hillary Clinton's Brothers Ask Firms to Finance Parties," *Wall Street Journal*, January 14, 1993, A18.

8. Valerie Richardson, "Tinseltown Going Gaga Over Inauguration of Clinton," *Washington Times*, January 17, 1993, A4.

9. Ibid.

10. Jerry Brown had retired from politics in 1983, after bizarre pronunciamentos had earned him the sobriquet "Governor Moonbeam." Paul Tsongas had retired from the Senate in 1984, after being diagnosed as suffering from lymphoma. The other presidential hopefuls were Senator Bob Kerrey and Tom Harkin. Neither had shown much fizz.

11. Jack W. Germond and Jules Witcover, *Mad as Hell: Revolt at the Ballot Box, 1992* (New York: Warner Books, 1993), 175.

12. Ibid., 176.

13. Ibid., 185.

14. Charles F. Allen and Jonathan Portis, *The Comeback Kid: The Life and Career of Bill Clinton* (New York: Birch Lane Press, 1992), 194.

15. Germond and Witcover, *Mad as Hell*, 189.

16. Art Harris, "Gennifer Flowers," *Penthouse*, December 1992, 68.

17. Jeffrey H. Birnbaum, "Clinton Received a Vietnam Draft Deferment for an ROTC Program That He Never Joined," *Wall Street Journal*, February 6, 1992, A16.

18. Germond and Witcover, *Mad as Hell*, 193.

19. Ibid., 199.

20. Allen and Portis, *The Comeback Kid*, 202.

21. Ibid., 203.
22. Ibid., 236.
23. Germond and Witcover, *Mad as Hell*, 266.
24. Rowland Evans and Robert Novak, "Record Doesn't Support Claim That Clinton Backed Gulf War," *Chicago Sun-Times*, March 4, 1992, 29.
25. Allen and Portis, *The Comeback Kid*, 237.
26. And, incidentally, the vast majority of young men in his generation never served a day in uniform; according to the Vietnam Veterans of America Foundation, less than 30 percent of Clinton's generation served in the military. Perhaps 10 percent served in Vietnam.
27. Editorial, "The Liberal Face Off," *Wall Street Journal*, March 5, 1992, A14.
28. Kenneth R. Minogue, *The Liberal Mind* (New York: Vintage Books, 1963), 1.
29. Governor Bill Clinton, remarks at Georgetown University, Washington, D.C., October 23, 1991.
30. Governor Zell Miller, Speech at the 1992 Democratic National Convention, New York, July 13, 1992.
31. David Maraniss, "After Latest Repudiation, Clinton Hopes Past Is Prologue," *Washington Post*, November 27, 1994, A1.
32. Germond and Witcover, *Mad as Hell*, 342-345.
33. Ibid., 345.
34. William Jefferson Clinton, Speech at the 1992 Democratic National Convention, New York, July 16, 1992.
35. Ibid.
36. Ibid.
37. Albert Gore, Speech at the 1992 Democratic National Convention, New York, July 16, 1992.
38. Germond and Witcover, *Mad as Hell*, 384.

CHAPTER 2

1. Howard Fineman, "Clinton's Team: The Inner Circles," *Newsweek*, October 26, 1992, 28.
2. "A Yank at Oxford," *Sunday Times*, October 25, 1992, Features Section.
3. Yankelovich Clancy Schulman, "The 60's Generation: A Profile," April 1986.
4. Charles F. Allen and Jonathan Portis, *The Comeback Kid: The Life and Career of Bill Clinton* (New York: Birch Lane Press, 1992), 201.
5. "Washington Dateline," Associated Press, April 10, 1993.

CHAPTER 3

1. Zbigniew Pelczynski, interview, October 1993.
2. George Archibald, "Clinton at Oxford," *Washington Times*, October 25, 1992, A1.
3. Ibid.

4. Nick Rufford and David Leppard, "A Yank at Oxford," *Sunday Times*, October 25, 1992, Features Section.

5. John Ranelagh, *The Agency: The Rise and Decline of the CIA* (New York: Simon & Schuster, 1986), 251-252.

6. In itself this was an amusing and instructive story. The Marxist Kopolds still did not approve of the dissident Havel. Also there was a news report that the United States Embassy "nixed" a visit between the Kopolds and the president "after the extent of the family's communist connections became clear."

7. David Pryce-Jones, *The War That Never Was: The Fall of the Soviet Empire 1985-1991* (London: Weidenfeld & Nicholson, 1995), 74.

8. John Kenneth Galbraith, "Reflections: A Visit to Russia," *New Yorker,* September 3, 1984, 54-61.

9. Pelczynski, interview, October 1993.

10. Rufford and Leppard, "A Yank at Oxford," Features Section.

11. Kopold, interview with author, October 1993.

12. Ibid.

13. Ibid.

14. "Of Barricades and Ivory Towers: An Interview with T. W. Adorno," *Encounter*, September 1969, 63-65.

CHAPTER 4

1. Archibald Cox gave this notion its most famous formulation when after the student takeover of Columbia University he, as a Harvard law professor mediating with the students, called them "the best informed, most intelligent, and most idealistic generation this country has ever known." [*National Review*, September 16, 1988, 14.]

2. Fred Barnes, "Revenge of the Squares," *New Republic*, March 13, 1995, 23-26.

3. Kenneth Kenniston, *Youth and Dissent: The Rise of a New Opposition* (New York: Harcourt Brace Jovanovich, 1971), 312.

4. "Notable and Quotable: Bill Clinton," *Wall Street Journal*, January 21, 1993, A14.

5. "Educating Ira," *Economist*, May 15, 1993, 32.

6. Mickey Kaus, "The Policy Hustler: The Politicized Economy of Robert Reich," *New Republic*, December 7, 1992, 17.

7. Strobe Talbott, "Rethinking the Red Menace," *Time*, January 1, 1990, 7.

8. Kaus, "The Policy Hustler," 18-22.

9. Jonathan Alter, "Winter of Discontent," *Newsweek*, January 24, 1994, 23.

10. Elizabeth Drew, *On the Edge: The Clinton Presidency* (New York: Simon & Schuster, 1994), 65-66.

11. White House Press Briefing, February 16, 1993.

12. James Simon Kunen, *The Strawberry Statement: Notes of a College Revolutionary* (New York: Random House, 1969), 4.

13. Ulick O'Connor, *The Yeats Companion* (London: Mandarin Paperbacks, 1991), 11.

CHAPTER 5

1. Howard Fineman, "Big Times in Little Rock," *Newsweek*, January 24, 1994, 24.
2. L.J. Davis, "The Name of Rose," *New Republic*, April 4, 1994, 14.
3. Mario Vargas Llosa, *A Fish in Water: A Memoir* (New York: Farrar, Straus & Giroux, 1994), 32.
4. David Maraniss, *First in His Class: A Biography of Bill Clinton* (New York: Simon & Schuster, 1995), 394.
5. Michael Kelly, "The President's Past," *New York Times Magazine*, July 31, 1994, 20-22.
6. Donald Yacoe, "Defendants Plead Guilty in Pay-to-Play Case," *Bond Buyer*, March 6, 1995, 1.
7. James Ring Adams, "What's Up in Jakarta?" *American Spectator*, September 1995, 28-32.
8. Christopher Knowlton, "Of Bibles, Bonds, and Billions," *Fortune*, February 12, 1990, 112.
9. James Ring Adams, "Clinton's Bert Lance?" *American Spectator*, October 1992, 20.
10. Fineman, "Big Times in Little Rock," 24.
11. "Mrs. Clinton's Role in Lawsuit Settlement Questioned," Associated Press, February 3, 1994.
12. R. Emmett Tyrrell, Jr., "The Arkansas Drug Shuttle," *American Spectator*, August 1995, 17.
13. Greg Hitt, "Inquiry: S&L Laundered Drug Cash," *Arkansas Democrat-Gazette*, July 28, 1995, 8A.
14. John H. Fund, "Bred in a One-Party State," *Wall Street Journal*, August 15, 1994, A10.
15. Ibid.
16. Ibid.
17. John H. Fund, manuscript prepared for *Wall Street Journal* but not published.
18. Fund, "Bred in a One-Party State," A10.
19. Ibid.
20. Harry S. Ashmore, *Arkansas: A History* (New York: W.W. Norton & Co., 1984), 162-163.
21. Ibid., 192.
22. Gwen Ifill, "The 1992 Campaign: Clinton Defends His Character to Supporters," *New York Times*, April 21, 1992, A20.
23. Daniel Wattenberg, "Love and Hate in Arkansas," *American Spectator*, April/May 1994, 32.

24. Meredith L. Oakley, *On the Make: The Rise of Bill Clinton* (Washington: Regnery Publishing, Inc., 1994), 162.
25. Interestingly, William L. Webster, the former Missouri attorney general, pled guilty to felony charges of conspiracy and embezzlement in federal district court in 1993 for just this sort of misuse of state printing equipment, office resources, and state employees. [Virginia Young, "Webster Still Denies Injury Fund Misuse," *St. Louis Post-Dispatch*, June 5, 1993, 1A.]
26. Oakley, *On the Make*, 173-174.
27. Ibid., 327-328.
28. Ibid., 358.
29. James Ring Adams, "The Obstructionists," *American Spectator*, April/May 1994, 29-30.
30. Adams, "Clinton's Bert Lance?" 18-24.
31. Rex Nelson, interview with author, August 23, 1995.

CHAPTER 6

1. "Whitewater; Curiouser," *Economist*, July 9, 1994, 29.
2. Later the *American Spectator* reported that Hillary Clinton engaged in bank fraud in 1985 and engaged in a conspiracy to obstruct justice that extended up to January 5, 1996, when her billing records mysteriously materialized in the White House. The piece, written by James Ring Adams and me, claimed to be based on substantiating documents and telephone logs. Again, the press did not report the story, though Mrs. Clinton was being subpoenaed the week the piece was published. No one in the press even asked to see our documents!
3. Jeff Gerth, "Clintons Joined S&L Operator in an Ozark Real-Estate Venture," *New York Times*, March 8, 1992, 1.
4. Jeff Gerth with Stephen Engelberg, "Head of Failing S&L Helped Clinton Pay $50,000 Personal Debt in 1985," *New York Times*, December 15, 1993, B8.
5. Daniel Wattenberg, "Cash Voting," *American Spectator*, December 1994, 60.
6. Jerry Seper, "Clinton Loans Raise New Questions," *Washington Times*, July 15, 1994, A1.
7. Meredith L. Oakley, *On the Make: The Rise of Bill Clinton* (Washington: Regnery Publishing, Inc., 1994), 522.
8. Seper, "Clinton Loans," A1.
9. Sara Fritz, "S&L Funds Used For Clintons, Probers Say," *Los Angeles Times*, February 4, 1994, A28.
10. John Soloman, "Donations to Political Funds Were Used to Pay Off Clinton Loans," Associated Press, July 13, 1994.
11. "Washington Dateline," Associated Press, July 13, 1994.
12. Marilyn W. Thompson, "Clinton Loans for '90 Gubernatorial Race Leave Tangled Trail for Whitewater Probe," *Washington Post*, August 30, 1994, A1.

13. Marilyn W. Thompson, "Role of Arkansas Bank Assumes Added Importance in Whitewater," *Washington Post*, February 1, 1995, A2.
14. David Brock, "Living With the Clintons," *American Spectator*, January 1994, 25.
15. Lisa Schiffren, "Bill and Hillary at the Trough," *American Spectator*, August 1993, pp. 21-22, and Becky Brown, interview with author, May 19, 1995.
16. Brock, "Living With the Clintons," 24.
17. Paul Bedard, "Watkins Cites Pressure to Fire," *Washington Times*, January 18, 1996, A1.
18. David Brock, "The Travelgate Cover-Up," *American Spectator*, June 1994, 30.
19. Ann Devroy and Ruth Marcus, "Golf Outing Sinks White House Aide," *Washington Post*, May 27, 1994, A1.
20. Douglas Jehl, "Clinton Aide's Copter Bill Raised to $13,000," *New York Times*, May 29, 1994, 15.
21. General Accounting Office report of December 9, 1993 interview with David Watkins.
22. "White House Defends Hillary Styling Fees," *Washington Times*, May 29, 1993, A3.
23. Robert Novak, "She Continues to Seek Control," *Chicago Sun-Times*, March 14, 1994, 29.
24. Rowan Scarborough, "Passes Stalled by White House Aides," *Washington Times*, March 23, 1994, A1, and Frank J. Murray and Rowan Scarborough, "Clinton Demotes Associate Counsel," *Washington Times*, March 24, 1994, A1.
25. John McCaslin, "Inside the Beltway," *Washington Times*, June 28, 1994, A8.
26. David Maraniss, *First in His Class: A Biography of Bill Clinton* (New York: Simon & Schuster, 1995), 325.
27. Frank J. Murray and Jerry Seper, "Clinton Stalls on Records, Leach Charges," *Washington Times*, January 4, 1994, A1.
28. Jerry Seper, "Whitewater Figure Denied Immunity," *Washington Times*, November 28, 1994, A1.
29. Ruth Marcus, "Much Disregard for the Truth," *International Herald-Tribune*, August 23, 1994.
30. Elizabeth Drew, *On the Edge: The Clinton Presidency* (New York: Simon & Schuster, 1994), 384.
31. Susan Schmidt, "Prosecutor Building Case Against Ex-Justice Official," *Washington Post*, November 30, 1994, A2.
32. Drew, *On the Edge*, 379.
33. Hearing of the Senate Banking Committee, July 29, 1994.
34. Matt Labash, "Buy George," *American Spectator*, October 1994, 30-34.
35. This is an unusual cause of demise. According to the U.S. Consumer Product Safety Commission only an estimated seventy-five persons die in falls from buildings annually, and a third of them are children under ten.
36. "Whitewater; Curiouser," *Economist*, 29.

CHAPTER 7

1. Virginia Kelley, *Leading with My Heart* (New York: Simon & Schuster, 1994), 18.
2. David Maraniss, *First in His Class: A Biography of Bill Clinton* (New York: Simon & Schuster, 1994), 26.
3. Ward Pincus, "Oft-Wed Father Left Clinton with a Tangled Family Tree," *Arkansas Democrat-Gazette*, August 15, 1993, 15A.
4. Kelley, *Leading with My Heart*, 73.
5. Ibid., 74.
6. Ibid., 73, 110, 84.
7. Maraniss, *First in His Class*, 98.
8. Meredith Oakley, *On the Make: The Rise of Bill Clinton* (Washington: Regnery Publishing, Inc., 1994), 30.
9. For years Clinton and his mother recounted stories of Dude Clinton's fights with Virginia. They told of Billy at twelve calling the police. Never before had this dramatic altercation been mentioned, not in public, nor in Billy's divorce affidavit. All that is stated in that document is, "The last occasion in which I went to my mother's aid, when he was abusing my mother, he threatened to mash my face in if I took her part." And biographer Oakley adds, "Nothing in his testimony indicates that young Billy was able, or even attempted, to stop Roger Clinton's beatings." [Oakley, *On the Make*, 30.]
10. David S. Broder, "Beware the 'Trust' Deficit," *Washington Post*, February 24, 1993, A19.
11. George E. Condon, Jr., "Clinton Is Hearing 'No' from Far-Flung Corners," *San Diego Union-Tribune*, July 14, 1994, A11.
12. Elizabeth Drew, *On the Edge: The Clinton Presidency* (New York: Simon & Schuster, 1994), 158.
13. Associated Press, "President and Pope Discuss Differences," *Chicago Tribune*, June 2, 1994, 1.
14. Paul Bedard, "Yeltsin's 'Nyet' Bruises Clinton As Summit Ends," *Washington Times*, July 11, 1994, A1.
15. Ann Devroy, "Clinton Finds No Explanation to Aide's Death; Probes Continuing On Apparent Suicide," *Washington Post*, July 23, 1993, A4.
16. Frank J. Murray and Michael Hedges, "'Rock of Gibraltar'; Close Aide's Suicide Leaves President, Staff Puzzled," *Washington Times*, July 22, 1993, A1.
17. Devroy, "Clinton Finds No Explanation," A4.
18. Daniel Wattenberg, "Love and Hate in Arkansas," *American Spectator*, April/May 1994, 33.
19. Jack Nelson, "Angry Clinton Rebukes His Whitewater Critics," *Los Angeles Times*, December 21, 1995, A1.
20. Douglas Jehl, "Job Plans of Clinton Aides Renew Debate on Lobbying," *New York Times*, December 8, 1993, A22.
21. Editorial, "Mr. Clinton Spins the Lobby Door," *New York Times*, December 9, 1993, A30.

22. "The Whitewater Inquiry; Transcript of President's News Conference on the Whitewater Affair," *New York Times*, March 25, 1994, A18.

23. Douglas Jehl, "Clinton Calls Show to Assail Press, Falwell and Limbaugh," *New York Times*, June 25, 1994, A1.

24. Reuters, "Excerpts From Clinton's Comments on Cynicism and the Press," *New York Times*, June 25, 1994, 12.

25. Jonathan Schell, "Haircut: A Tale with a Life of Its Own," *Newsday*, July 18, 1993, 31.

26. Jehl, "Clinton Calls Show," A1.

27. Kelley, *Leading with My Heart*, 14.

28. Betty Glad, *Jimmy Carter: In Search of the Great White House* (New York: W.W. Norton & Co., 1980), 101.

29. Adam Meyerson, "Mr. Kaplan, Tear Down this Wall," *Policy Review*, Fall 1993, 4.

30. Ibid.

CHAPTER 8

1. During his 1974 challenge to Hammerschmidt, Clinton was referred to as "the boy" by friend and foe alike. [David Maraniss, *First in His Class: A Biography of Bill Clinton* (New York: Simon & Schuster, 1995), 334.]

2. Michiko Kakutani, "Retracing a Path That Led to the Presidential Trail," *New York Times*, February 10, 1995, C30.

3. Meredith L. Oakley, *On the Make: The Rise of Bill Clinton* (Washington: Regnery Publishing, Inc., 1994), 128.

4. Richard Reeves, *President Kennedy: Profile of Power* (New York: Simon & Schuster, 1993), 14.

5. Frequently, I have noticed the Chronic Campaigner has a pushy, doting mother; he is, upon careful inspection, often a mama's boy.

6. This was her cause before she ever had a child. Then after she paused to have one—relying on the state of Arkansas to provide a nanny—she became ever more authoritative on the subject of children's rights and their claims against their parents, at least against those parents who stayed home to raise them.

7. Gwen Ifill, "Clinton Resists Being Labeled a Liberal," *New York Times*, July 28, 1992, A11.

8. Martha Sherrill, "Hillary Clinton's Inner Politics," *Washington Post*, May 6, 1993, D1.

9. John Brummett, *High Wire: From the Back Woods to the Beltway: The Education of Bill Clinton* (New York: Hyperion, 1994), 282.

10. Bill Clinton, speech before the American Society of Newspaper Editors, Dallas, April 7, 1995.

11. Thomas J. McGrew, "FTC Moves to Political Left," *Legal Times*, April 18, 1983, 13.

12. John F. Harris, "Clinton Asks Support for Policy Review," *Washington Post*, April 9, 1995, A11.

13. "HUD to End Inquiries Into Protests of Its Proposals," *New York Times*, September 3, 1994, 7.

14. Bob Woodward, *The Agenda: Inside the Clinton White House* (New York: Simon & Schuster, 1994), 247.

15. Lisa Schiffren, "Bill and Hillary at the Trough," *American Spectator*, August 1993, 20-23.

16. Woodward, *The Agenda*, 32.

17. William H. Honan, "Books, Books and More Books: Clinton an Omnivorous Reader," *New York Times*, December 10, 1992, C15.

18. Michael Duffy, "The State of Bill Clinton," *Time*, February 7, 1994, 26.

19. Reuters, "Clinton Recalls Pickup Trucks and Dating," February 8, 1994.

20. Leah Garchik, "He's a Sentimental So and So," *San Francisco Chronicle*, June 21, 1993, B5.

21. Steve Marshall, "Emergency Officials Like FEMA Response," *USA Today*, July 16, 1995, 8A.

22. Gwen Ifill, "Clinton Defends His Character to Supporters, *New York Times*, April 21, 1992, A20.

23. Oakley, *On the Make*, 48.

24. Douglas Jehl, "Growing Up in the Melting Pot Called Hope, Ark." *New York Times*, July 7, 1994, A12.

25. Maureen Dowd, "Beached," *New York Times*, June 19, 1994, Section 6, 18.

CHAPTER 9

1. Connie Bruck, "Hillary the Pol," *New Yorker*, May 30, 1994, 60.

2. Ibid.

3. Leslie Bennetts, "Pinning Down Hillary," *Vanity Fair*, June 1994, 109.

4. Martha Sherrill, "The Education of Hillary Clinton," *Washington Post*, January 11, 1993, B2.

5. Becky Brown, interview with author, May 19, 1995.

6. David Maraniss, *First in His Class: A Biography of Bill Clinton* (New York: Simon & Schuster, 1995), 319-320.

7. Ruth M. Adams, introduction for Hillary D. Rodham, 91st commencement of Wellesley College, Wellesley, Massachusetts, May 31, 1969.

8. Martha Sherrill, "The Rising Lawyer's Detour to Arkansas," *Washington Post*, January 12, 1993, B2.

9. Hillary D. Rodham, address, 91st commencement of Wellesley College, Wellesley, Massachusetts, May 31, 1969.

10. Michael Shain, Doug Vaughan, and Pat Wechsler, "Inside New York," *Newsday*, May 4, 1993, 13.

11. Rodham, Wellesley address, May 31, 1969.

12. Ibid.

13. James F. Blumstein and James Phelan, "Jamestown Seventy," *Yale Review of Law and Social Action*, Spring 1970, 55.

14. Ibid., 58.

15. Daniel Wattenberg, "The Lady Macbeth of Little Rock," *American Spectator*, August 1992, 28.
16. Ibid.
17. Ibid.
18. Ibid., 29.
19. Donnie Radcliffe, *Hillary Rodham Clinton: A First Lady for Our Time* (New York: Warner Books, 1993), 39, 42.
20. Maraniss, *First in His Class*, 257.
21. Rodham, Wellesley address, May 31, 1969.
22. Herb Caen, "Poor Herbert's Almanac," *San Francisco Chronicle*, November 12, 1992, B1.
23. Maraniss, *First in His Class*, 255.
24. Sara Rimer, "Columbia's Rebels Retake Campus for a 20th Reunion," *New York Times*, April 25, 1988, B1.
25. Ibid.
26. "All Things Considered," National Public Radio, August 11, 1993.
27. Laura Mansnerus, "After Her 'Public Torture,' Lani Guinier Finds Acclaim and 'Solidarity' in Many Places," *New York Times*, September 3, 1993, A17.
28. Leslie Bennetts, "Pinning Down Hillary," *Vanity Fair*, June 1994, 109.
29. Rimer, "Columbia's Rebels," B1.
30. Ibid.
31. Ibid.
32. Martha Sherrill, "The Retooling of the Political Wife," *Washington Post*, January 13, 1993, D2.
33. Maraniss, *First in His Class*, 321.
34. Meredith Oakley, *On The Make: The Rise of Bill Clinton* (Washington: Regnery Publishing, Inc., 1994), 497.
35. Bruck, "Hillary the Pol," 66.
36. Sherrill, "The Retooling of the Political Wife," D2.
37. Maureen Dowd, "Hillary Rodham Clinton Strikes a New Pose and Multiplies Her Images," *New York Times*, December 12, 1993, E3.
38. Alice Thomson, "The Power Perm," *Times* (London), July 7, 1993, Features Page.
39. Her husband defended the name revision to a *New Yorker* writer thus: "She told me she was nine years old when she decided she would keep her own name when she got married." Youth of the 1960s take the judgments of a nine-year-old seriously [Bruck, "Hillary the Pol," 64.]
40. Jill Gerston, "A Closetful of Classics," *Los Angeles Times*, November 20, 1992, E1.
41. Ernie Freda, "Washington in Brief," *Atlanta Journal and Constitution*, February 3, 1993, A4.
42. Rebecca Borders, "Bill's Cousin Cornelius?" *American Spectator*, May 1996, 27.
43. Lois Romano, "The Clintons' House of Cards," *Washington Post*, December 3, 1993, G3.

44. Michael Kelly, "Saint Hillary," *New York Times Magazine*, May 23, 1993, 63.

45. Maureen Dowd, "Hillary Clinton Says She Once Wanted to Be a Marine," *New York Times*, June 15, 1994, B8.

46. Martha Sherrill, "Hillary Clinton's Inner Politics," *Washington Post*, May 6, 1993, D2.

47. Jeffrey Stinson, "Hillary Clinton Takes a Role as Husband's Closest Adviser," Gannett, December 26, 1992.

48. Evans & Novak, "Posts Held Hostage by Diversity Cops," *San Diego Union-Tribune*, January 23, 1993, B8.

49. David Brock, "Where Was Hillary?" *American Spectator*, September 1994, 21-24.

50. "Hillary Clinton Benefited from Shady Deal in Old People's Homes," *Sunday Times*, February 13, 1994, 1.

51. Brock, "Where Was Hillary?" 23-24.

52. As McDougal remembered the negotiations to the *Los Angeles Times* in 1993, Governor Clinton jogged by his office one morning in 1985, said personal costs had become onerous, and asked that Rodham be put on retainer. "McDougal said he recalled the event vividly because he was so uncomfortable in the meeting—not over the retainer issue, but because throughout that morning conference, Clinton sat sweating in McDougal's new leather desk chair, an expensive gift from his wife," chronicles the *Times* in its November 7, 1993 edition.

53. Neil A. Lewis, "Top Justice Official Testifies of Limits on Foster Inquiry," *New York Times*, August 11, 1995, A1.

54. Sherrill, "The Retooling of the Political Wife," D2.

55. James Ring Adams and R. Emmett Tyrrell, Jr., "The Case Against Hillary," *American Spectator*, February 1996, 26.

56. Hillary Rodham Clinton, *It Takes a Village: And Other Lessons Children Teach Us* (New York: Simon & Schuster, 1996), 319.

57. Christopher Hitchens, "Minority Report," *Nation*, February 21, 1994, 223.

58. Bruck, "Hillary the Pol," 76.

59. Lynn Sweet, "Rosty Twinkles Over 'Marvelous Witness,'" *Chicago Sun-Times*, September 29, 1993, 6.

60. Paul Bedard, "Hillary's Health Care Reform Task Force Cost $13.8 Million," *Washington Times*, November 10, 1995, A3.

61. Marian Burros, "Hillary Clinton Seeking to Soften a Harsh Image," *New York Times*, January 10, 1995, A1.

62. Bruck, "Hillary the Pol," 88.

63. Barton Gellman, "Clinton's Relationship with the Military Hurting, but Healing," *Houston Chronicle*, April 4, 1993, A14.

CHAPTER 10

1. David Brock, "Living with the Clintons," *American Spectator*, January 1994, 21.

2. Michael Duffy, "The State of Bill Clinton," *Time*, February 7, 1994, 24.

3. "The conflicting, and often contradictory, forces within contemporary liberalism," is how Thomas Byrne Edsall diagnosed the condition. [*New York Review of Books*, October 7, 1993, 6.]

4. Richard L. Berke, "States' Top Democrats Get Appeal for Patience," *New York Times*, June 27, 1993, 22.

5. Ann Devroy, "A Bonding Experience at Camp David," *Washington Post*, February 5, 1993, A1.

6. Deborah Orin, "A Cigar?" *New York Post*, February 3, 1993, 4.

7. Martin Sieff and Ronald A. Taylor, "Clinton Team Denies Outreach to Vietnam," *Washington Times*, February 5, 1993, A1.

8. Keith Bradsher, "A Clinton Aide's Farewell to Clients: Keep in Touch," *New York Times*, February 5, 1993, A1.

9. Ann Devroy, "Clinton Fires White House 'Worker Bees,'" *Washington Post*, February 7, 1993, A19.

10. Micky Kaus, "Washington Diarist," *New Republic*, March 7, 1994, 46.

11. Leslie H. Gelb, "Clinton As Carter?" *New York Times*, April 25, 1993, Section 4, 17.

12. Michael Kinsley, "Clinton's Trouble," *New Republic*, August 9, 1993, 6.

13. Dan Balz and Ann Devroy, "First Days Offer Clinton 'Powerful Lessons,'" *Washington Post*, January 31, 1993, A1.

14. David Von Drehle, "Beginner's Luck or President's Prowess? Dazzled Capitol Wonders if Clinton Can Keep Lighting Up the Board," *Washington Post*, March 26, 1993, A1.

15. Ibid.

16. George F. Will, "'Details to Follow,'" *Washington Post*, April 4, 1993, C7.

17. Douglas Jehl, "Clinton Nominations Come Slowly and with Many Setbacks," *New York Times*, January 30, 1994, 20.

18. United States Department of State List of Chiefs of Mission as of December 31, 1993.

19. Frank Gaffney, "The Meltdown of Security Clearances," *Washington Times*, March 29, 1994, A15.

20. Rowan Scarborough, "Passes Stalled by White House Aide," *Washington Times*, March 24, 1994, A1.

21. Tom Raum, "Washington Today: Passing the Torch and the Problems," Associated Press, January 20, 1993.

22. Mark Stencel, "Verbatim," *Washington Post*, January 21, 1993, A21.

23. Ann Devroy, "Clinton Says He Bears 'Full Responsibility' for the Outcome," *Washington Post*, April 21, 1993, A15.

24. Anne Gowan and Sean Piccoli, "But Was It 100 Days that Looked Like America?" *Washington Times*, April 28, 1993, E1.

25. William Lowther, "Eyes on Clinton's Ear," *Mail on Sunday*, April 11, 1993, 5.

26. Mr. and Mrs. L. D. Brown, interview with author, May 1995.

27. Lois Romano, "The Reliable Source," *Washington Post*, April 22, 1993, D3.

28. Margaret Carlson, "Remaking of the President," *Time*, May 17, 1993, 41.

29. Ibid.
30. Richard Benedetto, "55% Approve of Clinton's Performance," *USA Today*, April 28, 1993, 1A.
31. Thomas L. Friedman and Maureen Dowd, "Amid Setbacks, Clinton Team Seeks to Shake Off the Blues," *New York Times*, April 25, 1993, A1.
32. David S. Broder, "Panetta: President in Trouble on Hill," *Washington Post*, April 27, 1993, A1.
33. Michael Duffy, "That Sinking Feeling," *Time*, June 7, 1993, 25.
34. Lloyd Grove, "Clinton's Bad Case of the Blah-Blahs," *Washington Post*, May 12, 1993, B1.
35. Curiously, weeks later—June 30 to be precise—a writer for *Newsday* was inspired to refute charges that Air Force One's long delay on the runway at LAX inconvenienced air traffic, though *Newsday*'s writer admitted that two runways were closed down for almost an hour and he quoted an air-traffic controller stating the obvious, namely, that Clinton's haircut was an immense inconvenience. Equally curious, a year later, on June 24, Boy Clinton amid a self-pitying lamentation over his foul treatment by the press uttered this stretcher: "I could give you a lot of examples. A year ago there was a widely reported story that I kept airplane traffic waiting an hour in Los Angeles to get a haircut in an airport. That wasn't true either." [Reuters, "Excerpts from Clinton's Comments on Cynicism and the Press," *New York Times*, June 25, 1994, 12.] Well, what "wasn't true either"? That he got the haircut? That he snarled air traffic? Here is a classic if trivial example of Boy Clinton's urge for obfuscation; a full year after the fact he still is doggedly at work enshrouding in confusion a straightforward example of his impulsiveness.
36. Lois Romano, "The Reliable Source," *Washington Post*, May 18, 1993, E3.
37. Michael Kelly, "Saint Hillary," *New York Times Magazine*, May 23, 1993, 22.
38. The press's urban sophisticates tittered when the White House revealed that the Clintons had hired a "distant cousin." Once again, the Arkansas Snopes may have had the laugh on the press. Careful investigation shows no relationship between him and Cornelius. Documents from David Watkins and Vince Foster show both men to have been surprised when the White House claimed Cornelius as a Clinton cousin. The only Arkansas relation of Cornelius that Rebecca Borders could find in writing about her in the May 1996 issue of the *American Spectator* was a grandmother. Borders concludes that the twenty-four year–old blonde was no cousin to Bill but was, nonetheless, very "close."
39. Paul Bedard, "Watkins Cites Pressure to Fire," *Washington Times*, January 18, 1996, A1.
40. Duffy, "That Sinking Feeling," 22.
41. Laura A. Kiernan, "Running on TV: Clinton Makeup Job," *Boston Globe*, May 27, 1993, 17.
42. Thomas L. Friedman, "Clinton, Saluting Vietnam Dead, Finds Old Wound Is Slow to Heal," *New York Times*, June 1, 1993, A1.
43. Lawrence McQuillan, "Gergen Brings Experience and Different Views," Reuters, May 29, 1993.

44. "War, Crises, Politics... and 3 Quick Holes," *New York Times*, June 3, 1993, A20.
45. Michael Kelly, "Words and Deed; The Guinier Affair Aggravates Clinton's Credibility Problem," *New York Times*, June 6, 1993, E1.
46. John Lancaster, "Accused of Ridiculing Clinton, General Faces Air Force Probe," *Washington Post*, June 8, 1993, A1.
47. Elaine Sciolino, "Arm Bosnians? Clinton Didn't Mean It," *New York Times*, June 23, 1993, A6.
48. Jane Gross, "Clinton's Lost Half-Brother? To Neighbors, He's Just Leon," *New York Times*, June 22, 1993, A12.
49. "President Finally Speaks to Man Claiming Kinship," *New York Times*, June 26, 1993, A6.
50. Richard Morin and Ann Devroy, "President's Popularity Continues to Weaken," *Washington Post*, June 30, 1993, A1.
51. R.W. Apple, Jr., "The Guinier Battle; President Blames Himself for Furor Over Nominee," *New York Times*, June 5, 1993, A1.
52. Ibid.
53. Richard Reeves, *President Kennedy: Profile of Power* (New York: Simon & Schuster, 1993), 52.
54. Duffy, "The State of Bill Clinton," 24.
55. James Simon Kunen, *The Strawberry Statement: Notes of a College Revolutionary* (New York: Random House, 1969), 27.
56. In 1995 documents came to light revealing that even the president had a hand in Thomason's grab for the Travel Office. Clinton recommended Thomason's company, TRM, to White House aides with the notation "these guys are sharp."
57. Frank J. Murray and Michael Hedges, "'Rock of Gibraltar,'" *Washington Times*, July 22, 1993, A1.
58. David Von Drehle, "Friend Who had Clinton's Ear and Heart," *Washington Post*, July 24, 1993, A1, and Ann Devroy, "Clinton Finds No Explanation to Aide's Death," *Washington Post*, July 23, 1993, A4.
59. Suspicions about Foster's frame of mind were transformed into suspicions about the circumstances of his death as more evidence of government bungling came out and Special Prosecuter Robert Fiske's report on the death seemed to doctor some evidence. For instance, it made assertions about the testimony of Foster's executive assistant, Deborah Gorham, that contradicted her FBI statement. Suspicions gave way to conspiracy theories when discrepancies among official accounts of the condition of the corpse became apparent. Then, too, for years there remained straightforward questions that never got answered: the origin of the gun, why the suicide's fingerprints were not on it, how it remained neatly in his hand after recoiling from the soft palate at the back of his mouth where he fired it, and why, on recoil, it did not damage his teeth. Supposedly, Foster had walked seven hundred feet into a park, reclined on a hillside, and fired that gun in his mouth. Yet the bullet was not found nor were skull chips and

brain matter, and the soles of his shoes were free of soil and grass clippings. Witnesses disputed the amount of blood found and other grisly details such as the position of an exit wound. All in all there continued to be reasons to doubt that the truth was getting out.

60. Douglas Jehl, "Without a Home, Clinton Is a Rolling Stone," *New York Times*, July 18, 1993, A1.

61. Once our Troopergate story was published Clinton apparatchik Betsey Wright persuaded Ferguson to deny the contents of the first call through an affidavit signed not by him but by his lawyer. It was a maneuver that confused many in the press into thinking that the president had never offered jobs for anything. His second call offering jobs for information was never addressed. Two days after Ferguson's lawyer promulgated his affidavit Ferguson refuted its contents, repeating to the *Los Angeles Times* that Clinton had discussed federal jobs for Perry and himself. Of course by then the press's confusion was beyond repair.

62. Michael Isikoff and Ruth Marcus, "Clinton Tried to Derail Troopers' Sex Allegations," *Washington Post*, December 21, 1993, A1.

63. Ruth Marcus, "First Lady Lashes Out at Allegations," *Washington Post*, December 22, 1993, A1.

64. Terrence Hunt, "Clinton Denies Troopers' Sex Allegations, Calls Them 'Outrageous,'" Associated Press, December 22, 1993.

65. William C. Rempel and Douglas Frantz, "Troopers Say Clinton Sought Silence on Personal Affairs," *Los Angeles Times*, December 21, 1993, A1.

66. David Maraniss, *First in His Class: A Biography of Bill Clinton* (New York: Simon & Schuster, 1995), 440-441.

67. Editorial, "First in His Class," *New Republic*, February 27, 1995, 9.

68. Brock, "Living with the Clintons," 18-30.

69. Sally Quinn, "Clinton's 'Hidden' Handicap," *Washington Post*, January 30, 1994, C1.

70. Robert Shogan, "Ex-Arkansas State Worker Says Clinton Harassed Her," *Los Angeles Times*, February 12, 1994, A21.

CHAPTER 11

1. Peter J. Steinberger, "Why Clinton Will Lose," *Wall Street Journal*, November 29, 1995, A14.

2. Clifford Krauss, "Energy Nominee Faces Battle on Feminist Group," *New York Times*, July 17, 1993, 6.

3. Christopher Georges, "The Devil in the Details," *Washington Post*, August 15, 1993, C2.

4. Paul Gigot, "Why Liberals Should Thank Clarence Thomas," *Wall Street Journal*, July 8, 1994, A10.

5. David S. Broder, "The Candidate Problem," *Washington Post*, November 8, 1995, A17.

APPENDIX A

Mr. J.A. Compton
Dept. S Rm. 4N20
P.O. Box 1925
Washington, D.C. 20013

Dear Sir:

I am writing in regards to an advertisement recently seen in the New York Times,(4-1-54), advertising opportunities available for employment with your agency.

Currently employed in the Executive Protection Unit of the State Police, State of Arkansas, I am a twenty-nine year old white male with experience in the criminal justice system of the state totaling ten years. My first contact with the process came in employment in 1974 with the Department of Corrections. Since then my work has included service with one of the larger municipal police agencies and most recently with this department. My principal activities have been in the area of narcotic and dangerous drug enforcement. This has included both covert conspiracy and diversion investigations as well as covert operations including local, state and federal level violators.

At a point approximately two years ago in my tenure with this agency I received an opportunity to enter the executive protection area through service with the Governor's Security Unit. Having received college hours in Political Science along with Criminal Justice I had an abiding interest in the inner workings of government. Since there is a natural closeness to the everyday activities of government I have been afforded a unique chance to see this first hand not only at the state level but the national as well. In travelling with the two Governors I have served under I have been able to use my foreign language skills, especially Spanish, and have further developed my interest in foreign affairs especially United States-Soviet relations. In this area I have furthered my language capabilities by earning college credits in the Russian language including understanding of the Cyrillic alphabet.

During my tenure in the protection unit I have remained involved in the drug enforcement area as well. While in enforcement I received education that I would from the Department of Justice's Drug Enforcement Administration, including basic and advanced Narcotics and Dangerous Drugs as well as conspiracy and diversion schools. While in the investigative school I received the Administration's Scholastic Achievement Award in Miami, Florida.

Governor Bill Clinton of Arkansas recently appointed me to a state committee studying alcohol, dangerous drug and substance abuse. I am currently serving on this committee concerning the state of abuse and our aggressive or educational program to combat it in our state. Concerning this area I have authored several position papers and continue to write in other areas.

(A) Letter trooper L. D. Brown wrote to the CIA in response to a CIA employment advertisement and at the suggestion of his boss, Governor Bill Clinton.

April 3,1984
Page two

Governor Clinton has been an inspiration for me to further my
career in government service and in particular to explore the
possibilities of employment with your agency. My language skills,
enforcement backround in narcotics operations, coupled with my
personal association with government as well as participation
in it have also led me to this correspondence. Your consideration
and return correspondence would be appreciated.

Thank you,

[signature]

Larry Douglass Brown
Little Rock, Arkansas

CENTRAL INTELLIGENCE AGENCY
SOUTHWEST PERSONNEL REPRESENTATIVE
PO BOX 50611 DALLAS, TEXAS 75250
214-767-8850

19 April 1984

Mr. Larry D. Brown
4724 Fairlee Drive
Little Rock, Arkansas 72209

Dear Mr. Brown:

Thank you for your recent expression of interest in the employment opportunities of the Central Intelligence Agency.

Your personal data has been reviewed and it appears appropriate to begin the next step in our application process. Please find enclosed an admission ticket for our Professional Applicant Test Battery (PAT-B), to be administered on 5 May 1984 at the University of Arkansas at Little Rock.

I would appreciate a collect call from you to confirm the above test date.

Again, thank you for your interest in our organization. I look forward to receiving your call.

Sincerely yours,

Kent Cargile

Personnel Representative /sc
Central Intelligence Agency

Enclosure

(B) Correspondence from CIA Personnel Representative Kent Cargile to L. D. Brown.

CENTRAL INTELLIGENCE AGENCY
SOUTHWEST PERSONNEL REPRESENTATIVE
PO BOX 50811   DALLAS, TEXAS 75250
214-767-5890

28 June 1984

Mr. Larry D. Brown
4724 Fairlee Drive
Little Rock, Arkansas 72209

Dear Mr. Brown:

I would appreciate a collect call from you, at your earliest
convenience, to discuss the status of your application.

Sincerely yours,

Kent M. Cargile
Kent M. Cargile
Southwest Personnel Representative

CENTRAL INTELLIGENCE AGENCY
SOUTHWEST PERSONNEL REPRESENTATIVE
PO BOX 50611 DALLAS, TEXAS 75250
214-767-8850

5 September 1984

Mr. Larry D. Brown
4724 Fairlee Drive
Little Rock, Arkansas 72209

Dear Mr. Brown:

Your application papers for employment with the Central Intelligence Agency have been forwarded to our Headquarters in Washington, D.C. for consideration.

After adequate time for review, you will receive definitive word from Headquarters as to whether or not there are presently any employment opportunities fitting your background and qualifications.

If you receive a tentative job offer, you may expect a lengthy period of processing before a firm offer will be made. During this period, you will be invited to visit our Washington Headquarters, at government expense, where you will be interviewed by officials of the component interested in employing you. You will also complete the remainder of your processing.

I am pleased to nominate you for employment with the Central Intelligence Agency. Whether we have an opening at this time or not, I enjoyed talking with you and wish you only the best in the future.

Sincerely yours,

Southwest Personnel Representative
Central Intelligence Agency

Appendix A

PROFESSIONAL APPLICANT TEST BATTERY

Examination Admission Ticket

EXAMINATION DATE · 5 May 1984

TEST CENTER   Room A101, Student Services Building, University of
Arkansas at Little Rock, 33rd and University Streets

Ms. Fanye Porter, Test Administrator

KENT M. CARGILE   317

THIS TICKET MUST BE PRESENTED FOR ADMISSION

CANDIDATE'S SIGNATURE

(C) Examination Admission Ticket given to L. D. Brown to take
Professional Applicant Test as a requisite of his entry into the CIA.

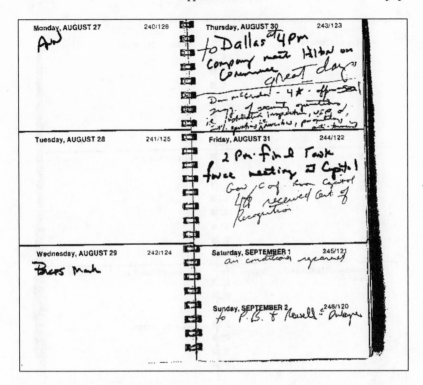

(D) A selection of L. D. Brown's Day Books. Note 30 August, the day he meets with "Dan McGruder" in Dallas. Later Brown returns to the entry and notes the name of Barry Seal as his contact. Note also Brown's scrawl in Cyrillic of approximate dates of flights, 23 October and 24 December.

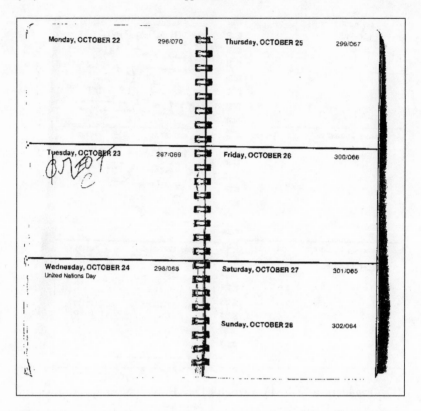

Monday, OCTOBER 22   296/070   Thursday, OCTOBER 25   299/067

Tuesday, OCTOBER 23   297/069   Friday, OCTOBER 26   300/066

Wednesday, OCTOBER 24   298/068
United Nations Day

Saturday, OCTOBER 27   301/065

Sunday, OCTOBER 28   302/064

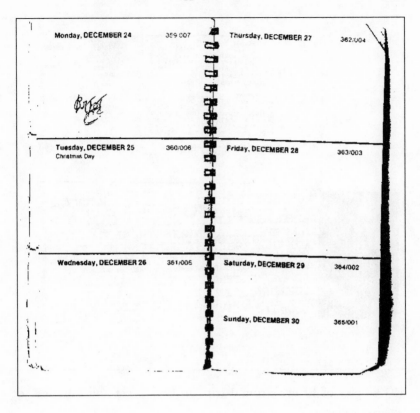

Monday, DECEMBER 24 359/007

Tuesday, DECEMBER 25 360/006
Christmas Day

Wednesday, DECEMBER 26 361/005

Thursday, DECEMBER 27 362/004

Friday, DECEMBER 28 363/003

Saturday, DECEMBER 29 364/002

Sunday, DECEMBER 30 365/001

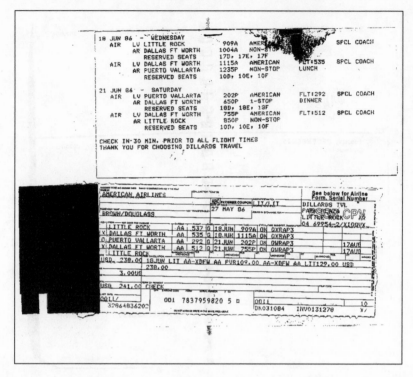

(E) Copies of Brown's round-trip airplane ticket and itinerary to Puerto Vallarta.

1995   **L.D. BROWN GRAND JURY STATEMENT**

My name is Larry Douglass "L.D." Brown. I was born in 1955 in Greenville, Mississippi. When I was very young, my family moved to Pine Bluff, Arkansas, where I grew up. I attended the University of Arkansas for one year, and later, I attended the University of Arkansas, at Pine Bluff and at Little Rock.

My first law enforcement job was at the Tucker State Prison. I worked there as a field sergeant for approximately three years. In about 1977, I was hired as a police officer with the Pine Bluff Police Department.

In 1980, I was hired as an Arkansas State Trooper. I have been an Arkansas State Trooper since that time. My present rank is Corporal. I currently am assigned to the highway patrol.

Back in 1980, when I first started as an Arkansas State Trooper, I worked on narcotics cases in St. Francis County. Later, I was transferred to Little Rock, where I continued to work narcotics cases.

In approximately August 1982, I began working on the Governor's security detail. At that time, the Governor was Frank White.

In 1982, the Governor's security detail consisted of about 11 Arkansas State Troopers whose job it was (1) to provide security to the Governor at the Mansion; (2) drive or otherwise provide transportation to the Governor when he traveled outside the Mansion; (3) provide security to the Governor when he appeared in public; and (4) provide other appropriate services to the Governor's immediate family, such as security and transportation.

(F) L. D. Brown's Grand Jury statement given under oath.

Troopers on the security detail might also be responsible for answering phones on occasion at the Mansion, or performing routine errands for the Governor and/or his family, like delivering a speech or picking up packages and things like that.

Members of the Governor's security detail were assigned in shifts. There were always two troopers working during each shift, except for the midnight shift, which involved only one trooper. The Governor's security detail would travel with the Governor, and/or his family, outside of Little Rock, or even outside of the state.

I worked for Frank White's security detail until he lost his bid for re-election to Bill Clinton. In about December 1982, the Clintons began the process of moving into the Governor's Mansion. I believe that this was the first time that I met Governor Clinton and his family. Governor Clinton decided that he would like me to stay on his security detail, and I agreed.

In January 1983, I drove Governor Clinton to his inauguration. Many of the troopers on the security detail did not like to travel. I did. As a result, I volunteered frequently to accompany Governor Clinton whenever he traveled outside Little Rock. I soon developed a close relationship with Governor Clinton and Mrs. Clinton too.

When Frank White was Governor, he usually had a trooper with him whenever he left the Governor's Mansion. Bill Clinton was not like that. Governor Clinton often would leave the Mansion without an escort.

I worked on Governor Clinton's Security detail until June

2

1985. During that time, I became very close to the Governor and his family. No other trooper on the detail was as close to the Clintons as I was during that time.

I do not intend to discuss here the personal matters of the Clintons. Because of my relationship with Governor and Mrs. Clinton, I saw and learned of various private matters.

I met my wife while working on Governor Clinton's security detail. She was employed in the Mansion as Chelsea Clinton's nanny when I met her. Later, I was able to help my wife's mother get a job at the Governor's Mansion as well.

During the time I worked for Governor Clinton's security detail, I observed Governor Clinton leave the Mansion and go jogging. Governor Clinton frequently went for a run without any troopers accompanying him. Sometimes, he would finish his run at some other location in Little Rock and call back to the detail to pick him up.

In June 1985, my relationship with Governor Clinton changed. At that time, I had had conversations with Governor and Mrs. Clinton about being appointed to the position of Assistant Director at the state crime lab. During a series of conversations with Governor and Mrs. Clinton, they promised me an appointment to that post, which had just become vacant. As it turned out, however, I was not appointed to the position of Assistant Director. I talked to Governor Clinton about the situation and was not satisfied with his explanation as to why I did not get the position. I felt deeply hurt and disappointed with the way things had worked out

3

regarding the Assistant Director position and the way the Clintons had dealt with me concerning it.

On June 21, 1985, I asked to be transferred off of the Governor's security detail. I decided that it would be best not to work for the Clinton's anymore. I was then assigned to the auto theft unit of the Arkansas State police.

Shortly after I left the detail, around the end of June 1985, Colonel Goodwin, the then director of the Arkansas State police, asked me if I would meet with Betsey Wright and Jim Clark. Betsey Wright was a political aide to Governor Clinton, and Jim Clark had just been appointed to be the Director of the state crime lab. I met Betsey Wright and Jim Clark at Betsey Wright's home on Hill Road.

At the meeting, Betsey Wright told me that she was concerned that I was "mad" at Governor and Mrs. Clinton. At one point in the conversation, Betsey Wright said to me words to the affect of: "Well, you're not going to say anything." By that, I understood that she was concerned with the possibility that I might make public statements regarding the Clintons that could embarrass them, which she knew that I could do. I told Wright and Clark that I just wanted to be left alone.

Following that meeting with Wright and Clark, I came to feel that Governor Clinton and his aides viewed me as a possible threat to them.

For the next several years, I had a distant, but cordial, relationship with Governor Clinton. I became the President of the

4

Arkansas State Police Association in approximately late 1985. In
that capacity, I had occasion to be involved in legislative
efforts, lobbying and the like. From time to time, I would be at
the State Capitol working on matters concerning the Arkansas State
Troopers.

In 1989, Governor Clinton and I had a political dispute
concerning a piece of legislation. Governor Clinton had asked for
my support, and the support of the Arkansas State Police
Association, for his controversial tax increase proposal. The tax
bill was in trouble in the Arkansas House, and Governor Clinton
needed our organization's support to help pass the bill.

During the legislative effort to pass the tax bill, I met with
the Governor. He asked for my support of the bill. He promised me
that if our organization helped pass the bill, he would introduce
legislation in a special session of the legislature providing for
a pay raise for troopers. I agreed to support his tax bill, and
our organization's efforts helped the bill pass. The bill passed
by one vote in the Arkansas House.

Later that fall, Governor Clinton called a special session of
the Arkansas legislature. The Governor did not place a trooper pay
raise bill on the legislature's call, as he had promised repeatedly
that he would. The special session never considered a trooper pay
raise bill. This was contrary to the Governor's promise to me.

Throughout 1989, I had been telling my organization that the
Governor had promised us a pay raise bill in the special session.
Our organization had spent considerable effort and resources in

5

trying to win support for the expected pay raise bill. When I realized that the Governor was reneging on his promise to the Arkansas State troopers and me, I made a statement to the press indicating that I felt the Governor had broken a promise to the troopers. This was in late October 1989.

When Governor Clinton became aware of my public statements regarding a trooper pay raise bill, he became extremely upset with me. Later, we had a meeting with Governor Clinton at the Mansion. I think this meeting was a couple months after the late October statements. At the meeting, Governor Clinton was indignant that I had gone to the press and suggested that he had broken a promise. At the conclusion of the meeting, the Governor asked that we put our differences behind us and that we work together for a pay raise bill in the next regular session of the legislature. I agreed, and a pay raise bill did pass in 1991.

I recall seeing an encounter between Governor Clinton and David Hale at the state Capitol. I was in an area that I call "the tunnel," which is a drive-through, pick-up point under the steps of the east side of the state capitol building. I was talking to Governor Clinton alone. There were other people in the general area, as there usually are when the Capitol is open for business. We had been talking for a few minutes. During our conversation, Clinton saw David Hale in the area. He turned away from me to talk to Hale. The Governor's back was to me as he spoke to Hale. I heard Governor Clinton say to David Hale words to the affect of: "We need to raise some money. You're going to have to help us out." I do not recall if Hale said anything in response, but I could see his facial expression. He appeared surprised and taken aback. Governor Clinton turned back to me and finished our conversation shortly. I left. I do not recall if David Hale remained in the area to continue talking to Clinton or not.

I remember the encounter between Clinton and Hale, because of the timing and location of the exchange, and because I felt Governor Clinton had put Hale on the spot in a way that was unusual. I also felt that Hale was visibly uncomfortable with Clinton's remarks.

I have tried to remember when this encounter between Governor Clinton and David Hale occurred. I do not have an exact date or month that I can be 100% certain of. I believe that the encounter occurred in the time period of 1985-1986. I don't think I was in the Governor's security detail at the time. I do recall that I was at the Capitol frequently during the month of January 1986, because there were matters concerning the troopers that I was working on and that I recall discussing with Governor Clinton personally.

7

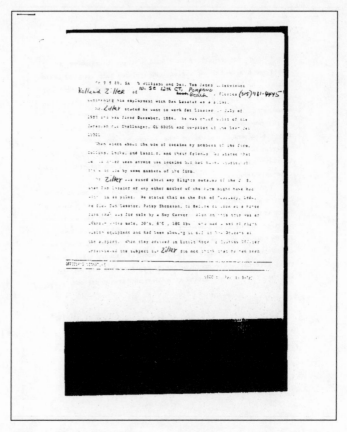

(G) DEA report of Dan Lasater's flight to Belize with Patsy Thomasson, who is now on the White House staff.

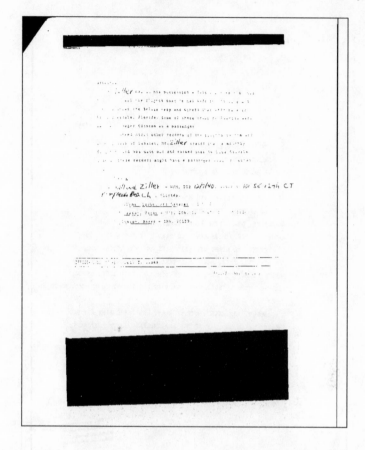

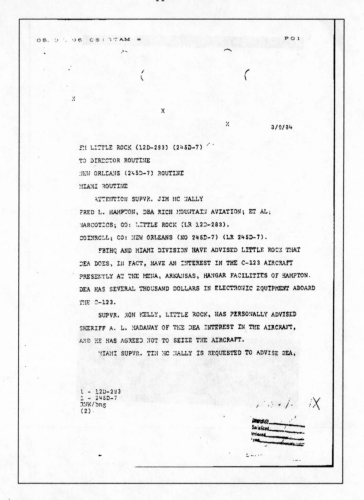

(H) FBI Teletype information on Barry Seal's C-123K.

OC. 27. 90 08:37AM ✳   P03

PAGE TWO LR 12D-283 UNCLAS

MIAMI THAT RED HALL, A COLUMBUS, OHIO, DRUG SMUGGLER AND

ELECTRONICS EXPERT IS PRESENTLY PERFORMING SOME TYPE OF

ELECTRONICS WORK ON THE C-123, SUPRA.

▓▓▓▓▓▓▓▓▓▓▓▓▓▓▓▓▓▓▓▓▓▓▓▓▓▓▓▓▓▓ ALSO DETERMINE

FROM DEA, MIAMI: (1) WHY AIRCRAFT MOVED TO MENA, ARKANSAS,

FROM FLORIDA; AND (2) IS RED HALL DOING WORK FOR BARRY SEAL

OR DEA ON THE C-123.

    LITTLE ROCK IS CONTINUING ITS INVESTIGATION IN CAPTIONED

MATTER TOWARD CONSPIRACY CASE AGAINST HAMPTON AND SEIZURE OF

HAMPTON'S ASSETS IN MENA, ARKANSAS.

    MIAMI SUTEL RESULTS TO NEW ORLEANS, LITTLE ROCK, AND

FBIHQ.

BT

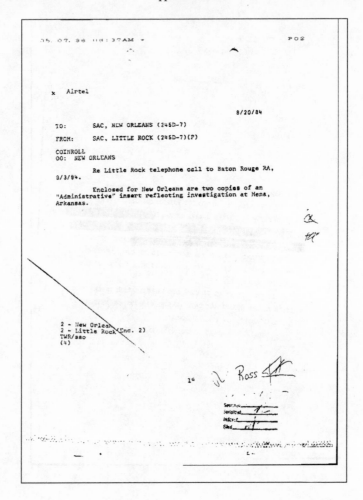

x   Airtel

8/20/84

TO: SAC, NEW ORLEANS (245D-7)

FROM: SAC, LITTLE ROCK (245D-7)(P)

COINROLL
OO: NEW ORLEANS

        Re Little Rock telephone call to Baton Rouge RA,
8/3/84.

        Enclosed for New Orleans are two copies of an
"Administrative" insert reflecting investigation at Mena,
Arkansas.

2 - New Orleans (Enc. 2)
2 - Little Rock (Enc. 2)
TWR/sao
(4)

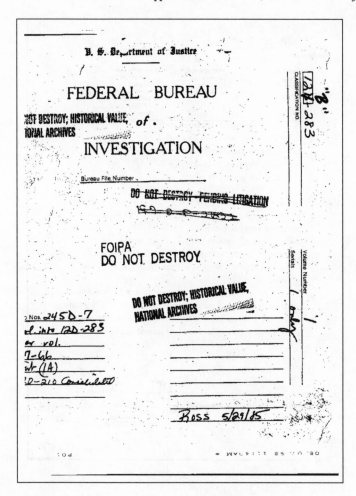

(I) FBI internal memo with more information on Seal's plane.

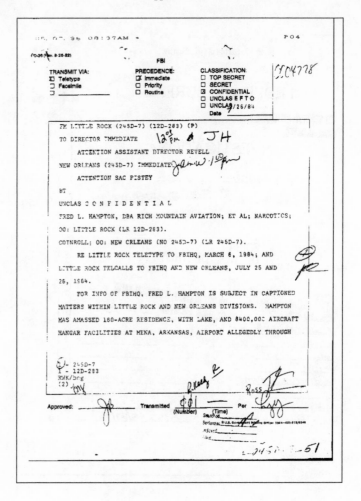

FD-36 (Rev. 8-26-82)

FBI

TRANSMIT VIA:
☐ Teletype
☐ Facsimile
☐ _____

PRECEDENCE:
☐ Immediate
☐ Priority
☐ Routine

CLASSIFICATION:
☐ TOP SECRET
☐ SECRET
☐ CONFIDENTIAL
☐ UNCLAS E F T O
☐ UNCLAS
Date _____

EC0478

PAGE TWO LR 245D-7 UNCLAS C O N F I D E N T I A L
NARCOTICS SMUGGLING. IRS HAS EXTENSIVE FINANCIAL INVESTIGATIVE
DATA RE HAMPTON WHICH IS IN PROCESS OF BEING MADE AVAILABLE
TO FBI LITTLE ROCK THROUGH IRS INVESTIGATIVE DISCLOSURE
PROCESS.

ON JULY 24, 1984, HAMPTON INVITED POLK COUNTY SHERIFF
A. L. HADAWAY TO HAMPTON'S ATTORNEY'S OFFICE IN MENA AND
THEREAFTER RELATED THE FOLLOWING TO SHERIFF HADAWAY:

ALSO PRESENT DURING A PORTION OF THE CONVERSATION WAS
A LOCAL NEWSPAPER REPORTER. HAMPTON THEREAFTER PLAYED A
VIDEO RECORDING OF A CABLE NEWS NETWORK (CNN) REPORT OF AN
ALLEGED CIA OPERATION WHICH ALLEGEDLY SHOWED INVOLVEMENT OF
SANDANISTA REBELS IN INTERNATIONAL COCAINE SMUGGLING MARKET.
HAMPTON ALSO FURNISHED SHERIFF HADAWAY A COPY OF A MIAMI
HERALD NEWSPAPER ARTICLE (UNDATED) CONCERNING THE SAME MATTER.
HAMPTON THEREAFTER ADVISED THE SHERIFF THAT THE THREE AIRCRAFT
PRESENTLY AT THE MENA AIRPORT AT HAMPTON'S HANGAR WERE, IN
FACT, CIA AIRCRAFT, AND THAT HE (HAMPTON) WAS MAINTAINING THE
AIRCRAFT FOR THE CIA. HAMPTON STATED THAT THE MILITARY TYPE
AIRCRAFT (CAMOUFLAGED PAINT WITH NO NUMBERS) WERE THE ACTUAL
CIA AIRCRAFT USED IN THE OPERATION SHOWN ON THE CNN VIDEO.

Approved: _____ Transmitted _____ Per _____
(Number)   (Time)

☆ U.S. Government Printing Office 1984-421-912/9248

FD-36 (Rev. 8-28-82)

FBI

206330

TRANSMIT VIA:
- ☐ Teletype
- ☐ Facsimile
- ☐ _____

PRECEDENCE:
- ☐ Immediate
- ☐ Priority
- ☐ Routine

CLASSIFICATION:
- ☐ TOP SECRET
- ☐ SECRET
- ☐ CONFIDENTIAL
- ☐ UNCLAS E F T O
- ☐ UNCLAS

Date _____

PAGE THREE LR 245D-7 UNCLAS C O N F I D E N T I A L

IT SHOULD BE NOTED THAT THIS AIRCRAFT WAS OBSERVED, IN CON-
NECTION WITH LITTLE ROCK'S ONGOING INVESTIGATION, AT HAMPTON'S
HANGAR ON JULY 19, 1984, AND INDIVIDUAL EXITING THIS AIRCRAFT
WAS BELIEVED TO BE BARY SEAL, SUBJECT OF NEW ORLEANS "COINROLL"
INVESTIGATION.

SHERIFF HADAWAY HAS ADVISED THAT HAMPTON HAS FURNISHED
HIM THIS INFORMATION SO THAT THE SHERIFF AND LAW ENFORCEMENT
OFFICIALS WILL BE AWARE OF HAMPTON'S ACTIVITIES WITH THE CIA
IN CONNECTION WITH NARCOTICS SMUGGLING.

FBIHQ SHOULD NOTE THAT SHERIFF HADAWAY HAS BEEN
EXTREMELY COOPERATIVE AND HAS WORKED CLOSELY WITH LITTLE
ROCK FBI AND DEA IN MANY SENSITIVE NARCOTICS CASES, SUCH AS
CAPTIONED MATTERS. SHERIFF HADAWAY HAS CONTACTED FBI LITTLE
ROCK WITH ABOVE INFO AND IS CONSIDERING SEIZURE OF AFORE-
MENTIONED THREE AIRCRAFT AS HE DOES NOT BELIEVE THE CIA
WOULD OPERATE WITH A PERSON SUCH AS HAMPTON, AND FURTHER
THAT IF IT WAS SOME OPERATION WITH THE CIA, THAT HAMPTON
SHOULD NOT BE TELLING EVERYONE ABOUT IT. SHERIFF HADAWAY
OPINES THAT HAMPTON IS ATTEMPTING TO MASQUERADE HIS OWN DRUG
SMUGGLING ACTIVITIES WITH THIS ALLEGED CIA CONNECTION.

Approved: _____ Transmitted _____ Per _____
                        (Number)   (Time)

☞ U.S. Government Printing Office: 1984—421-613/8245

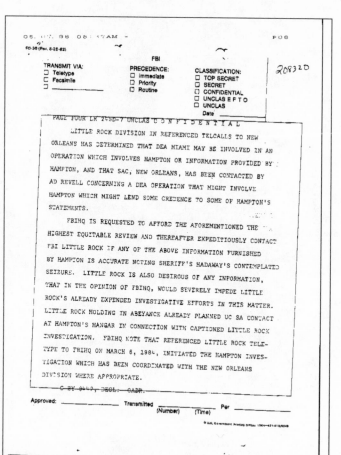

05. .. 96 08: 7AM   P08
FD-36 (Rev. 8-26-82)

                              FBI
TRANSMIT VIA: PRECEDENCE: CLASSIFICATION: 208320
☐ Teletype   ☐ Immediate   ☐ TOP SECRET
☐ Facsimile   ☐ Priority   ☐ SECRET
☐ _____   ☐ Routine   ☐ CONFIDENTIAL
                                         ☐ UNCLAS E F T O
                                         ☐ UNCLAS
                                            Date

PAGE FOUR LR 245D-7 UNCLAS C O N F I D E N T I A L

LITTLE ROCK DIVISION IN REFERENCED TELCALLS TO NEW
ORLEANS HAS DETERMINED THAT DEA MIAMI MAY BE INVOLVED IN AN
OPERATION WHICH INVOLVES HAMPTON OR INFORMATION PROVIDED BY
HAMPTON, AND THAT SAC, NEW ORLEANS, HAS BEEN CONTACTED BY
AD REVELL CONCERNING A DEA OPERATION THAT MIGHT INVOLVE
HAMPTON WHICH MIGHT LEND SOME CREDENCE TO SOME OF HAMPTON'S
STATEMENTS.

FBIHQ IS REQUESTED TO AFFORD THE AFOREMENTIONED THE
HIGHEST EQUITABLE REVIEW AND THEREAFTER EXPEDITIOUSLY CONTACT
FBI LITTLE ROCK IF ANY OF THE ABOVE INFORMATION FURNISHED
BY HAMPTON IS ACCURATE NOTING SHERIFF'S HADAWAY'S CONTEMPLATED
SEIZURE. LITTLE ROCK IS ALSO DESIROUS OF ANY INFORMATION,
THAT IN THE OPINION OF FBIHQ, WOULD SEVERELY IMPEDE LITTLE
ROCK'S ALREADY EXPENDED INVESTIGATIVE EFFORTS IN THIS MATTER.
LITTLE ROCK HOLDING IN ABEYANCE ALREADY PLANNED UC SA CONTACT
AT HAMPTON'S HANGAR IN CONNECTION WITH CAPTIONED LITTLE ROCK
INVESTIGATION. FBIHQ NOTE THAT REFERENCED LITTLE ROCK TELE-
TYPE TO FBIHQ ON MARCH 6, 1984, INITIATED THE HAMPTON INVES-
TIGATION WHICH HAS BEEN COORDINATED WITH THE NEW ORLEANS
DIVISION WHERE APPROPRIATE.

C BY 9447, DECL: OADR.

Approved: _____ Transmitted _____ Per _____
                                        (Number) (Time)

☆ U.S. Government Printing Office: 1984-421-418/9548

APPENDIX B

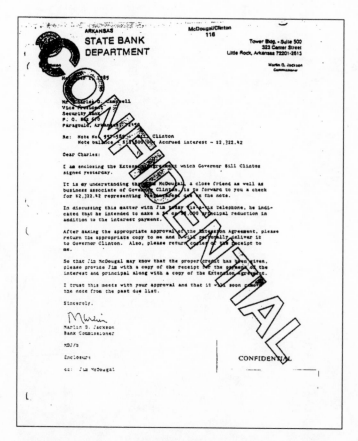

Marlin Jackson's letter on State Bank Department stationery to the loan officer of his former bank, intervening for renewal of the 1980 loan to Hillary that originated at James McDougal's Bank of Kingston (later Madison Bank and Trust). Jackson was president of

Security Bank of Paragould, which picked up Hillary's loan when federal bank examiners cracked down on Madison Bank. Jackson became state bank commissioner before his former bank refinanced Hillary, and he claimed he had no role in the transaction. This letter shows, to the contrary, that he continued to be a key player in the Clintons' finances, personal and political, even after taking his state position.

APPENDIX C

(A) At Yale Law School in 1970, Hillary Rodham helped found the *Yale Review of Law and Social Action* "to present forms of legal scholarship and journalism which focus on programmatic solutions to social problems." She served on the board of editors for the first issue, which ran articles entitled "Rent Strikes and the Law," "Feeding the Poor," and "Lawyers and Revolutionaries." The second issue, on which she worked as an associate editor, devoted fifty pages to the New Haven Superior Court murder trial of a Black Panther, Lonnie McLucas, accused of killing a suspected informer. The trial, in which McLucas was convicted of conspiracy but not murder, was the prelude to the murder conspiracy trial of Bobby Seale and seven other Black Panthers; the trial convulsed New Haven and Yale throughout that spring. Among the illustrations, the editors chose to run the above three drawings of pigs, identified as members of the San Francisco police tactical squad.

(By way of background, a Black Panther speaker at Yale in April 1970 had discussed the West Coast case with these words:

> The brother is charged with four counts of attempted murder of four pigs. And I don't think that's wrong. Because everybody knows that pigs are depraved traducers that violate the lives of human beings and that there ain't nothing wrong with taking the life of a motherfucking pig.

The statement drew loud boos from many in the audience [see John Taft, *Mayday at Yale* (Boulder, CO: Westview Press, 1976), 58–59].)

U. S. SMALL BUSINESS ADMINISTRATION

PORTFOLIO FINANCING REPORT

PART A - SMALL BUSINESS CONCERN DATA

IDENTIFICATION	PREFINANCING INFORMATION
Name SUSAN H. MCDOUGAL, d/b/a MASTER MARKETING, A SOLE PROPRIETORSHIP	Fiscal Year Immediately Prior To Date Of Financing (Date) _____ N/A
Street Address 1310 Main Street	Number of Employees: Total
City Little Rock County Pulaski	Managerial / Skilled / Unskilled or Semi-skilled
State Arkansas ZIP Code 72201	Gross Revenue for the Year / Profit or (Loss) for the Year
Date Business Established 1986	Taxes for the Year: Total / Federal / State / Local
Form of Business: Corporation___ Partnership___ Proprietor Y (Check one)	Total Assets / Net Worth (Deficit) / Retained Earnings (Deficit)
Standard Industrial Classification Code: 7311	Borrowing: Total / Short-term / Long-term
Employer Identification Number:	

PART B - FINANCING INFORMATION

Date Of This Financing 4-3-86

Total Amount Of This Financing $300,000.00

Total Amount Disbursed This Date $300,000.00

Purpose Of Financing (Use of Proceeds)

working capital

INSTRUMENT(S) EVIDENCING THIS FINANCING AND AMOUNTS APPLICABLE TO EACH

Debt Only

$300,000.

Interest Rate(s):

12%

Debt with Equity Features

-0-

Equity Only

-0-

Discount -0-   Fees -0-   Commissions -0-   Other Charges -0-

Where one or more of the instruments is considered an "Equity Security" as defined by Section 107.302 (b) of SBA Regulations, make the appropriate entries:
(a) Actual ownership 0 % (b) Potential ownership 0 %
(c) Total Actual and Potential 0 %
"Is the financing covered by this Portfolio Financing Report the first financing by this Licensee?
☒ Yes ☐ No
Has SIZE STATUS DECLARATION, SBA Form 480, been completed?
☒ Yes ☐ No
Has ASSURANCE OF COMPLIANCE, SBA Form 652D, been completed? ☒ Yes ☐ No
Immediately prior to the financing covered by this Portfolio Financing Report, did this small business concern have an outstanding financing balance with this Licensee?
☐ Yes ☒ No

If yes, the balance prior to this financing was $

Are management services being provided or to be provided by the licensee to this small business concern?
☐ Yes ☒ No
If yes, is there a formal contract or agreement covering these services?
☐ Yes ☐ No
If yes, a copy of the contract or agreement should be furnished to SBA with the filing of this report.
Where this report includes an equity interest, is this small business concern required to repurchase its equity interest from the licensee? ☐ Yes ☒ No
If yes, a copy of the contract or agreement should be furnished to SBA with the filing of this report.

NAME OF LICENSEE Capital-Management Services, Inc.

LICENSEE NUMBER 0 6 0 6 5 2 0 7

PART C - VERIFICATION

The information contained above is certified to be complete and correct to the best of my knowledge and belief.

Date 4/3/86   Signature _____

Title President

SBA FORM 1031 (3-75) USE PREVIOUS EDITION UNTIL EXHAUSTED

(Use the reverse side if more detail is necessary)

(B) Copy of Financing Report and check for $300,000 from David Hale's Capital-Management Services, Inc., to Susan McDougal, made out to her non-existent Master Marketing Co. This is the loan that Hale testified he had been pressured personally to make by then-Governor Bill Clinton. According to Hale, Clinton told him his own name couldn't appear on the loan, but then offered Whitewater Development Co. shares as security.

CAPITAL-MANAGEMENT SERVICES, INC.
PHONE 501-664-8613
1910 NORTH GRANT, SUITE 200
LITTLE ROCK, ARKANSAS 72207

000458
81-779/820

April 3 19 86

PAY TO THE ORDER OF   SUSAN H. MCDOUGAL d/b/a MASTER MARKETING $300,000.00

Three-hundred-thousand and no/00-------------------------------- DOLLARS

PULASKI BANK
AND TRUST COMPANY
LITTLE ROCK, ARKANSAS

FOR   LOAN   Linda Sue Hale

⑈000458⑈ ⑈082007791⑈ 3 040 577⑈

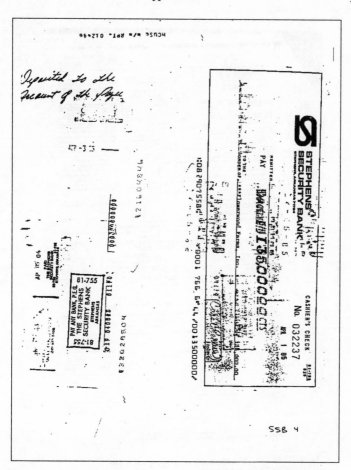

(C) The paper trail that could bring down the Clintons.

(1) Loan of $135,000 to James McDougal from Stephens Security Bank of Stephens, Arkansas. Check is dated 1 April 1985, but disclosure form gives maturity date of 3 April 1986. Stated purpose is to make improvement at McDougal's Flowerwood Farms development. Federal investigators have heard testimony that Hillary Clinton gave her personal guarantee to the loan.

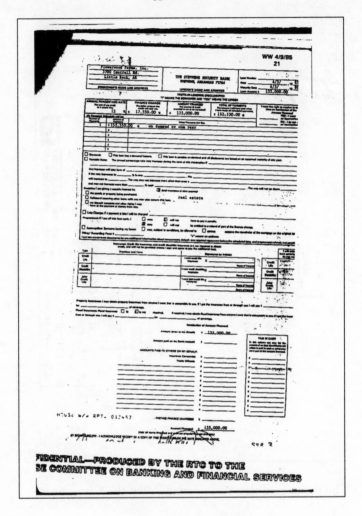

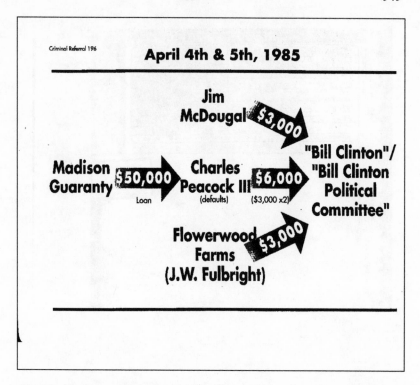

(2) Chart shows that House Banking Committee concludes that McDougal diverted the money to other uses, including campaign contributions to Bill Clinton.

(3) Richard T. Smith, president of Stephens Security Bank, calls McDougal, asking for loan to be repaid. He cites pressure from federal bank examiners.

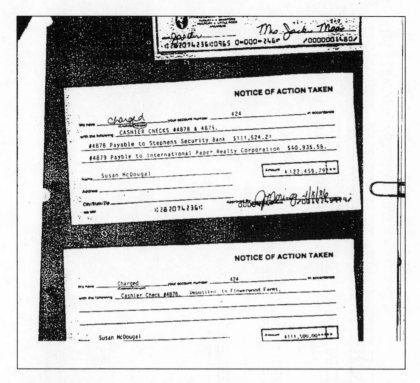

(4) McDougal uses money from Hale's $300,000 loan to Susan to pay off Flowerwood Farm debt, taking pressure off Hillary. Hale made a payment on 3 April 1986, the due date of the Flowerwood loan from Stephens Security Bank.

HOUSE W/W RPT. 012467

SSB 8

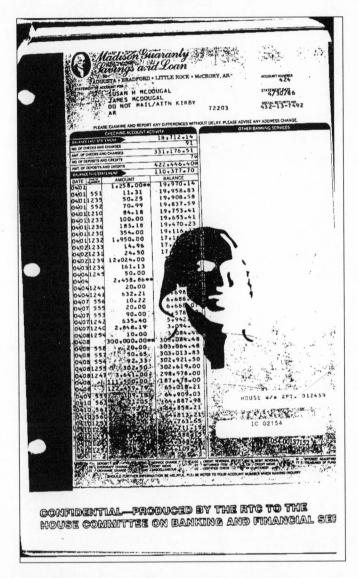

(5) Money from rest of the loan also helps out the Clintons, paying off $24,455 owed to Ozarks Reality, their Whitewater broker, for more than a year.

INDEX